BLACK MEN
Obsolete, Single, Dangerous?

Books by Haki R. Madhubuti (Don L. Lee)

Tough Notes: A Healing Call for Creating Exceptional Black Men
Claiming Earth: Race, Rage, Rape, Redemption: Blacks Seeking a
Culture of Enlightened Empowerment
Dynamite Voices: Black Poets of the 1960s
Black Men: Obsolete, Single Dangerous? The Afrikan American
Family in Transition
From Plan to Planet: Life Studies: The Need for Afrikan Minds
and Institutions
Enemies: The Clash of Races
A Capsule Course in Black Poetry Writing (co-author)
HeartLove: Wedding and Love Poems
Groundwork: New and Selected Poems of Don L. Lee/
Haki R. Madhubuti from 1966-1996
Killing Memory, Seeking Ancestors
Earthquakes and Sunrise Missions
African Centered Education (co-author)
Book of Life
Directionscore: New and Selected Poems
We Walk the Way of the New World
Don't Cry, Scream
Black Pride
Think Black
Releasing the Spirit: A Collection of Literary Works from
Gallery 37 (co-editor)
Describe the Moment: A Collection of Literary Works from
Gallery 37 (co-editor)
Million Man March/ Day of Absence: A Commemorative Anthology
(co-editor)
Confusion by Any Other Name: Essays Exploring the Negative
Impact of "The Blackman's Guide to
Understanding the Blackwoman" (editor)
Why L.A. Happened: Implications of the '92 Los Angeles Rebellion (editor)
Say that the River Turns: The Impact of Gwendolyn Brooks (editor)
To Gwen, With Love (co-editor)

BLACK MEN
Obsolete, Single, Dangerous?

The Afrikan American Family in Transition:
Essays in Discovery, Solution and Hope

Haki R. Madhubuti

Third World Press, Chicago

BLACK MEN

Third World Press
Publishers since 1967

Printed in the United States of America

08 07   20 19 18 17 16 15

Library of Congress Catalog Card Number: 89-51325

ISBN: 0-88378-135-2 (alk. paper)

Cover illustration by Calvin Jones
Cover concept and design by Gina M. Allen

In Memory of

Malcolm X (El-Hajj Malik El-Shabazz)

Hoyt W. Fuller

Two mountains who left fertile valleys

James Baldwin   M. Carl Holman   John O. Killens

Mickey Leland   Harold Washington   Bob Marley

Max Robinson

Dedication

To Black Women

To the millions of Black people
who have given their lives
in our struggle for liberation

For the example of the brothers of the
National Black Wholistic Retreat Society

Jesse Carter   Chester Grundy   David Hall

John Howell   Kamau Jawara   Jack Thomas

and

Nelson Mandela

Bob Law   Lu Palmer   Don Johnson

Acknowledgments

This book could not have been completed without the ground-breaking works of Robert Staples, Marcus Garvey, Hoyt W. Fuller, Bobby Wright, Gwendolyn Brooks, Frances Cress-Welsing, Neely Fuller, James E. Blackwell, Charles V. Willie, E. Franklin Frazier, W.E.B. Du Bois, Vivian Gordon, Nathan and Julia Hare, Wade Nobles, Maulana Karenga, Chancellor Williams, Ayi Kwei Armah, Harold Cruse, Cheikh Anta Diop, Jeff Donaldson, Abena Joan Brown, Margaret Burroughs, Hannibal Afrik, Murray DePillars, Harriette Pipes McAdoo, Useni Eugene Perkins, Na'im Akbar, Conrad Worrill, Kalamu ya Salaam, Gil Scott-Heron, Barbara Sizemore, Olomenji, David Lemieux, Richard Wright, Malcolm X, Asa Hilliard, Jacob Carruthers, Imari A. Obadele, Carter G. Woodson and others. Their research and/or actions helped to shape my thesis. However, I am totally responsible for any misinterpretation of their works or errors that may appear in this book.

I must also give a sincere thanks to my editor Christine Minor. Her help has been invaluable and her eye keen. Thanks also to Gina Minor (marketing & production), Tonya Thompson (typesetting) and Kelvin Dance (editing).

H.R.M.

Note:

I used a capital "B" when referring to Black people. The word "Black" is descriptive, but also it is a political and cultural term that identifies people of Afrikan descent at a world level. See the chapter "Nothing Black But a Cadillac."

In spelling Afrika I use "k" rather than "c" because for many activists the "k" represents an acknowledgment that "Africa" is not the true name of that vast continent. When I speak of Afrika, I'm bringing an Afrikan-centered view to my meaning. Therefore, the Afrika spelled with a "k" represents a redefined and potentially different Afrika, and also it symbolizes for me a coming back together of Afrikan people worldwide. Let it be understood that when I speak of Afrika and when most whites think of "Africa," we are coming from two different worldviews.

"A well-educated Black has a tremendous advantage over a well-educated white in terms of the job market. And, I think sometimes a Black may think that they don't really have the advantage...but I've said on occasion—even about myself—If I were starting off today, I would love to be a well-educated Black because I really believe they do have an actual advantage today."

Donald Trump
on R.A.C.E. (an NBC special)

"This is a very dangerous statement, especially since it wasn't challenged by anyone."

Haki R. Madhubuti

"A rich white boy can say anything he wants to in this world—no matter how ignorant it is."

A Black Female Student

The pain is in the eyes. Young Black men in their late twenties or early thirties living in urban America, lost and abandoned, aimlessly walking and hawking the streets with nothing behind their eyes but anger, confusion, disappointment and pain. These men, running the streets, occupying corners, often are beaten beyond recognition, with scars both visible and internal. These men, Black men — sons of Afrika, once strong and full of the hope that America lied about — are now knee-less, voice-broken, homeless, forgotten and terrorized into becoming beggars, thieves or ultra-dependents on a system that considers them less than human and treats them with less dignity and respect than dead dogs. I am among these men. I will *never* forgive white people for what they have done to Afrikan-American men, women and children. This is our story, and this time *we are not asking for* or waiting on *apologies* and *handouts*.

H.R.M.
1990

Contents

Introduction
A View from the Second Sunset

Why this Book

I consider myself primarily a poet. I'm a poet in the Afrikan griot tradition, a keeper of the culture's secrets, history, short and tall tales, a rememberer. As a Black poet, I have a certain sense for language, both its beneficial and destructive powers. Therefore, as a writer who is well aware of his own cultural heritage, I am extremely affected by anything that alters that heritage.

In America, not only has my Afrikan heritage been altered (a polite description), but also Afrikan American people have been mentally (and in many cases physically) disfigured. We are not who we used to be. I am keenly aware that all people change. However, we've been transfixed, made motionless by others, transformed into people who are often unrecognizable from our original Afrikan selves. We are people who, by and large, have been taught to deny reality as we hurriedly try to fit into somebody else's worldview.

I wrote this book because I sensed a need in the United States for a new truth — a truth not based on false histories, false assumptions, false arguments or false realities. In a *Newsweek* essay (1-21-80), the scientist/writer Isaac Asimov wrote about the "cult of ignorance" in this country. He said, "The strain of anti-intellectualism has been a constant threat winding its way through our political and cultural life, nurtured by the false notion that democracy means that 'my ignorance is just as good as your knowledge.'"

Ignorance about the state of Black people in America is appalling. However, what is even more appalling is that few people in the dominant culture even give a damn, and too many Afrikan American leaders have no idea how to improve the lives of their people.

This book is the result of a certain amount of frustration. I had grown tired of reading sociological and political reports alleging to address the Black condition. Most of these books, which were published by large trade or university presses and written by whites or negroes, contain only analysis without offering workable solutions for improving the status of

i

Black people. If explanation or examination was enough, after the tens of thousands of pages published over the last thirty years on the problems of Black people, Black families, Black women and Black men, we should be a free, conscious and developing people. This is not the case. It's like saying that the air is clean and the water is drinkable in Los Angeles.

Lack of Consciousness

One of the tragedies of Black life in America is that too many Black people never acquire insight into their own existence. *They just do not know who they are.* And, this confusion about *identity* and *source* is at the core of our ignorance. The Afrikans have a saying: "If you don't know who you are, any history will do." Welcome to America. This is the land where genocide was committed against nations of indigenous people; where New York was purchased with beads; where the abnormal defines normality; and where young people live and breathe on the words of burnt-out rock stars with their noses cut off.

Afrikan American people have little knowledge of themselves. We are products of a slave history, a Eurocentric worldview, that by definition cannot be developmental or inspirational. This history, for the most part, has been written, disseminated and taught by the sons and daughters of the people who raped Afrika of its people and wealth and literally sprinkled Afrikans around the world. They, while doing this, developed (created) in their politics, science, arts, economics, education and religion a rationale for Black destruction. This Eurocentric rationale provided the "intellectual and moral" basis for their taking of the world. Thereafter the world was divided into colors — Black, white and others.

Not Knowing and Not Wanting to Know

The education I received in the Black community was entirely different — in content and context — from that of whites. Not only was my "training" not a challenge, it was discouraging. The major piece of information I absorbed after twelve years of public education was that I was a problem, inferior, ineducable and a victim. And, as a victim, I began to see the world through the eyes of a victim.

I'll never forget how hard my mother worked to make ends meet for my sister and me. Our material lives were impoverished; we didn't have a television, record player, car, telephone or too much food. We acquired much of our clothing from secondhand stores, and I learned to work the streets very early. My life began to change when I was introduced to other worlds.

One year on my birthday, my mother took me to a five-and-dime store to buy me a gift. She bought me a blue plastic airplane with blue wheels, a blue propeller and a blue string on the front of the plane so that one could pull it across the floor. I was happy. That following week she took me and my sister to Dearborn, Michigan where she occasionally did "day work." Day work, for the uninformed, means Black women cleaning up white folks' homes. Dearborn, Michigan is where many of the movers and shakers who controlled the automobile industry lived. What I quickly noticed was that they lived differently. There were no five-and-dime stores in Dearborn at this time; there were craft shops. This is where the white mothers and fathers bought their children airplanes in boxes. In the boxes were wooden parts, directions for assembly, glue and small engines. Generally, the son would assemble the plane (which might take a day or two) and then take the plane outside and — guess what — it would fly.

This small slice of life is an example of the development — quite early — of two different consciousnesses. In my case and that of other poor youths, we would buy the plane already assembled, take it home and hope it rolled on the floor as if it was a car or truck rather than a plane. In Dearborn, the family would *invest* in a learning toy, and the child would put it together. Through this process, the child would learn work ethics and science and math principles. And, as a result of all that, the plane would *fly*. I was learning to be a consumer who depended on others to build the plane for me. The child in Dearborn made an investment, worked on it and, through his labor and brain power, produced a plane that flew. Translating this to the larger world, I was being taught to buy and to use my body from the neck down, while the white upper class boy was being taught, very early, to prepare himself to build things and run things, using the neck up. Two different worlds: my world — depending on and working for others, and his world — controlling his own destiny.

We have three billion-dollar businesses in the Black community: the church, drugs and consumerism. The Black church, basically, is the main spiritual, moral and cultural institution. It is not viewed as a business and, therefore, its economic benefit to the Afrikan American community is somewhat dubious. Drugs represent the backbone of the underground economy. Drug profits ($45 million last year in New York City) support a large chain of growers, suppliers, pushers and their families. However, the damage of the drug business to the Black community is disastrous, and it hovers over our community like a white plague. Obviously, consumerism is not a business. But, the extent to which Afrikan American consumers support businesses outside of their community as well as businesses located within but not of their community makes a profound economic statement.

A *people* cannot develop into a serious "autonomous" community without a financial base that initiates and provides for the community's creativity and resources.

White business since 1968 has been moving rapidly out of the inner cities as well as the country. Such exclusion of Blacks from available work, along with poor education, leads to a drop-out and give-up mentality. This country was built upon the backs of slave laborers. In the 20th century, America grew to its present state due to the development of small and medium-sized businesses. Today, according to the Small Business Administration, there are 19 million small businesses, and over one-half of them are family owned and operated. SBA has projected that over one-third of the new jobs created between the years 1990 and 2005 will require a college education; one-half of the jobs will require a minimum of 13.5 years of education.

Where does that leave Afrikan American people? Less than half of the Black students in the high school class of 1990 will finish; and of those who do, most will be under-educated. Couple this with the "outlawism" of big business and the 8.5 million unemployed white people, and it looks as though Black people will continue to be blamed for being lazy and not wanting to work. With Black male unemployment approaching 48%, the future doesn't look too inviting. Less than 4% of the jobs in the United States are manned by Black men. I'm not an economist, but I'm intelligent, and after reading *The Great Depression of 1990* by Ravi Batra, I think we are headed for a fall worse than that of 1929.

The destruction of Black men starts at birth, intensifies during boyhood, accelerates during the teen years and finalizes in early adulthood. I fear white people. This fear is based upon my interaction with them as well as my ongoing study of them, their history, psychology, politics, economics and culture. This fear comes from the experiences that Black people and other people of color have encountered in their contact with whites. Even the most naive understanding of European-American history should lead one to the conclusion that white people, as a collective body, have left huge scars of death and destruction on *all* of the people of the world whom they have "visited." Herein lies my fear: the one "creative act" at which few people have been able to beat white people is that of producing large death. We live among the chief killers in the world; I tried to document this in my last book of essays *Enemies: the Clash of Races*.

The world has gotten worse for Black men. A young Black man, according to the U.S. Census Bureau, has a 1-in-21 chance of being murdered as compared to a 1-in-333 chance for a white man of the same age. One out of two Black young people lives in poverty. The Black male prison population is over 50%, whereas our population in the country is around 13%. Of the six leading causes of death among the adult population, Black men lead the list in each category: homicide, heart attacks, cancer, suicide, strokes and accidents. The status of Black males in America is beyond the endangered species category.

At War?

A common saying among conscious Black men in regards to our current political, social and economic status in America is, "We are at war." I used to subscribe to such a theory myself. However, after many years of front-line activity in Black struggle and eleven years of research for this book, I've come to the conclusion that the relationship that Black and white men have is worse than war.

Nations fight wars. Nations prepare, execute and win or lose wars. Professional fighters fight personal wars. They prepare, execute and either win or lose. Even though we like to call ourselves the "Black nation," in fact, we are a heterogeneous body of Afrikan American men, women and

v

children searching for a better life. And, we are about as prepared to fight a war as we are to educate our children.

I think the best word to accurately describe the impact that the white nation is having upon Black people is *terror*. The Black community is being terrorized by whites at all levels of human involvement. The question that usually surfaces when I make this point is, "Are all white people terrorizing Black people?" It doesn't matter. What does matter is that the terror that is being inflicted upon the Black community is effective and has stopped most serious development.

Racism is not only alive and well in America, it is a growth industry. We need to understand that white world supremacy (racism) is a *given* fact of life in the world and is not vanishing. Therefore, we cannot, if we are intelligent, continue to use racism as an excuse to not execute our worldview. If this is clear, we will save a lot of hearts and minds that think we can change white people with conversation, spiritual sharing, money or astronomy.

White men and their women kick ass and dig graves all over the world. Mass media in the United States consistently portray Black men as the chief villains in this country. The best example of this portrayal is the last Presidential election. The fear of two Black men, Jesse Jackson and Willie Horton, helped to elect George Bush. America is drowning in drugs, and Congress and the President give $150 billion to the savings and loan industry and $8 billion to fight drugs. Evidently, the savings and loan industry's lobby is more effective than millions of ordinary lives being destroyed daily by drugs. The Black men murdered in Howard Beach and Bensonhurst are only very small examples of racially motivated crimes against Black people. Where is the lobby for the disenfranchised Blacks of America?

This book is not a cry for white help, white pity or even white understanding. Literally hundreds of books do that. After thirty years of active participation in the Black liberation movement in this country and the world, I'm convinced, without doubt or hesitation, that white world supremacy (racism) has to be seen as an organized and deliberated attack on all people of color. And, an effective defense against it must be incorporated into the teaching of every Black youth in the world.

John Kenneth Gallbrath in his book *The Nature of Mass Poverty* talks about people accommodating themselves to their condition. Poverty exacts its own reality. A poor person, like a poor family has to make his or her life out of what is available or what is left over from the well-to-do. This is, in part, the sort of terrorism about which I write. Often the only thing that can come from nothing is less than nothing. Poverty is, indeed, slavery.

As I was completing this book, the National Research Council issued its report *A Common Destiny: Blacks and American Society.* Here are some of its findings:

Economic Status: In income and earnings, Blacks gained fairly steadily relative to whites from 1939 to 1969. The percentage of people living in households with incomes below the poverty line has risen for both Blacks and whites in the past decade. Black poverty rates have been two to three times higher than those of whites at all times.

Residential Segregation: Residential separation of Blacks and whites has remained practically unchanged since the 1960s. The report notes that discrimination against Blacks currently seeking housing "has been conclusively demonstrated."

Education: "Segregation and differential treatment of blacks continue to be widespread in the elementary and secondary schools," the committee reported. College enrollment rates of all high school graduates declined sharply after 1977; while white rates have recovered, Black rates remain significantly lower than those of the 1970s. The odds of a Black student entering college within a year of graduating from high school are less than one-half the odds for a white student.

Political Participation: The proportion of Black federal, state and local public administrators rose from less than 1% in 1940 to 8% in 1980, but this figure is still less than Blacks' current 13% proportion of the U.S. population. Blacks still make up only about 1% of all elected officials.

Crime: "Black Americans are disproportionately victims of crime," the committee found. Blacks are twice as likely to be victims of robbery, vehicle theft and aggravated assault. "As long as there are great disparities in the socioeconomic status of blacks and whites, blacks will continue to be over-represented in the criminal justice system as victims and offenders," the committee stated.

Health: There are wide gaps in the mortality and morbidity of Blacks compared to whites at all ages except for individuals 85 and older. The odds that a Black baby will die shortly after birth are consistently twice as high as those for a white baby.

Child and Family Issues: The majority of Black children under the age of 18 live in families that include their mothers but not their fathers, while one in every five white children lives with just his or her mother. These figures are particularly significant considering the fact that female-headed families were 50% of all Black families with children in 1985, but they received only 25% of total Black family income. During the 1970s, one in every three Black children lived in poverty for at least seven of those 10 years; for white children the figure was one in 33.

I've tried to speak to all of these issues in this book. In the chapter "Never Without a Book," I write about the importance of literature. However, there are three books of which most people may not be aware; these books should be on every Afrikan American adult's "must study" list: *The Isis Papers* by Dr. Frances Cress-Welsing; *The United Independent Compensatory Code/System/Concept* by Neely Fuller, Jr.; and *The Destruction of Black Civilization* by Chancellor Williams.

This book is a call for serious Afrikan American men to
stand tall and dare to be great,
dare to move beyond the limited ideas of others,
dare to think for yourselves,
for the future.
dare to conceive a world where you
are more than a consumer,
a buyer,
a clown in purple
wearing odd clothes finding glory in not being
Black.
dare to stretch your imagination to where
beauty is the norm
rather than an ignorant accident
stomped upon in the stupor of quick
highs and lies masquerading as

truth.
dare to be beauty,
dare to be creative fire,
dare to be fathers, husbands,
dare to be quiet life fighters with a smile
dare...

H.R.M.

I. Changing Seasons

"It is always easier to proclaim rejection than actually to reject."

Frantz Fanon
The Wretched of the Earth

The B Network

brothers bop & pop and be-bop in cities locked up
and chained insane by crack and other acts
of desperation computerized in pentagon cellars producing
boppin brothers boastin of being better, best & beautiful.

if the boppin brothers are beautiful where are the sisters
who seek brotherman with a drugless head unbossed or beaten
by the bodacious West?

in a time of big wind being blown by boastful brothers,
will other brothers beat back backwardness to better & best
without braggart bosses beatin butts,
takin names and diggin graves?

beatin badness into bad may be urban but is it beautiful & serious?
or is it betrayal in an era of prepared easy death hangin on corners
trappin young brothers before they know the difference between
big death and big life?

brothers bop & pop and be-bop in cities locked up
and chained insane by crack and other acts
of desperation computerized in pentagon cellars producing
boppin brothers boastin of being better, best, beautiful
and definitely not *Black*.

the critical best is that
brothers better be the best if they are to avoid backwardness
brothers better be the best if they are to conquer beautiful bigness
Comprehend that bad is only *bad* if it's big, Black and better than
boastful braggarts belittling our best and brightest
with bosses seeking inches when miles are better.

1

brothers need to bop to being Black & bright & above board
the black train of beautiful wisdom that is bending this bind
toward a new & knowledgeable beginning that is
bountiful & bountiful & beautiful
While be-bopin to be
better than the test,
brotherman.

better yet write the exam.

Were Corners Made for Black Men to Stand On?

The larger question is what do a people do when the social, political and economic conditions under which they live are not only designed to limit their intellectual and material development, but are structured ultimately to kill them?

Every day, books, magazines, and newspaper articles are published with information detailing the "Decline of the Black Family," "The Crisis of Black Teenage Pregnancy, " "The Vanishing Black Male," "Brothers," and on and on. In much of the material published, the information is either rehashed sociological theories, excerpts from recent Ph.D. theses or articles from young hot-shot reporters looking for front-page bylines.

Black misery has always made good copy, yet there is much missing in this approach. There are answers, lies, music and many complexities in the lives of Afrikan Americans. However, the great majority of our people are not able to hear the survival songs.

Black people are not listening to the correct songs and their dance is increasingly becoming that of a beginner willing to accept "solutions" from the false musicians. It is not that Afrikan American people are inherently negligent in their search for life-giving and life-saving answers. The problem is the context and content of the answers that are presented. Social-political theory is passed off as "objective wisdom," as the world-view of Euro-Americans permeates Black life in ways that inhibit the majority of Blacks from functioning in their own best interests.

Cultural Absolutions

There are certain cultural resolutions that should be non-negotiable as a people pursues beauty and power. At the top of such a list is the necessity for the members of a people to know and be themselves (i.e., Afrikan Americans or Black people, all 30 million plus, must have a common and individual understanding of their history, traditions, accomplishments and mistakes).

3

Secondly, it is crucial that a people develop and listen first to its own "experts," seers and wise women and men. A people's worldview can be a major detriment in the construction of possibilities and future.

Thirdly, in the construction of a future, a people needs, as clearly as possible, to define and understand its enemy(ies).

Finally, a people needs to develop its own workable worldview (of all areas of human activity). In doing so, that people brings forth a leadership that is dedicated and willing to work incessantly to fulfill the constituents' wishes. Afrikan Americans at the national level do not have these cultural resolutions.

America 1989 is where millions of homeless people are dismissed with, "They are lazy and have too many babies;" where AIDS is the new megadeath, and its origin is falsely and maliciously placed in the Afrikan community. America is where most problems are treated by either taking drugs, over-eating, exercising, having sex, spending money, committing raw violence, reciting Sunday morning prayers, or staring at 110-channel television sets.

Material Value

Young unwed Black girls who give birth are no longer the exception, and young Black fathers have no idea of the "destruction" they bring forth with each of their seeds that matures to birth without proper nurturing. The U.S. is a country in which an educated person is measured by degrees, letters of reference and who one knows, rather than products produced. Value is determined by what one wears, where one lives, what one drives, where one parties and the type of employment one has.

America's trillion dollar budget supports an antiquated defense structure, while the poor of the land are redefined and ridiculed as their benefits are legislated downward. America's 36 % Black unemployment rate is considered tolerable as the Black underground economy expands and consumes those who least need it.

The West is canned food, processed knowledge, imitation grass and an economic system that rewards few. It also includes fake art, overly amplified "music," oppressive architecture, plastic shoes and a political system that operates for the wealthy. Many people endure 25-floor public housing, pencil-less classrooms, junk "food" and inadequate medical care. Malnourished children, material-minded adults, addictive religions and

4

political ideologies that condone a "Killing Field" attitude toward the unbelievers are viewed as normal. Black life is affected by overcrowded prisons, too few homes, over-stressed minds, fat bodies and a communicative network that legitimizes the easy, the quick and 30-second answers. America's context and content is built upon a subtle and effective ideology of White World Supremacy that few people understand. For those who do, many are unwilling to voice the call to resist.

Culture

As a people, our understanding of culture is severely limited. Black culture, as a force for survival and development, is given very little attention in the education of our young. However, the education that is transmitted (or not transmitted) is a product of the dominant white culture.

The politics and the economics that a people experience do not just appear, but are the unique results of that people's or somebody else's culture. The language, science and technology that bring meaning (or control) to a people's existence are also cultural.

One problem, of course, is that to most of us culture, as a concept, is abstract — that is, one does not actually observe culture. Yet, we all experience its manifestations, such as clothing, art, music, housing, weapons, films, literature, language, food, political, educational and social organizations and economic structures. Anthropologist Laura Thompson sees culture as

> ...the supreme creation of a human community, the product of its deep-seated urge to fulfill and perpetuate itself...it is primarily a group problem-solving device instituted by a human community to cope with its basic practical problems.

Aspects Of Culture

Dr. Thompson places great emphasis on the coping and problem-solving aspects of culture. However, it must be noted that among anthropologists and sociologists, there are differences of opinions as to conclusive definitions of culture. Edward T. Hall, in his *Beyond Culture*, states that most serious students of culture, however,

5

...do agree in three characteristics of culture: it is not innate, but learned; the various facets of culture are interrelated — you touch a culture in one place and everything else is shared and in effect defines the boundaries of different groups.

Hall goes on to point out that:

...Culture is man's medium; there is not one aspect of human life that is not touched and altered by culture. This means personality, how people express themselves (including shows of emotion), the way they think, how they move, how problems are solved, how their cities are planned and laid out, how transportation systems function and are organized, as well as how economic and government systems are put together and function.

Misconceptions

My focus on culture is to clear the air of serious misconceptions regarding cultural influence and hopefully to move our analysis beyond the trap of looking at race, politics and economics as isolated and unrelated entities. The way people view themselves and the extent to which they rise up out of any situation and decide their own course is a serious cultural question.

Culture, "shared understanding," is that medium in which values are transmitted from generation to generation. It is generally accepted that human behavior can be and is systematically observed, and that the variability of individuals is a result of inherited characteristics (biology) and life experience (culture).

A people's consciousness, the way they view and operate in the world, is shaped by their (or another's) culture. All of the answers are not certain, but it seems that culture can disable and kill as well as develop and give life.

The most prevailing consciousness among Black people today is one of survival. And this survival is not of a collective nature, in which individuals, communities and institutes work together to solve problems. Black survival, especially in the urban areas, is more Darwinian, a "survival of the fittest" attitude. Its proponents will use whatever means at their disposal to achieve their ends, regardless of the cost and pain to others.

6

It has often been stated that Black people in America represent the revolutionary vanguard. Indeed, we may be a vanguard, but revolutionary we are not — that is, if I understand the concept of revolutionary vanguard: a people who are bold and sophisticatedly violent while actively involved in replacing an unjust, corrupt system with one that is just and incorruptible.

De-revolution

The evidence does not support this concept, no matter how we wish to romanticize today's "revolutionary climate." If any climate exists, it is one of de-revolution. The political, educational, military and financial organizations of the U.S. have been actively involved — especially in the last twenty years, through the use of mass media, politics, sports and entertainment — in depoliticizing millions of Black people.

Ask the average Black person to articulate what he or she wants out of life, and you will get about the same answers the white middle class would give. However, the great majority of Blacks, who are not able to move to the middle class, end up settling for what they can get. Therefore, we have been forced into and have helped develop a culture of survival and/or dependency, not one of development.

The survival/dependent culture deals more with immediate needs rather than long-term needs. The ongoing search for food, shelter, clothing, sex, material artifacts, social status and fast weekends are what direct us and absorb our energies on a day-to-day basis. As a result, there exists very little time for serious development. Yet, the most hurting aspects of this is that if the time existed, there would still be few examples of genuine development.

Cultural Mentalities

The culture of survival/dependency breeds people who riot rather than plan progressive change or revolution. It develops people who react rather than act, beg rather than take, play rather than study and follow rather than lead. Let's take a closer look at these two cultural mentalities: 1) the revolutionary or progressive mentality is one that creates, builds and works for the long term; 2) the riot mentality is one that seeks instant gratification and is more destructive than constructive. The revolutionary would

7

take over a school system or build a school, while the rioter would burn the school down and give little thought to the results of that action.

The charts below are designed to more clearly characterize these two mentalities as they affect our development as a people. This comparison is not scientific. But it represents my conception of the highest and the most destructive responses of two opposing cultural orientations.

MAXIMUM CULTURAL DEVELOPMENT
Revolutionary Mentality

1. Study-oriented: reads, evaluates and debates books, newspapers, magazines and scholarly journals. Accepts the challenge of education.
2. Worker: looks for ways in which to actively work for self; may hold a job outside in order to sustain self and family. Self-reliant.
3. Organized and systematic. Efficient and diligent.
4. Progressively collective; conscious of others; cooperative.
5. Family-oriented: regards mate as partner in struggle; loves children. Values trust in relationships.
6. Land conscious: realizes that the only thing that nobody is making any more of is land.
7. Disciplined; strong, unyielding and energetic.
8. Serious. Practices fair play, order and punctuality. Honest and dependable.
9. Analytical and critical.
10. Frugal: buys mainly on need basis; saves.
11. Social life is developmental and involves children.
12. Creatively aggressive: will dare the impossible if it is possible.
13. Respects elders.
14. Dislikes incompetence and mediocrity.
15. Fights against Black-on-Black crime and understands that its root is white-on-Black crime.
16. Loves Black art, music and literature.
17. Can give and follow instructions. Encourages experimentation and criticism.
18. Committed to Black liberation, local, national and international.
19. Does not use drugs.
20. Politically active. Not crisis-oriented; acts on information rather

8

than reacts. Plans for the long term; alert; prepared for change.
21. Self-confident. Respects others regardless of race or culture.
22. Understands the economic forces that control our lives on a local, national and international level.
23. Rational in decisions and actions.
24. Rewards merit and achievement.

SURVIVAL CULTURAL EXISTENCE
Accommodationist/Riot Mentality

1. Does not read or study after "formal" education. Buys few books; reads mainly newspapers, sports pages or popular novels and magazines.
2. Works eight hours a day for someone else. Welfare conscious, get-it-for-nothing attitude.
3. Unsystematic and definitely not organized unless it is for someone else.
4. Backwardly individualistic: I, me, mine mentality.
5. Not family-oriented: regards mate as property; rates children low; generally single-minded; does not want children or responsibility of home life.
6. Not land conscious.
7. Actively fights against discipline.
8. Non-serious majority of time.
9. Not critical or analytical; prefers not to think for self.
10. Consumer junkie; if it's advertised, he's got it. Cannot distinguish wants from needs.
11. Loves social and night life (i.e., lives for the weekend, loves sexual conquests).
12. A defeatist; has few goals other than acquisition of material artifacts.
13. Puts elders in nursing homes and forgets them.
14. Gravitates towards incompetence and mediocrity.
15. Involved in Black-on-Black crime or is apathetic about the issue.
16. Loves any kind of music of the new generation.
17. Can give instructions but not follow them; avoids/rejects criticism.
18. Committed to self-liberation only.
19. Drug dependent — cigarettes, alcohol, hard drugs, etc.

20. Politically inactive; crisis-oriented; reacts.
21. Egotistical, ignorantly arrogant, has little concept of culture; feels he will be forever the racial underclass.
22. Naive about economics; unaware of the international nature of capitalism that touches all of our lives.
23. Rewards "yes" people.

Revolutionary Culture

It is obvious that there cannot be progress without a progressive and revolutionary culture working at its highest level. The rebellions of the sixties were both reactive and proactive. Much of the destruction that took place in the sixties was in the Black community. There are concrete reasons for this and if we are to move forward, we have to confront the truth. As I see it, these are the reasons that most Blacks don't struggle at a political level:

- Many Black people are satisfied with the way their lives are and fear radical change from any segment of society.

- Of those Black people who believe change is necessary, many don't know what to do about it and feel that their individual efforts are not worth much. Therefore, they do nothing but talk.

- Just about every Black family in the country has one or more personal traumas that consume their quality time (e.g., a son or husband in prison; a mother or family member seriously ill; basic economic survival, etc.).

- In most Black families, members can point to at least one family member, no matter how remote, who has "made it" in America and that person(s) is constantly used as the example of what we all can do with hard work, fortitude and initiative. This implies that Black failure is always individually instituted.

- A great many young Black adults are interacting on a day-to-day basis with white people either at school, work or

10

play and find it difficult to separate the evils that the white race has perpetuated against Blacks from their new found friendships. Somehow, the one or two white friends or mates exonerate the crimes of their people. Therefore, to many Blacks "people are just people," and organized white death squads fall in the category of unbelievable. A historical perspective of Black/white confrontations is generally unknown or dismissed.

• There is a failure of Black leadership to accurately inform.

Historical Perspective

It is clear that our cultural models must be sophisticated as well as revolutionary. The culture of accommodation, submission and riot is encouraged and glorified in the United States. The culture of material acquisition is normal and those that reject such obvious nonsense are regarded as abnormal. We are encouraged and, indeed, rewarded with trinkets and positions of pseudo-responsibility if we seek the "American dream" through the avenues of a survival culture.

The unplanned and "matter of fact" misuse and abuse of women exists in most cultures. The relegation women to procreation and housework is a universal practice. The West has sought to answer the question by providing an economy that demands that all work if they are to eat.

The white female's entrance into the economy, according to Marvin Harris' "America Now," displaced Black male and female workers and, in effect, hurt the Black family economically. Most Black women, however, have had to work; as a result, their relationships with Black men have been somewhat different. Some of the problems in stable Black homes begin to surface when the men lose their jobs and cannot find new employment.

It is axiomatic that a sexist culture will produce a sexist mind. To deny that sexism exists is to deny we breathe. No matter how enlightened one thinks he or she is, this sexism seeps into our actions daily.

Cultural Imposition

However, it is obvious to the enlightened that there are few jobs men do that women cannot. Cross-cultural studies have indicated time and time again that work women perform is not necessarily their choice but is culturally imposed. In most cultures, males dominate the process of defining cultural norms.

As we move into the 21st century, especially in a highly scientific and technological society that has changed from a labor intensified economy to one that functions with computers and technology, the distinctions between men's and women's work will evaporate. If the workplace is able to move to an enlightened state, perhaps similar actions will prevail in the home.

While spending three years in the United States Army, I learned a great lesson. I, like all the other men, had to make my bed, clean my work and sleep areas, do kitchen duty and perform other acts that had been defined by U.S. culture as women's work. It seems to me that if we could do so-called "women's work" in the Army, then we can do it in civilian life, especially if our mates are working full-time jobs also.

It is insensitive and callous for men to expect their wives or mates, who often work eight hours, to come home and cook the food, clean the apartment, feed their children and husbands, do the dishes, mop the floors, wash the clothes and perform other household chores. If Black women are to advance and develop, they need time for self-realization. The sharing of housework does not diminish a man's masculinity; rather, it affirms a man's sense of fairness, love and security.

Gender Distinctions

The bottom line is this: if we are to develop as people, enlightened education requires that gender distinctions be minimized to those areas where such distinctions are vital and necessary. Understand that I am not pushing for a gender-free society but a society where one is not oppressed due to sex, race, religion, etc.

It is obvious that women cannot be replaced as mothers, nor men as fathers, without serious and often detrimental disruptions of the family. The family is a priority, and one must be clear that the ideal family structure is one where partners (men and women) communicate. Parenting and home duties are not pre-defined as something only women do. Serious development is a family activity that must include all members of the family.

12

1. We need an immediate halt to the destruction of Black families. This means that: a) examples of stable families have to exist; b) family-making has to be taught; c) young people should be discouraged from getting married at an early age; d) all our institutions should stress the emotional, economic and political benefits of strong Black families; e) Black families currently in difficulty should seek adequate family counseling; f) family support networks (indigenous and state-supplied) need development.

2. Black families should be nonviolent. Domestic violence, whatever the reason, should be outlawed. The increasing problems of battered Black women, as well as all forms of rape that often go unreported, must be addressed: a) conscious men need to help unconscious men (e.g., workshops, sports outings, clubs); b) shelters for battered women and children need to be supported; c) help for Black men unable to control their aggression towards mates and children is needed.

3. The great majority of our art and creative production must stress: a) strong families; b) self-respect, self-reliance and self-protection; c) the love of self and one's people; d) the need for functional education at all ages; e) strong political involvement; and f) institutional development (e.g., schools, churches, political clubs, social clubs and self-defense units). It is clear that we must create a mass Black media that can turn the negative tide of the mass white media.

4. We have to organize and demand full employment, better housing and quality education that will prepare us for the 21st century. It is also clear that we cannot be totally dependent upon the state for all of our needs. We must always seek alternatives to what is "given" to us.

5. Strong, innovative young adult programs need to be instituted immediately. Our youth are forever looking for productive programs, but there are very few. Structured youth development in an atmosphere of love and discipline is urgently needed.

6. The adult and juvenile justice systems need a complete overhaul.

National Problem

Youthful aggression and violence are learned behavior, and cannot be blamed totally on "female-headed households" or the lack of male presence. What is missing is an all-encompassing developmental environment where adequate support systems exist. This is a national problem, and it is the federal government's responsibility to aid in the development of social policies and intervention procedures that will support current and new family structures.

Effective political and social organizing is all but impossible if we do not rebuild from the inside. Strong families are key to fighting crime as well as building a strong people.

The answers are not as difficult as we expect them to be; much work has already been produced in this area. It is imperative that the national associations of Black social workers and Black psychologists join hands and minds and design programs that will positively impact our people.

Our approach to knowledge, especially the written word, should be at as serious a level as our approaches to lovemaking and war. Remember that the only places in the Western world where large quantities of "pertinent" knowledge (information) are stored are in government, educational, military and corporate computerized data banks and libraries (books).

Black people, en masse, do not have free and unlimited access to the data banks, and our accessibility to libraries and books is automatically and seriously curtailed as young Blacks become increasingly disrespectful of the written word. The old saying, "The best way to hide something from black people is to put it in a book," is quickly becoming reality. We are fighting for the minds of our people as well as the just development of the world.

High School Reading

Think of the possibilities, if before graduation, all Black high school students had to study and digest the works of Richard Wright, Gwendolyn Brooks, Sterling Brown, Chester Himes, Margaret Walker Alexander, Langston Hughes, Maulana Karenga, Sonia Sanchez, Lerone Bennett,

Harold Cruse, Sam Yette, Chancellor Williams, Mari Evans, W.E.B. Du Bois and others. What would be the results of that?

That's our mission if we believe in the future of Black people. We must develop not only a literate generation but one which also is politically and culturally aware. Reading is a major life developing requirement.

General knowledge doubles itself about every six years, and scientific knowledge doubles every two to three years. There are approximately 56,000 books published in the U.S. each year and an unbelievable number of specialized magazines, scholarly journals and monographs. Newsletters and special interest papers also flood the market.

The U.S. may not be the most literate nation in the world, but it certainly has more information available to the general public than any other nation. The great majority of information that is freely circulated goes untouched by the Black community, either because of ignorance or non-concern. The need for a highly literate and analytical mind to deal with today's world is not considered as important as basketball or hairstyles. Until our priorities change, we will not be able to compete or complete our task.

Education Of Children

Mothers and fathers, on special days (and not so special days), buy your child a book instead of candy or toys. When birthdays come around, introduce your children to the beauty of words. Limit television and comic books. To do less speaks of death in its most lasting form — the slow but efficient erosion of the mind.

A mindless people is a people that joins rather than initiates, obeys rather than questions, follows rather than leads, begs rather than takes. To allow this state of affairs to continue is, indeed, a serious and profound comment on the state of our literacy. Let's move the brothers off the corners, put them back into serious learning situations, and introduce them to new definitions. A good place to begin is with a re-evaluation of what it means to be a Black man in this world. Therefore, a working definition of Black manhood is needed:

15

your people first. a quiet strength. the positioning of oneself so that observation comes before reaction, where study is preferred to night life, where emotion is not seen as a weakness. love for self, family, children, and extensions of self is beyond the verbal.

making your life accessible to children in meaningful ways. able to recognize the war we are in and doing anything to take care of family so long as it doesn't harm or negatively affect other Black people. willing to share resources to the maximum. willing to struggle unrelentingly against the evils of this world, especially evils that directly threaten the development of our people.

to seek and be that which is just, good and correct. properly positioning oneself in the context of our people. a listener, a student, a historian seeking hidden truths. one who develops leadership qualities and demands the same qualities of those who have been chosen to lead. sees material rewards as means toward an end and not an end in themselves. clean — mentally, spiritually and physically. protector of Black weak. one who respects elders. practical idealist, questioner of the universe and spiritually in tune with the best of the universe. honest and trusting, your word is your connector.

direction giver. husband. sensitive to Black women's needs and aspirations, realizing that it is not necessary for them to completely absorb themselves into us but that nothing separates the communication between us. a seeker of truth. a worker of the first order. teacher. example of what is to be. fighter. a builder with vision. connects land to liberation. a student of peace and war. statesman and warrior. one who is able to provide as well as receive. culturally sound. creative. a motivator and stimulator of others.

a lover of life and all that is beautiful. one who is constantly growing and who learns from mistakes. a challenger of the known and the unknown. the first to admit that he does not know as he seeks to find out. able to solicit the best out of self and others. soft. strong. not afraid to

16

take the lead. creative father. organized and organizer. a brother to brothers. a brother to sisters. understanding. patient. a winner. maintainer of the i can, i must, i will attitude toward Black struggle and life. a builder of the necessary. always and always in a process of growth and without a doubt believes that our values and traditions are not negotiable.

REFERENCES

Hall, Edward T. *Beyond Culture.* Garden City: Doubleday, 1977.

Harris, Marvin. *America Now.* New York: Touchstone Books, 1982.

Thompson, Laura. *The Secret of Culture.* New York: Random House, 1969.

Greed is Only the Beginning:
Leadership, Money, Persona and Hypocrisy

On the streets the word is "Greed is not enough." In fact, among the junior players, it's "Greed plus anything else you can get," or "Enough is never too much." Hopefully, these sentiments are shared by only a few people. But if one is to measure the greed factor by the judges, lawyers, stock brokers, politicians, and junior Black players that populate the state and federal prisons, it would seem that "we've only just begun."

I

Part of the problem in Black communities is that too many talented, gifted, professional, artistic and wealthy persons leave. Not only do many of these people seldom return, for the most part they do not make significant contributions (financial or otherwise) to their people.

A lifetime membership in the NAACP or $1,000 donation to the local Afrikan American museum, Black theatre or Black charity is not really a significant contribution if a person is truly well off. If we survey the number of Black doctors, lawyers, professionals, entertainers, sports figures and business persons whose yearly net worth is beyond $100,000, it becomes a national shame to view the demise of Black communities across America.

I get tired of reading each week or month in *Ebony*, *Jet* and *Black Enterprise* about the latest Black millionaire, or the newest negro to close the multi-billion dollar deal for white people. I've had enough of reading and hearing about Reggie Jackson's cars, Wilt Chamberlain's beds, Diana Ross' houses (and marriages to white men), Sydney Portier's Caribbean paradise, Eddie Murphy's parties, Walter Payton's guns, and Oprah Winfrey's diet. Where are the serious rich among our people who are concerned about the vast majority of Black people — those who are poor, ignorant and see no hope of advancement or improvement in their future?

Yes, we do have some exceptional Black people with money. Ed and Bettiann Gardner of Soft Sheen restored the Regal Theatre (a theatre in

19

the Black community) and are known for aiding the Black arts. Bill and Camille Cosby ran to aid Fisk University and are out front making significant contributions to their people ($20 million to Spelman College). Ossie Davis and Ruby Dee have always been at the starting line of giving back to the "roots" of their beginnings. However, it is sad to say there are tens of thousands of Black people in the United States with serious money, skills and talent who do nothing except talk bad about their own people and compete in the Western race for conspicuous consumption champions.

The real dilemma among most Blacks with money is that of *values*. Really, how many houses does one need; how many cars can one drive; how many vacations to Europe and the Caribbean in a year are needed; how many closets of clothes can one wear; how much money must one accumulate to be successful or prove a point; and how much jewelry is necessary to make a statement of *wealth*? The Black poor and middle class, by comparison, give more to the less fortunate of our people than the Black rich. Many will observe, "That's why they are rich." Don't buy into that answer. The Black rich and the white rich are different and respond differently to their respective communities. The two groups also view their responsibilities to their people differently.

The white rich start foundations, build art centers, finance new wings for museums and libraries, endow university chairs and create scholarships for the less fortunate of their people and others. The white rich finance all types of summer camps, help keep white businesses viable, start independent think tanks, support their writers, artists and musicians and buy sports franchises. The major business of the white rich is world control and dominance while legitimizing the white way of life. The white rich hide their money and entrust their futures to lawyers, bankers, accountants, stock brokers and a highly trained and professional armed forces.

II

I've listened to revolutionary rhetoric for thirty years, and I've been accused of leaving a little of such rhetoric around myself. I've heard some of our most progressive "seers" talk about the new brotherhood and sisterhood of Blackness. I've been involved in and sat through heated debates in Tanzania and Algeria, in Washington, D.C. and Los Angeles, in smoke-filled rooms at retreats in North Carolina and Chicago, deciding the fate of the Black race as if the "seers" had that power. We've talked about the important issues of our people while our respect and love for each other slowly faded with the sunset, being replaced with the big "revolutionary" picture.

I now know that not only is it possible to smile and lie at the same time, but many of us have been convinced that it's *logical*. Somehow, I think that in fighting our "enemies" we've created new "enemies." For example, at many predominantly "Black" or "historically Black" universities, the "New Negro" administrators run their institutions like 16th century plantations, as if the faculty are children and the students are babies. I worry about the current and next generation of Afrikan American students. For many of them to *think* for more than thirty seconds is a probable cause for brain damage. Yet, their examples (us) are often men and women (mainly men) who talk a good game and invent the "right" words, but whose day-to-day actions—private and public—would, in a head-to-head competition, put most soap operas out of business.

This issue of the private and the public persona needs to be examined because we know, *we really do know*, that Mayor Getup, in fact, is a confirmed drug addict or alcoholic behind closed doors. However, his public pronouncements against drugs and alcohol put him to the right of Nancy Reagan. Publicly, Attorney Smith is at the forefront of advocating the rights of women and children, but back on the ranch he physically and verbally abuses his family and female associates; and most brothers encourage such actions by saying or doing nothing. Each Sunday morning Rev. Dr. So-And-So shouts eloquently about the need for morality, but privately he chases little boys and can't keep his hands off of his stepdaughter. Dr. Akhtar is quick to preach honesty among the people, but under the covers he sells his people bogus insurance and vacations to whore houses in Europe and the Caribbean. In the public's eye Mayor The-Buck-Stops-Here presents himself as a serious stand up politician who can't be be bought, but he allows bombs to be dropped on Black people. And finally, Dr. Such-And-Such raves abundantly across the country about how egalitarian his business or department runs, but privately his people can't take a decent bowel movement without his permission in writing. This is the point: the persons we often see in leadership positions are not the real men or women we think they are, but are studied creations of *false and disguised images* which, more often than not, take

21

advantage of and will pimp off Blackness as quickly as they buy weekly lottery tickets. In fact, Black people are to this leadership a private lottery to be played whenever they wish — generally, every Sunday morning or around election time. *Integrity* has become a noun that is missing from our vocabulary, and the only *honor* that exists is among thieves and an incestuous leadership that has lost touch with reality. *And*, it must be made very clear that this leadership is made up of 98% Afrikan American men. Nationally, Black women are still tokens in Black leadership positions, and they are nonexistent at the international level.

The money that Black people earn in the U.S. (and most of our money comes from wages) stays in the Black community for about four hours. Again, it's a question of *values*, *beliefs* and *knowledge*. However, one should not be too critical of the Black poor and middle class when they see the Black "well off" with afterburners on escaping to live, work, shop and play with whites. The $200 billion Afrikan American economy that Black leaders so often brag about is not an economy based upon Afrikan Americans' production of goods, or the distribution of indigenous products or services. The $200 billion Black economy is based upon Black people working for white people. Such an "economy" would end if white people ceased to employ Afrikan Americans. The major "businesses' in the Black community are the *church*, drugs and crippling consumerism. However, this does not mean that such an economy cannot be improved upon and transformed to aid in our own rebuilding.

III

There are *two* types of Afrikan American people that make it "big" in the Western world. The first is the *thief* in $2000 suits, with an idea, a lot of get-up-and-go and a Ph.D. in street smarts. This person has a frontier mentality of shoot first and answer questions if caught. Many politicians, business persons and big time preachers would fall into this category. This Type I person is a born and cultivated hustler and is often highly intelligent; he or she understands the psychology of the oppressed and the needs of former slaves, negroes, coloreds, Blacks, Afrikans and new slaves and will take advantage of all of them if given the opportunity or, better yet, the opening. Life to him or her is a poker game.

Type I hustler's belief in himself or herself boarders on the psychotic. His or her ego far surpasses anything that the artist, musician, actor, writer or performer needs to be successful. Self adulation and the need to be surrounded with yes people is crucial to the success of this person. This person has the style of a Duke Ellington without the substance, the ambition of an Oprah Winfrey without the backing and the mind of a petty criminal that got lucky. His or her working belief is "catch a sucker, bump his head," and the motto of this hustler is "find the weakness, exploit the need; if possible, avoid checks — cash only."

The other person that generally makes it in the West is the true visionary that plows ahead against tremendous odds to bring beauty into this world. Such persons fall into several categories, but I will highlight only two.

Visionary A is the man or woman with talent who has had the good fortune of living in an environment where such talent is encouraged and cultivated. This person is generally very creative and gifted and shares his or her gift with others. This person may create as a writer, visual artist, dancer, actor, musician, inventor or designer. Persons in this group spend most of their time creating and working at their art, designs or inventions; most of them are successful in their creating. However, they give away too much, and it is far too easy to get to their *hearts*. They are loving and caring people, and if they do not come in contact with serious and fair minded business people, they may work themselves into an early grave — primarily because most of them have to work "outside" jobs in order to live and are "single" focused. They do not take care of their bodies. And their families are generally "second" to their creative work.

Visionary B is the same as Visionary A with one big exception. He or she has the added insight of understanding that talent and creative genius in America are like intelligent Presidential candidates, neither will make it without proper packaging, management and serious resources. Visionary B is the creative person who takes the arts one step further; she or he makes it possible for the art form or product to get to the people or consumer. These are the people who often sacrifice their own personal creative years for the big picture. Hoyt W. Fuller in his cultivation of young writers; Dudley Randall in his founding of Broadside Press; Naomi Long Madgett through her Lotus Press; Abena Joan Brown in her ETA Creative Arts Foundation; Safisha Madhubuti through New Concept Development Center (a school for children); Ossie Davis and Ruby Dee in their cultivation of young actors; Margaret and Charles Burroughs and the groundbreaking Du Sable Museum of African American History; and Maulana

Karenga in his creation of Kwanzaa, Kawaida theory and the Nguzo Saba (the seven principles of Blackness). These are just a few cultural stabilizers who need to be identified, listened to, supported, highlighted and honored.

Visionary B people understand the limitations America puts on the artist and serious thinker. They have a burning desire to create institutions and structural support for Afrikan Americans. Many of these visionaries came out of the heat of the Black Power/Civil Rights movement of the sixties. Most of them have defined their needs carefully so as not to find themselves in conflicts of interest between their own work and the works of the artists they support and promote. Most of them have confronted struggle in America on many levels and will not allow their principles to be compromised by short-sighted clowns disguised as concerned Black people. Most Visionary B people live a comfortable "middle class" life but are without serious money. This brings me to the real concern that confronts us: it's not that we don't have leadership; we have the wrong leadership. It's a leadership devoid of ideas, resources or consistent following. It's a leadership that has been consumed by its own greed, its own ego, its own limitations. It's a leadership that ceases to be bold and, worse yet, ceases to listen to bold and creative people who are within their culture but outside of their cult.

IV

I am deeply concerned about the corruption, cynicism, dishonesty, power abuses, sexism and incompetence in our own ranks. I am concerned about our leaders looking evil in the eye and smiling with palms up. I'm concerned about our tendency to tap dance rather than take moral and ethical positions because it means that we must act morally and ethically. I am concerned about Afrikan American people who control large, urban school systems and who have proven beyond a doubt that things *can* get worse. I am concerned about Afrikan American people who have serious personal assets and don't share resources or knowledge with the less fortunate of our people. I am frightened by the "deals" and "treaties" we make — in the name of the people — with the enemies of the world, as we lie to our children about possibilities and future.

But what really digs into my gut is how we lie to each other. The 1989 versions of negroes are much bolder than they've ever been, and they are taking over Black Studies departments, Black universities, Black businesses, Black politics, Black organizations, Black media and Afrikan nations. Things are not right in the Black world. Show me two progressive Afrikan nations, and I'll show you ten that are an embarrassment to the memory of Nkrumah, Du Bois and Queen Ann Nzinga. The political and economic status in most Afrikan nations borders on lunacy. Show me two conscious Black Studies departments, and I'll show you five that are a joke; and if they were not our joke, they would not exist at any serious university. For example, there are people seeking employment in Black Studies who have *never* been involved in serious research of the Afrikan world community. Most of these people got into Black Studies as the last possibility for a university position, and while there they work their behinds off trying to get into other departments. For every three committed Black politicians I can name twenty who will sell their mommas if the deal is right. (Look at the 1989 Mayoral election in Chicago.) Show me an honest politician, and I'll show you someone who is unelectable because honesty, integrity, virtue, goodness, rightness and other ingredients of a *whole* people are quickly fading from our lives. They have been replaced with an arrogant pimpism that has aided in the subtle, but effective, destruction of our community.

What I'm trying to make clear to others and myself is that serious, honest, incorruptible, ethical and competent men and women are in the clear minority in Black America. Such people need to be identified, encouraged, supported, rewarded and protected. Black thinkers are constantly caught between a hurricane and a volcano. For example, to constructively question or criticize Afrikan American leaders like Jesse Jackson, Louis Farrakhan, Coretta Scott King, Benjamin Hooks or the *Big Black* in any city is not looked upon by this leadership or the majority of Black people as the responsibility or duty of serious thinkers and activists. Rather, such actions often are reduced to a *betrayal of the race*. Black people who think or, more accurately, those who think and disagree with the accepted line, no matter how inadequate a policy or program may be are always suspect and locked out. The reaction of the public to the criticism of accepted Black leadership often is personal, overlooks the possible validity of the criticism, and reduces a public problem to a personal one. As long as our condition is reduced to the egos of a few insecure men and women, there can *never* be progress or development.

25

Leadership by personality is cultism, and we all know where that can lead us. I hope that we've not forgotten Jonestown.

That which is missing in much of our leadership and community is a moral and rebuilding consciousness. We need a home-based regeneration. This act of re-creation must come from home-based activity in all walks of life. This will not be an easy task but one that demands that absolute best from all of us. John W. Gardner, in his important book *Morale*, states, "What makes a collection of people a society is the cohesiveness that stems out of shared values, purposes, and belief systems. When the inner cohesion dissolves, nothing remains." I contend that our "inner cohesion," or what I call *inner spirit*, has eroded with the acceptance of "integration," a national welfare system and a Euro-American worldview of success and possibilities. We have lost *our way*.

Regaining the incentive is not impossible. We need direction and a redefined purpose (i.e., focused lives that are based upon shared values, common needs, individual commitments, an understanding of the future and a willingness to accept light rather than weakening darkness). We need family, leadership and institutions. I often say that Black people in the Western Hemisphere are the real miracle on this landscape, and we need only to recapture our original music to survive this war. However, as we enter the 21st century, survival clearly is not enough. We've survived since we've been in the West. The crucial need today is for measurable progress and development for the majority of our people and not just for the talented few.

We need a new leadership that truly believes in our community and is willing to invest its time, resources and spirit in rebuilding. Again, quoting Gardner:

> There is risk for those who take the lead in rebuilding. People who act and initiate make mistakes. People seeking the path to the future often wind up in blind alleys. Those who have the confidence to act creatively to regenerate the society must also have the humility to know the danger of overestimating what they can accomplish.

However, on the brighter side, somehow I don't think Sonia Sanchez will betray thirty odd years of work, struggle and creative production for a job. It does not seem to me that Mari Evans — no matter how difficult it gets — will ever go back on forty years of Afrikan-centered work for a literary prize. For the twenty-five years that I've known Dr. Barbara Sizemore and Dr. Duke Jenkins, they have never displayed anything less than love and Afrikan-centered professionalism in their work. If Dr. James Turner and Dr. Ronald Walters give their word, it is done. It is inconceivable that Gwendolyn Brooks, after fifty years of teaching us all, would do anything to repudiate her work. Dr. Frances Cress-Welsing has lost jobs, patients, a school and her health due to the principles by which she lives. We need a whole new ethos that states, emphatically and subtly, that Afrikan American people can do whatever we need to do to advance ourselves. And like other successful cultures, our relationships with other people must be interdependent rather than dependent. If there is to be dependency, let it be within our culture.

When a community loses its foundation (philosophers, writers, poets, visual artists, skilled workers, musicians, professionals, dancers, business people, teachers), there is little left on which to build. The illusory benefits of integration and federal/state welfare, and the acceptance of both as panacea, have had disastrous effects on our people. The strength needed to wage this war is quickly fading into the moonset. There must be a renewed dedication to the values and principles that have enabled us to survive the worse holocaust ever to hit a people. Resistance must be our call, structured activism our plan, conscious sharing our method, a working presence our model — anything less is tantamount to surrender and certain death. This rebuilding must start immediately in those areas that we have the capacity to change: family, leadership and community-based institutions.

History, accurately understood, is very important in our struggle. As former chattel slaves in this country, it is absolutely foolish and stupid to turn to former slave masters for answers, serious aid or empathy in our struggle against them. Black struggle has been like trying to hold onto a slippery bottle of clear, lifesaving water; one may steal a drink or two, but in America the real requirement for liberation is the remaking of the mold in which the container was cast. Such a challenge, it seems, will take a lifetime and then some to complete. But that doesn't mean we should all go into debt, give up, and join the killers of the world.

Many of the activists who were initiated by fire into the Black movement in the sixties have only recently begun to understand the conditions for *true* and *lasting* liberation for Afrikan American people. A people is as strong as its institutions, and the primary institution of any strong people is the family.

Black people's status in the United States is worse than that of many Third World nations. We cannot continue to fool ourselves into believing that white people and others are concerned about our best interests. Two suggestions: 1) Black people in America need to elect an Afrikan American Congress. We need a new leadership that is not self-appointed or made for us by others. We need a new and bold leadership that *truly* will work in the best interests of the *majority* of Black people. Wherever Black people exist in large populations, we should elect representatives to air our views and decide our fate — similar to the function of the U.S. Congress; 2) All *aid* coming to the Black community from the white community should be looked upon and received as *foreign aid*. In 1988 Israel and Egypt received over $4 billion from the U.S. in foreign aid, and few people accused the people in those two countries of being lazy, unemployable or uneducable. Any aid — whether it's food stamps, AFDC, scholarships, grants or food — should be taken out of the category of welfare. We have *never* received our just due for contributing to the wealth of this country. All "welfare" has done is made many of our people into beggars and/or dependents. We never received the promised "40 acres and a mule;" the amount we are owed in reparations is in the trillions of dollars. The Afrikan American Congress would decide on this and other urgent matters facing our people. (Also see *Reparations Yes!* by Lumumba, Obadele and Taifa.)

Individually, we all have to become larger persons — persons who seek and demand *quality* rather than *weakening quantity*, persons who whisper good things to others rather than happy-hour gossip. We must become individuals who encourage, inquire about and, when possible, *help each other while working to eliminate dependency on other people.*

If I've read our philosophers and theologians correctly, what they are saying is, "*Do right.*" If I've correctly digested the Afrikan idea, it is about the transformation of a *can't do* philosophy to a *must do* philosophy. If the work of Garvey, Du Bois, Washington, Nkrumah, Muhammad, King, and Malcolm X means anything, it means not accepting anything less than our best. If I've learned anything from Gwendolyn Brooks, Margaret Burroughs, Margaret Walker, John H. Clarke, Queen Mother Moore, Ossie Davis and Ruby Dee, it is to be progressively consistent in my politics and profoundly kind in my manners. This is what I've learned from those who have survived the sixties and who continue to labor day after day after day, without reward or thank you.

The only voice that can sustain a people is the *inner cultural wisdom* of that people. We've bought and paid doubly for the Eurocentric image; let's now try the Afrikan-centered substance and quality — bring it into our homes, jobs, campuses, prisons, pulpits, politics and institutions. Let us cease being the great waiters and make *quality* our guiding word and winning production our goal.

We must be motivated *activists*. We exist in a world that does not respect people who do not speak up and fight for what is rightfully theirs. We must be able to rejoice in the world in which we find ourselves. It may be true that we've had little voice in the making of this world, but that doesn't mean we will *not have a hand in its reconstruction*.

Fighting in the Dark:
The Negro's Philosophy of Life

1) Ignorant of self, filled with self-hatred and has no *idea* of who he or she is. Runs from knowledge that may alter such feelings.

2) Believes that white people follow their own laws, rules, ethics, pronouncements and declarations. However, the negro will follow white laws, rules, ethics, pronouncements and declarations — even to his own detriment.

3) Believes that in the United States a person's color, hair, religion, politics, wealth and the way he/she speaks English are immaterial and not important to non-Black individuals and institutions.

4) Believes that money can buy one's freedom and liberty.

5) Believes that the answer to the negro's problem is lots of prayer and "who-you-know," Chicago style. Trusts white people and believes that most of them are fair minded on the race question.

6) Believes that a job/position with a Fortune 1000 company is security and progress and that those who do not have such are either lazy, lacking ambition or living in the sixties.

7) Believes that true democracy exists in the United States and that capitalism is the best economic system.

8) Advocates capital punishment, gun control, prayer in schools, anti-quota laws and anti-abortion legislation.

9) In a world ruled by unified groups, the negro is the world's most confirmed individualist. Believes that a person will eventually come and save him.

10) Believes that the mass media (press, television, radio) are fair, unbiased and free.

On The Streets:

A Chicago Cop's Inside Voice

In writing this book, I was missing one voice. It was the voice of the men who are charged with tackling the most difficult problems confronting the Afrikan American community on a daily basis. It was the voice of the men who have to be social workers, educators, protectors, enforcers, friends, enemies, doctors and lawyers: policemen.

I know a few cops. Many of the brothers who were a part of the Civil Rights and Black Power struggle of the sixties are now in law enforcement. In fact, many of the men were responsible for starting the Chicago Afro-American Policemen's League. However, I was not only looking for a person that I had personal knowledge of, but one who was younger than I and was currently working the Chicago streets. My search was a short one; the person I decided to approach for an interview had been in and out of my life for about twenty years.

David Lemieux has been active in the Pan-Afrikanist/Black Nationalist community in Chicago for at least twenty-three years. In the early days he was immediately noticeable because of his skin color; he could almost pass for white. He was one of the few brothers in struggle who was lighter than I, and his hair was totally straight. He also reminded me of myself at his age, he's about eleven years younger than I. Also, like many other light-skinned Blacks, he was forever trying to prove to himself and others (mainly darker-skinned brothers) that he was *really* Black. He was always the first to volunteer for the most difficult tasks. He would take chances that others wouldn't even think about. He was always studying and trying to stay ahead of the "enemy."

David was into weapons. We become close by going to the range together. I was amazed at his proficiency with all types of weapons, from hand guns to assault weapons. With weapons he seemed to be in his natural element. What I had learned in the military about weapons and the "art" of war seemed to have been born in David. When David decided to become a police officer, I was one of the men he consulted. I felt then, as I do now, that he would make a fine Afrikan American police officer. After seven years in the Chicago Police Department, he has thoroughly convinced me that he made a good decision.

As this interview details, he has not forgotten *who he is*, but the realities of the streets have forced him to be more serious and contemplative in his approach and response to the heterogeneous Black community. He is less romantic about being able to solve the very complex problems that Black people face in this country. As he pondered each question, I noticed that his youthful and quick responses of old had been replaced with slow and deliberate answers, more like interpretations or explanations rather than answers set in self-righteous stone.

It was clear that his seven years as a Chicago policeman had taken its toll. His growth was unmistakable, not only in terms of physically aging (strands of gray hair and lines in his face), but also in the wisdom of how he continued to approach each day with a glimmer of hope and spirited determination. He still feels that he can make a difference. Police work and social work are known for their high stress factor. The burn out rate among all police — Black and white — is very high. David had definitely become a "brother-in-blue" among the men and women who shared the uniform. However, he maintains and even nurtures his community relationships. He has not lost touch with those who taught him the way of Black manhood.

This interview was in the works for about six months. We talked at length many times, with me taking handwritten notes. In the final interview we used a tape recorder, and that is what is published here with very little editing. My gratitude to David Lemieux is unlimited.

David: My name is David Lemieux. I'm thirty-six years old. I've been a police officer in Chicago for the last seven years. Prior to becoming a police officer, I worked construction for about seven years. I've had all the miscellaneous boy jobs. I've been a file boy, stock boy, delivery boy, bus boy. I got into the construction industry because at one time I was involved with a group of Hebrews that were going back to Africa to live, and we all decided among us that we would each have some sort of trade. I chose to be a carpenter. Obviously, I never made it to Afrika.

To go back a little bit more, when I was sixteen years old, I was in the Black Panther Party. Way back then the farthest thing from my mind was being a police officer. The police were certainly considered our enemy for several reasons. First, they were the police and they represented the military arm of the government, and secondly, most of them were white, and we recognized basically that Caucasians were our enemy. So, the police department was never an organization that I would consider aligning myself with. As I got older and observed the situation in the community and how the community was being destroyed from the inside out, as well as from external pressure, I wanted to do something about that. I've been involved with different people, different groups of brothers at different times, and we thought that perhaps we could move on certain problems in the community on our own and be successful. That never really worked out very well. Unfortunately, the way things are set up, when a private citizen tries to remedy some of the problems in his community, if he takes overt action, he places himself in more jeopardy than the good that he's trying to accomplish is worth. That's just the way it is right now because there's not enough support from the community; and such actions only work when the community at large is behind this sort of thing.

I'd considered becoming a police officer way back. I think that the police test was given in '76 and it cross my mind to take it, and I said, "No, that's ridiculous." The test was given again in '81. By this time I was twenty-eight or twenty-nine years old. I took the test because I've always been military in my spirit. I've always wanted to do things, put my hands on things, sometimes put my hands on people. I've considered myself a soldier or a warrior for the race since I was thirteen years old. I was not in the military. I came of age during the Vietnam years, and I certainly wasn't going to Vietnam. My politics rejected that. So, I saw the police department as possibly a vehicle that I could use to legitimize being armed. I've been armed almost all the time since I was sixteen. I figured that I could use the police department as a vehicle to legitimize that basic need, but much further than that, to give me a chance to intervene on some of the problems that are in our community. So, I took the test, and I was fortunate enough that I didn't have to wait a long time to be called. Within about a year's time I was at the academy.

Now, going to the police academy was very much like going back to high school. It involved some of the same indignation that I would have imagined they have in the military. They try to get you very involved in the group, being a member of their department brotherhood in blue and all that. Most of the stuff falls, pretty much, on deaf ears. At the age of twenty-nine, I had a realistic appraisal of where Black people stood in

35

relation to other people and made it through the academy. I did well at some things there.

I won an award in shooting, which is no big thing to me. It was nice being in front of other people who are not accustomed to seeing Black men excel at that sort of thing. I was assigned to a district on the southside of Chicago. I worked in uniform for a year and did some of the more mundane police work like writing reports, traffic accidents and giving out parking tickets, but also I did start to make some pretty decent arrests. I wanted to be in plain clothes from the time that I came on the job. I saw that it was something that I could do. In about a year's time, after almost daily harassing some of the people who were in charge of the plain clothes unit in the district, they finally assigned me to the tactical unit, and I've been working tact for the most part for the last six years. What we do mainly is narcotics and violent crimes. We deal with the more serious crimes that are called "part one," which are the felonies, and we deal with the narcotics and also a little gambling and prostitution.

Haki: How did becoming a police officer affect your relationship with your family? How did it affect your relationship with other brothers and friends?

David: As far as my friends were concerned, I was blessed in the fact that I did discuss my decision with people that I've known for years, people in what I would describe as the Afrikan community, people with the same politics as my own and the same philosophy that I have. I thought at first I'd meet a negative reaction, that people would say, "How can you do that?" But, the reaction that I get more often than not is, "We need more brothers like you on the force. We need people that think the way that you do because we're certainly not going to get the service that the community is in bad need of from people who don't have any interest in what happens to us. At the very least, the other people will be indifferent to our needs, and at worst, they'll be hostile to our needs, which will make our existence even worse." So, for the most part, people in the community that I spoke with prior to coming on the job were supportive. Now, as far as family is concerned, they weren't thrilled about it — because of the danger of the job more so than anything else. I haven't run into any philosophical problems with anybody. It was mainly just the danger. It is dangerous — although I felt more in harm's way while working construction than I have on this job.

Haki: What is the relationship that you have with the other police officers?

David: That's a good question. I have a circle of people that I work around that I would say know me pretty well or that I have a very good rapport with. I would say that I am considered somewhat of an oddity because of the way I act and express myself and because of the way I dress. A lot of things that are taken for granted in the cultural and Pan Afrikanist community are considered odd by outsiders. We get very isolated because we only deal with people who are about the same things that we're into. Well, on this job I'm around people who are the antithesis of everything that we represent. I'm not just talking about the other police officers who may have an adversary attitude about what I believe in, but I'm also talking about the people in the community that I come in contact with. In general, I get along. I think I'm well liked, or at least I should say, "I'm well respected," even though I'm sure that those who don't like me respect me because of my work. I make a lot of arrests and I make them with a clean conscience. When I jail people, these are people that the community need not have around. I never had any problem with that. I think that in six years I've made one or two arrests that I wish that I could have gone and unarrested. Considering I've probably made a thousand arrests, that's not bad.

Haki: Out of the thousands of people that you've arrested, what percentage of them are Black men and what ages are these Black men? And what percentage are white men?

David: I work almost exclusively in the Black community. White boys don't come through our community to commit crimes. In six years, I've arrested ten white people. The reality is that the crimes in our community are committed by Black people against Black people.

I have tried to consciously observe what is happening to us as a people for at least twenty-two years. I became involved in the movement when I was thirteen; I was still in grade school. I'm thirty-six now. That's well over twenty years of Black street experience. I have observed with

37

vested interest what's happening to our people and what's happening to our community. It would seem to me that our exposure to this alien culture in the United States has had the effect on our people that reminds me of these science fiction movies where they drop an atomic bomb somewhere and you see all these people running around with four arms and three legs — mutations. It would seem that our exposure to this constant war against our whole spirit, psyche and self-esteem has created almost generations of mutants of people. There's almost nothing else left to build on. It's like the eggs that you buy in the supermarket; a hen can sit on an egg until she dies, and no chick will ever come from it because it no longer has the necessary ingredients to promote life; it has a clear sticky fluid that looks like life fluid and a yellowish mass that looks like yoke, but it doesn't contain the genetic information to produce life. This is what I think has happened in a large degree to our community. A lot of the of the genetic information to promote life has been destroyed. There has been so much death and disease and unhealthiness. I'm not just talking about physically, mentally, spiritually, emotionally or materially, but at every possible level. There has been too much death generated in our community — in the minds of our children, elders and everybody in between. Generations of losers are created.

Many Black adults find it very difficult to locate fertile ground for creative and life-giving thoughts and actions. An example is this: I arrested a guy for burglary one time. This brother had gone downstairs to his neighbor's apartment, kicked in the door, stole his neighbor's stereo set, took it upstairs, and set it up in his house. Well, his neighbor comes home and calls the police, and after our little investigation, we were able to get inside and find out that his equipment was right at this other guy's house. Now, this was not a dope dealer gone bad. This was not, "He owes me some money." It wasn't anything like that. It was simply, "I will go downstairs and steal what's in this guy's house and take it to my house." Well, both the victim and the offender were in their early twenties. I had the offender in the room and I was talking to him, and I was pretty new on the job. As a matter of fact, I was still in uniform back then. I haven't been in uniform for about five years. And I talked to him, "Now brother, listen. Think about what you've done. You've gone downstairs, you've stolen this stuff from your neighbor. Maybe you don't understand the relationship that Black people should have to one another." Now, I'm saying all this to him. This is the police, the uniformed police standing here giving this brother a lecture on Black awareness. That's what I was doing. I said, "Even if you don't understand how we should relate to each other as a community, you should at least figure, 'Well, he's my next door neighbor. I'll watch his back, he'll watch my back.' If nothing else, there would be some kind of relationship there. You're a young brother in your twenties. He's a young brother in his twenties. I'm sure that whatever you have you had to strive for and struggle to get and he had to do the same thing." So, I'm talking to this brother like this, saying all what I consider to be the most sensible things. I talked to him for a while — fifteen, twenty minutes, and when I finally paused, he said, "Are you through?" I said, "Yeah." He said, "Let me tell you what I think about what you just said." And he spit on the floor; he actually spit on the floor. He said, "Man, fuck some Black people!" Now, see that attitude, that's not the rare attitude; that's the common attitude. It would be OK if you only ran into this now and then.

Haki: Common attitude among whom?

David: The community at large does not have race consciousness or Black consciousness. I mean, we are always aware of our Blackness in the sense that we are aware of the difference in the way we look from the way that some other group of people look, but as far as our Blackness as a positive bond to one another, no. That's not the general feeling of the community. I would say that feeling did manifest itself when Harold Washington was elected. It was because of something we could focus on as a community. Our Blackness is the most permanent circumstance to anything that happens in our life. But, it is not perceived that way by the community at large, certainly not in a positive way.

Haki: What do you think is the cause of this? Do you see any redeeming factors that could possibly turn this around?

David: What disturbs me most about my perception of other Black men across the board is that despite the movement of the '60s, despite better access to information about ourselves, it still appears to me that we do not love ourselves for what we are. Black Americans, Black people that live in the United States, people of Afrikan descent that live here still reject those things in us that are most Afrikan. We still do not like "nappy" hair, "dark" skin, "thick" lips, "broad" noses, those very essential personal traits about Blackness. Afrikan characteristics are rejected. However, most Black people have "nappy" hair, "dark" skin, "full" lips. So, those very things which are most common among us are still the most unloved.

The reason that I am mentioning this is because I don't see that as superficial; I see that as something very, very deep. You still have Black women coming up to a child saying, "Oh, you got good hair, or "Oh, you got bad hair." This is some stuff that goes all the way back to slavery, all the way back to our initial encounter with the Europeans. I think that the lack of racial self-esteem is at the core of everything. Certainly, we can speak about the historical causes of enslavement and of our presence here. I don't have to document that. The final outcome of our experience here has been this very personalized self-hatred having to do very much with the way we look. Ironically, I am very light complexioned. And, because an issue is made out of complexion in our community, I have very personal experiences with the way our people assess each other based on color. When someone tells a dark brown-skinned woman because they see her with a very light-skinned man, "Oh, you all will have pretty babies," they are not saying that because of any reason other than the fact than that if this darker-skinned person has a child with this person who is lighter than her, there's a chance that the offspring's going to be lighter at least than the woman who bares it. That's sick, that's very sick. I don't think white people do that at all. I just don't see that. There is a perception of beauty that's based on symmetry and certain things among Europeans. Maybe if two attractive white people were together perhaps someone would say to them, "Yes, you all are going to have attractive children." But, a dark-skinned brother could be with a light-skinned woman that looks like a toad and someone is gonna say to him, "You all are going to have pretty children," because that child may be lighter. Or, a dark-skinned sister could be with a light-skinned man that looks like a toad, and someone is going to say, "Ah, you all are going to have some pretty babies," simply because in his mind there is a belief that the complexion is gonna change. Well, I've never heard a white man say about a white woman, "She's too white." I've never heard that. Now, I've worked around white men. I've worked construction. I've worked around plenty of them. We use to work on job sites, and white women walked pass the job sites, and the men would stand out there and look at them and whistle at them and stuff. Not once, and I was listening to them, that's for damn sure, but not

40

once did I hear a white man say to another white man, "Man, she's too white." Not once. But, I wish I had a dollar for each time I heard a Black man say, "She's too Black," or every time I heard a Black woman say, "He's too Black." Now, keep in mind there is a segment of our community that is not like that, obviously. But, in general, who do most Black people think are the most beautiful Black women? Jane Kennedy, yellow woman. What's this Miss America lady — Vanessa Williams, little yellow woman. I'm not faulting these sisters for their complexion; I'm light-skinned. We're not in control of how our complexions come out, but it's the way that our people approach the standards of beauty which are still white, European and anti-Black. It's not a thing of we appreciate this and we appreciate that. We appreciate this at the exclusion of that, you know, and that's not good.

Haki: Getting back to the Black men...specifically, what do you see as the major problem? What is the state of young Black men in Chicago?

David: I would say confused. No, you're only confused if you're pondering a question and you don't know what's going on. The confusion comes when you're seeking a solution without any success. So, "confused" wouldn't be a good word. It's horrible, it's horrible.

Haki: What do you mean "horrible"?

David: It's horrible in the sense...Our people, our young people don't love the things about themselves that are already there. In other words, our young Black men don't have any — you know, this sound so trite — no positive heroes, but there's really no other way to put it. I mean, money is admired. Obvious consumption is admired. It's like the dope dealers set the standards for acquisitions.

Haki: And what about a man like Jesse Jackson or Louis Farrakhan as freedom fighters?

David: Well, you know it would seem that young Black men in their late teens and early twenties don't pay a lot of attention to people like Jackson and Farrakhan. Well, to give an example, I had a button once with Farrakhan's picture on it, and I asked the guy who it was. He said,

41

"I know who that is, that's Jackie Wilson." You know, I mean I was surprised he even knew who Jackie Wilson was. We're so unaware of what we have to be proud of.

Haki: Why do you think that the unawareness exists?

David: We stopped making education that was relevant to us as a people an issue. Black history, Black culture and Black achievement ceased to be important. The information of what we have to be proud of is not getting out to our children. Consequently, they grow up not being proud of anything remotely connected to themselves.

Haki: The majority of the young men that you deal with, are they from single parent homes, foster homes or two-parent homes?

David: I'd say many of them come from single-parent homes. I deal mostly with single parents, mainly women.

Haki: What about single females?

David: Most of the unaware are single Black females although this lack of self-knowledge and this lack of self-esteem seems to be throughout the community. See, I work in the district that encompasses what we would call the low end into the high end. It encompasses Woodlawn, Park Manor, South Shore, Jackson Park, Highlands. So, the community that I work in has on one block homes that cost three hundred and fifty thousand dollars, and two blocks away there are people that are living six in one little room with rats and roaches and the whole deal. So, all the economic levels of our people are represented in the community that I work in, but this attitude or lack of understanding of who we are and what we should be about seems to run through both communities.

It is true, yes, that there's a disproportionate number of homes that are headed by single Black females, and there are a lot of Black men that grow up without fathers. I don't even like the word image — a father reality, a male, a positive male reality. I mean, that person doesn't have to be the children's biological father, just any positive male reality. This is a man; these are the expectations of the man; this is how the man should be. Well, that's just not happening enough in our community. We think we're men

42

once we start screwing. Our young men become sexually active possibly earlier than other groups of young men. I can only talk about us. I don't know what goes on in the white community, but I know in our community we become sexually active certainly earlier than we should be, and it's totally opposite of the way of traditional African culture. For example, in traditional African culture, the young men are prepared for manhood. Now, what that means is whatever responsibility that men have to fulfill in that society, whether they are hunters, or farmers whatever it is that men do in that particular society, the young men are trained for this by other older men, not just their own fathers but, groups of men, groups of elders — and the same with the women. Whatever it is that women do in the society, whether they are hunters, fisherman or farmers, they're prepared for those responsibilities by other women who have obtained status already. In our community, in general, young brothers are on their own. The major teachers are the streets.

Haki: At what age do you see young men hitting the streets on their own?

David: Well, I'm seeing a lot of fourteen-year-olds and fifteen-year-olds that are living by themselves. What I mean is fourteen-year-olds and fifteen-year-olds already, as we say, think they are grown. They feel as though they're adults. They may be responsible for some of their basic needs. Certainly, there's not great responsibility being taken for the education and protection of these young men. If their needs were being met, they wouldn't be out there roaming the streets at fourteen and fifteen years old, instead of in school where they are supposed to be.

Haki: What do you see as the major problem with Black men?

David: The drug problem is so out of control. It cuts up people coming and going. I tell these little dope dealers that I lock up all the time that I understand why anybody wants to acquire money. You need money in this society to take care of yourself. You need money to buy things with. Nothing is given away free. It's something that you want badly. They are not going to give you transportation. They are not going to give you a car. They are not going to give you decent clothing. They are not going to give you decent shelter. So, if you want to elevate your life-style, you do need money.

Dope is a way to make money, make no mistake about it. But, what I tell them is, "Dope is making a few Black people rich and a whole lot of Black people miserable." Of course, keep in mind what I said earlier about the guy that spit on the floor. I still say this stuff now. I'm sure it has as about as much of an effect now as it did then. It's just that maybe these guys don't feel like my temperament is as stable as it use to be, that maybe if they spit on the floor something might happen to them. But the thing with drugs and the reason that it is drawing so many people is the lure of money. At one time you thought that the dealer was real smart, that the dope dealer did not use his product. Because cocaine is such a prestige thing, you get all these dope dealers self-destructing because they make their money, but they also start using their product, which insures the fact that they are going to go under eventually.

None of this is doing the community at large any good at all. You get the teenagers thinking this shit is great. They see these brothers in these Corvettes and Blazers, you know, nineteen, twenty years old, making several thousand dollars a day. It's very hard to explain this to a fifteen or sixteen-year-old who has never had anything and who all of a sudden has an opportunity to make a lot of money. Not only does he have an opportunity to make a lot of money, but it has been so glamorized that, of course, no one ever thinks that they are going to get caught. And see, that's another thing, we haven't even talked about the penitentiary mentality. I stopped this brother one night, and this was a narcotics investigation, which is mostly what I do. This brother told me that the penitentiary makes a man out of you. Now, this brother is like twenty-three years old. He was standing there. He had his little girlfriend with him. I was so enraged, I was trembling. "You mean to tell me that your freedom just being totally taken away from you and put in a cage is something that makes a man out of you?" The ability to endure hardship may attest to our toughness. Sometimes it just attests to our numbness.

Haki: What do you think he meant by that?

David: He meant that he thought that it was a real test to his mettle to go to the penitentiary and survive. And I said, "Man, that's ridiculous." I asked him if he had younger brothers and sisters. He said he had some

44

younger brothers. I said, "Would you want them to go to the penitentiary?" His answer was, "Well, if they did something and got caught, they could go." And he meant that. He was serious as I am.

Haki: What do you think is happening in the penitentiary?

David: Now, keep in mind I have not been inside any penal institutions. I've been locked up in some of those lock-ups overnight. I have never sat in county for weeks and months and certainly never been in Stateville. I know people who have. From what I see, from what I hear on the street, the fear of the penitentiary is no big thing because the penitentiary is *so* full of Black men, so full of people that people know, it's like a reunion. "Oh, Reggie, what's happening? That's right, you did that robbery, right? Yeah, ok." There's dope in the penitentiary. There's everything else in the penitentiary. Sometimes it becomes a blur whether the community is a extension of the penitentiary's life-style or the penitentiary is an extension of the community's life-style. That's real bad. We have come to accept enslavement as a reality of our existence and not reject it. It's like people who think they have to have bacon and eggs for breakfast every morning. They'll eat bacon and eggs even if they don't taste it. They eat it because it's just a habit. Being incarcerated has become a habit with a large segment of Black men and it's just accepted.

Haki: What group of Black men do you see that exist in our community who have any effect on young Black men? What about the preachers? Ministers are generally considered the male leaders along with the politicians. How do young street men see and deal with that?

David: I'm going to probably step on a lot of toes here, but I think at this point with the eighties attitude, ministers are starting to carry a real stigma of homosexuality. It's like no one is a man. There are churches with large followings and there are ministers that have nothing to do with any homosexuality, I'm sure.

It seems to be an older generation of people that are more involved in the church. I don't see many people flocking to the churches. Keep in mind these observations about the community are always with exception. There will always be groups of us who will go forward and not be beaten down, but I look at the community at large and I really try not to oversimplify. I really, truly believe that the worst problem in our community is a lack of self-esteem as a race. People that really care about who they are are not going to take just anything, they are not gonna take abuse from other people, and they are not going to abuse themselves.

Haki: What about the gang problem?

David: The gangs, as mentioned earlier, are men between the ages of fifteen and twenty-five. Well, it's really extended to Black men between fifteen and forty-five, but at least between fifteen and twenty-five you are in your warrior state. You are also in an immature state because you haven't been on the planet long enough to be wise and to be experienced, so you have a lot of energy that really needs someone to direct it. And that's why it is important to have a culture that's intact as opposed to one that isn't. You have this whole huge group of Black men that have no direction. I'm saying that fourteen to twenty-five-year-olds are not old enough to make quality decisions based on their own experience, and there's no one directing them and no examples for them to make quality decisions based on someone else's wisdom. The gangs are an appeal to people because they are something that someone can belong to. A gang is something that's identifiable. It's something that creates, something that has an element of danger and something that instills fear in other people. Power is an important thing to young people who have been pushed out of society.

Haki: What about this old fear factor? What do you think young men are scared of?

David: Well, I hate to say this, but it sure seems like our people fear the white man. Sometimes in the way of just doing police work...the things that Black citizens will say to Black police officers that they won't say to white police officers. It's like people in the community will treat Black police and white police very different. They fear the white police. They don't necessarily fear Black cops. There are good reasons for them to fear a whole lot of police of color, believe me. They fear the white police, I think, because they don't feel as though they have any win at all with white police, whereas with Black officers they feel they can get over. Again, this is because of our lack of self-esteem. They don't accept the fact that we will the same power. I hate to put it that way, but they sort of reject that. This is not all the time; make no mistake about it. You say, "What do our young men fear the most?" When I say, "The white man," I don't mean the white police necessarily. It just seems that our rebelliousness is directed toward each other and not toward anything else. We fear white people.

Haki: What's the feeling of male cops toward female cops? Have female cops been a force in terms of young Black males? Have they been effective?

David: That's a very relevant issue for me. I've worked with several female police officers. I worked with the first Chicago female officer to be killed in the line of duty. There is such a hellacious disrespect for Black women among Black men and especially among so called "Black" police officers. If they were really Black, they wouldn't disrespect the sisters. Negro police treat Black women horribly. They treat them terribly — sometimes, I think, even worse than the white boy because I think that the white boy has a different idea about women than we do. Not that their perception is necessarily correct, but it's just different and it may not be manifested in as harsh a matter. I think many Black men see themselves in adversary relationships with Black women. It's like a constant battle, and that will be manifested on this job. If a female officer is in an adversary relationship with a Black man, then it will undoubtedly replay itself on the job.

Haki: So, you're saying the Black female officers have the qualifications and capabilities of being a good police officers as far as you're concerned. You do not have problems with them?

David: Not at all. I could talk for a long time about the science, the logistics, or whatever of police work. It's a whole different thing; it's a whole different world, but it is our world. It's something that our community is deeply involved in. It's just like anything else. If you have someone who's a jerk, he's going to be a jerk as a police officer. If you have a nonconscious *negro* who doesn't like himself and doesn't like other Black people, then he's going to be brutal, rude, disrespectful; he's going to make all the same mistakes that the white boy makes. And he's going

47

to hurt us worse because our expectations are greater. If you have someone who's conscious, then you're going to get better service. That's with anything. If you go to the library to get a book, and the librarian doesn't like Black people, you're gonna have a problem.

Haki: What about getting back to Afrikan American men and the question about drugs and gangs?

David: Well, it always sounds like the catch all answer, but the community has to reject drugs. I do know enough about how that has worked in places where it is legal. I think England has some sort of setup where they register their heroin addicts and they go and get their treatments and medication. Something like that may reduce the crime that surrounds narcotics. I say reduce it, not eliminate it.

Haki: Is it worse than alcohol?

David: Yes, I think it's certainly worse than alcohol.

Haki: So, if you legalize marijuana, heroin and so forth, then someone is always in the laboratory making up a new drug.

David: Yes.

Haki: So, you're always going to have a drug problem unless you go to the core of the problem. And the core of the problem is poverty, lack of self-esteem, ignorance and powerlessness. You have politicians saying, "Lets get rid of drugs," etc., etc., but once they get out of the limelight, they shoot-up too. There are few serious examples.

David: Well, they are certainly not serious about drugs. I don't feel that the governmental agencies even on a local level are really serious because they are so out-of-tune with what we have to deal with. I mean, I know it's a problem. I realize that it's a big problem in the white community too. It's not like this is something that's exclusively ours. The reason why it's such a big issue now is because it's become a problem in the white community. It's getting a lot of attention, but as to them being really serious? I can't see it. I think there are some individuals that are serious about it, but do I think that the nation is institutionally serious about it? No.

Haki: What about the courts? Are the defendants predominantly Black?

David: When you go in the court room you think white people don't commit crimes because you hardly see any. I mean, you do see some, but the courts, just like the jails, are full of Black men and women.

Haki: More Black men than any other group?

David: Yes, but I would say I've arrested more women in the past year than I did in the first five.

Haki: Why is that?

David: Narcotics, dope, the status. It's the good life "shit." I mean, these sisters like running with these dope dealers and riding in somebody's Corvette, and they like going to these little lounges and places, sitting up there with the guy with the gold. He'll buy them this and he'll buy them that, but also when the police pull up behind their car, they also sit and let the guys hand them the dope because they think that the police won't find it. But see, we got something for that — that's called "female officers." That doesn't mean anything. I've made some very hostile lectures to some of these young sisters. I say, "OK, y'all think this shit is cute? You'll be sitting in Dwight Penitentiary looking crazy, thinking about how you wasted your young life sitting in somebody's jail 'cause you think it's fun to ride around with this jerk here who's selling poison to the community." Then too, there are more and more women using drugs.

Haki: Any concluding remarks?

David: White people and their systems have us locked in between a rock and a hard place. We cannot depend on them to pull us out of the quick sand they put us in. Even though whites deserve most of the blame, we are not completely clean. If we are to survive, we have to dig deep, we have to take long breaths, we have to be honest around our own weaknesses and corruption. I guess what I'm trying to say is that I don't have all the answers, but I do know that if we don't care for ourselves and do not act in ways that demand respect from others, there is no hope. We've got to clean up home first, and try to understand the very complex ways of the world.

Haki: Thank you.

AIDS: The Purposeful Destruction
of the Black World?

If there was one subject I was sure that I would not write about, it was AIDS (Acquired Immune Deficiency Syndrome). Like most misinformed, confirmed heterosexuals, I was convinced that AIDS was a white middle-class homosexual disease that, at worse, would only touch Black homosexuals. I also felt that the AIDS reports coming out of Afrika were exaggerated, and that white people were doing what they normally do with things that had gotten out of hand, *blame the victim*. As the saying goes, "ignorance is bliss." Well, in this case ignorance kills; and AIDS, unlike anything else that has invaded the Black World or any world, has the potential of devastating the Afrikan population unlike any weapon we've known since the Afrikan holocaust, the enslavement of Afrikan people by Europeans.

My enlightenment occurred because of five unrelated incidents. About two years ago, Dr. Frances Welsing sent me some of her research, including the book *A Survey of Chemical and Biological Warfare* by Cookson and Nottingham, published in 1969. This text details the type of biological and chemical research and warfare being carried on in the Western world. Their work centered on chemical agents for riot control and the rise of biological agents as weapons that could be dispatched unexpectedly on the "enemy." In many ways, the book is a frightening exposé on the early genetic/biological research of mad men parading as scientists. All of this research was/is being supported by the United States, Canada, Britain and West Germany. The crucial thing is that the authors document the early experimentation with viruses that would attack the immune systems of people.

The second and most jarring incident occurred at a national conference where a dear friend admitted during a presentation that her brother had just recently died of AIDS. This friend is a very strong person, a product of the Black Liberation struggle of the sixties and one who does not weaken easily. I could only share her pain from a polite distance, but it was something that I could not forget.

51

In 1988, I received, by mail from the publishers, a copy of Michael Meiers' *Was Jonestown A CIA Medical Experiment?* This 575-page book is the first serious text to look at the Jonestown murders as murders, implying that they were CIA ordered. Mr. Meiers, without doubt or hesitation, theorizes that the 900 people killed (most of whom were Black) were unknowingly involved in a CIA-sponsored human behavior experiment. His documents suggest that "Jim Jones was involved with the CIA and that the medical laboratories at Jonestown were much too large to be consistent with the professed religious purpose of that group." He provides reason to believe that "the purpose of Jonestown was to establish a controlled environment in which a large number of persons could be brainwashed into the act of ultimate self-denial, mass suicide." He also points out that U.S. Representative Ryan, who was also killed at Jonestown, was an "active critic and investigator of CIA activities." Meiers raised too many questions to be ignored.

The next message of death was closer to home. Max Robinson, a friend and brother in struggle, the first Afrikan American news anchor on national network television, became very ill and was isolated in a hospital outside of Chicago. Upon seeing him, I was inwardly crushed by his loss of weight and his emaciated look. It was difficult to keep the tears back. However, Max did not tell me that he had AIDS, and he was in good spirits; according to him, he was improving quickly and would be able to go home soon. I let it go at that, and two months later — without my seeing him again — Max was dead. It was his wish that people know he died of AIDS and that he did not contract it through the *assumed avenues* of drug use or homosexual activity. Max was a woman's man to the bone (one of his problems), and he did drink a great deal. However, he wanted his death to mean something and hoped that his community would begin to respond more positively to the current crisis. He knew that the topic of AIDS was such a taboo in the Afrikan American world that even he, as strong as he was, could only share it with a few family members and trusted friends.

The final alert came Federal Express. A friend from the West Coast sent me a video tape of the work being done by Dr. Theodore A. Strecker. With the tape, he sent piles of other written documentation that convinced me that AIDS is not the next mega-killer, but is *now* ravishing the Black world from Zaire to Haiti, from Zambia to Chicago, from Uganda to Brazil, from Malawi to New York and San Francisco. Here are some of the major misconceptions about AIDS documented in Dr. Strecker's "The Strecker Memorandum" that we need to be immediately aware of:

1) AIDS is a man-made disease.
2) AIDS is not a homosexual disease.
3) AIDS is not a venereal disease.
4) AIDS can be carried by mosquitoes.
5) Condoms will not prevent AIDS.* (This goes against the findings of other research.)
6) There are at least six different AIDS viruses loose in the world.
7) There will never be a vaccine cure.
8) The AIDS virus was introduced into Afrika by the World Health Organization (WHO).
9) The AIDS virus can live outside the body.

Dr. Strecker has unearthed evidence that the AIDS virus was created in a laboratory at Fort Detrick, Maryland from smallpox and hepatitis B vaccines. It is now certain that the World Health Organization introduced the vaccine that contaminated east and central Afrika with the AIDS virus.

Dr. William Campbell Douglass, a fourth-generation physician and the National Health Federation's "Doctor of the Year" in 1987, agrees with Dr. Strecker's assertion that AIDS is man-made. In his book, AIDS: The End of Civilization, he states:

> The world was startled when the *London Times* reported on its front page, May 11, 1987, that the World Health Organization (WHO) had "triggered" the AIDS epidemic in Africa through the WHO

---

*More than one out of every 200 condoms were found to be defective in laboratory tests, a UCLA study has found. The defective condoms either allowed water or air to escape, failed strength tests or leaked the AIDS virus, the Los Angeles Times reports. Brands that allowed the virus to escape, either through pinholes, tears or pores in the rubber membrane, included the Lifestyles Conture Trojan Naturalube, Trojan Ribbed and Contracept Plus. "All condoms may not be equally effective in preventing [AIDS] transmission," the report said. Nevertheless, it's still safer to use even the worst-scoring condom than no condom at all. (Briefing, "Some condoms leak AIDS," September 17, 1989 issue of the Chicago Sun-Times).

smallpox immunization program. The only people in the free world not surprised by the *London Times* front page exposé were the Americans — because they never heard about it. It is chilling to think that our press is so controlled that the most momentous news break since the assassination of President Kennedy didn't even make the sports section, much less the front page *of any American daily paper, radio or television news.*

According to the *London Times* of May 11, 1987 in an article, "Smallpox Vaccine Triggered AIDS Virus" by Pearce Wright:

> Although no detailed figures are available, WHO information indicated that AIDS league table of Central Africa matches the concentration of vaccinations...The greatest spread of HIV infection coincides with the most intense immunization programmer, with the number of people immunized being as follows: Zaire 36,878,000; Zambia 19,060,000; Tanzania 14,972,000; Uganda 11,616,000; Malawi 8,118,000; Ruanda 3,382,000 and Burundi 3,274,000.

Pearce Wright also notes that Brazil was also "covered in the eradication campaign," and that about 14,000 Haitians on United Nations assignment to central Afrika were also infected. Mr. Pearce also states, "Charity and health workers are convinced that millions of new AIDS cases are about to hit southern Africa. After a meeting of fifty experts near Geneva this month it was revealed that up to 75,000,000, one-third of the population, could have the disease within the next five years." And, we know that due to the inhumane nature of the South Afrikan white supremacy system, the Afrikans will be "contained." This containment will "intensify its (AIDS) outbreak by confining the groups into comparatively small, highly populated towns where it will be almost impossible to contain its spread" among Afrikan people. There have been over 50,000 deaths in Afrika already and *it is conservatively believed that close to 75,000,000 Afrikan people could be infected.*

Dr. William C. Douglass, writing in the December 1987 edition of *Health Consciousness* in an article entitled "WHO Murdered Africa," states emphatically that the World Health Organization used Afrikans as the testing ground for the man-made deadly virus AIDS. He points out that this green monkey business was a lie to confuse the world and make small of the epidemic while blaming its origins on Afrikans. Nothing

54

could be further from the truth. Dr. Douglass, quoting from the World Health Organization (WHO), volume 47, pp. 251, 1972, states: "An attempt should be made to see if viruses can in fact exert selective effects on immune functions. The possibility should be looked into that the immune response to the virus itself may be impaired if the infecting virus damages more or less selectively, the cell responding to the virus." The major question being asked is, "Why should anyone want to do this?" I think that the answer is rather simple if one reads this release from Moscow, published in the *Herald Examiner*, June 6, 1987:

> Soviets Charge U.S. Has Germ Weapon To Kill Blacks MOSCOW — U.S. Information Agency director Charles Wick said he broke off talks yesterday with the chief of a Soviet news agency that claims the CIA has a biological weapon for killing blacks. Wick told a news conference at the U.S. Embassy that he received a cable from Washington on Thursday about a dispatch from the Novosti news agency that asserted the Central Intelligence Agency had developed an "ethnic weapon." Summarizing the story, Wick said it claimed that CIA agents "employ war gases in the developing countries" and that "the latest stride in this field is the ethnic weapon, morbific bacteria which is lethal for the Africans but harmless for those of European extraction."

We do know that much of this biological/chemical research re-emerged (much of it started during World War II in Germany) after the rebellions of the 1960s, when white men viewed their cities going up in flames set by Black men and could do nothing. Well, part of their answer, as always, was, "How do we *eliminate* (not solve or understand, but eliminate) the problem?" In the United States, according to these people, Black people — more specifically, Black men — are the problem.

Dr. William C. Douglass is absolutely certain that the AIDS virus did not originate in monkeys, and he states, "In fact it doesn't occur naturally in any animals...AIDS started practically *simultaneously* in the United States, Haiti, Brazil, and Central Africa. (Was the green monkey a jet pilot?) Examination of the gene structure of the green monkey cell proves that it is not genetically possible to transfer the AIDS virus from monkeys to man by natural means." Dr. Theodore Strecker's research clearly shows the connection between the National Cancer Institute (NCI) and the World Health Organization in creating the AIDS virus. Dr. Douglass states:

...they combined the deadly retroviruses, bovine leukemia virus and sheep visna virus, and injected them into human tissue cultures. The result was the AIDS virus, the first human retrovirus known to man and believed to be 100 percent fatal to those infected."

Maybe the reader has doubts about this information, and the one question that continues to tag at him or her is, "Why has AIDS been viewed as a homosexual, and now drug-user, disease when in Afrika it was obviously a heterosexual disease?" I think that the answer is not difficult; the two groups that a great many people in the population do not care about and would not be overly-concerned if they disappeared are homosexuals and drug-users. Their logic is that since AIDS is a homosexual and drug-related disease, then — because "I'm not homosexual, don't use drugs, and don't care for either group — I'm safe. Anyway, AIDS is probably the wrath of God against their evil ways." As I said earlier, such nonsense can get one killed and should be left to the mindless bigots and racists that blame the world's ills on everybody except themselves.

I could go on giving example after example about the eminent danger of AIDS, but I'm sure I made my point. Tony Brown in his syndicated column raised the question and asked another one:

Is it a coincidence that Ft. Detrick, which is where Col. Huxsoll's biological warfare research is being done, is also the site of AIDS research? This coincidence certainly fuels the rumor, whether true or not, that the AIDS virus was genetically engineered at Ft. Detrick and aimed at the same groups that Hitler tried to exterminate in WWII: Blacks (Hitler considered Jews to be non-Whites, among other things); homosexuals; prisoners; and drug addicts. The AIDS epidemic of today is also concentrated worldwide and in the United States among the same groups — if you substitute Blacks for Jews (on whom there is ample genetic research for biological weapons). Another coincidence?

Two other recent books on this man-made disease are *AIDS: Biological Warfare* by retired Lt. Col. T.E. Bearden, and *AIDS and the Third World*, by the PANOS Institute. Also see "AIDS Update," an article by Frank Murray in the September/89 edition of *Better Nutrition*; this article explores a holistic approach to "curing" AIDS.

56

In the white world when it comes to warfare, there are very few *coincidences*. That is why the United States has war colleges, one of the largest standing armed forces in the world, think tanks, and thousands of secret research projects underway at universities and private companies coast to coast. There also exist in this country a spineless media system and a corporate structure that will maintain its power, "by any means necessary." I do not have an answer to this one, except — *educate* yourselves, be understanding of those that are ill and, as always, be *activists* about this and any other death that threatens our community. As we face life, we cannot let the horrors in this world stop us. *Seek preventative health and each day fight for that which is good, just and right, regardless of what others are doing.*

REFERENCES

Bearden, T.E. *AIDS: Biological Warfare*. Greenville: Telsa Book Company, 1988.

Campbell, William. *AIDS: The End of Civilization*. Clayton: Valet Publishers, 1989.

Cookson, John and Nottingham, Judith. *A Survey of Chemical and Biological Warfare*. New York: Monthly Review Press, 1969.

Douglass, William C. "WHO Murdered Africa," *Health Consciousness*. December, 1987.

Michael Meiers. *Was Jonestown A CIA Medical Experiment?* Lewiston: The Edwin Mellen Press, 1988.

The Panos Institute. *AIDS and the Third World*. Philadelphia: New Society Publishers, 1989.

"The Strecker Memorandum" by Theodore A. Strecker (tape and written documents), 1986.

"This is a Bio-Attack Alert" by Theodore A. Strecker, 1986. The Strecker Group, 1216 Wilshire Boulevard, Los Angeles, CA 90017. (213) 548-3198

Wright, Pearce. "Smallpox Vaccine Triggered AIDS Virus," *The London Times*. England. May 11, 1987.

Black Men: Obsolete, Single, Dangerous?

Where is the Future?

It was late Friday on a hot July night that the temperature rose to 101 degrees, driving mothers, fathers and children out of projects and tenements to front stoops, parks, bar stools and small back-alley crap games. Anything to deal with the heat. Johnny J., T.C. and Bigfoot were throwing sevens for small change in the back of the Godfather No. 2 lounge on Chicago's west side.

At about 1:00 a.m., lights from two directions hit their game, and they were ordered to "hug the ground" by two white male cops and one Black female cop. One of the white cops told all three to get up and spread eagle against the wall of the Godfather lounge and ordered the Black woman cop to search the Black men. As the woman went up and down Bigfoot's pants legs he moved as she touched his penis and commented "ain't that a bitch." At that moment, the Black woman cop — hearing only the word "bitch" and feeling his movement — fell backwards, pulled her 38 special, and proceeded with surgeon's accuracy to blow the right side of Bigfoot's head off. The Black woman cop was congratulated, promoted, decorated by her superiors and detailed to another Black community. All three Black men had records, and T.C. and Johnny J. were given three years for resisting arrest. What had been described as "justifiable homocide" was in the real world "one less nigger," murdered not by a white or Black male cop, but by a Black woman cop. Few saw the significance of this act.

Bigfoot, at twenty-five, was in the prime of his life and *never* had a chance. To die at such a young age and at the hands of a Black woman remains a mysterious irony that will plague us as we move into the 21st century. What may be the ultimate and most profound reality of our current situation may well be that some of the mothers that bring life may indeed be the mothers or daughters of mothers that aid Black men and white men in the removal of Black men from this part of the earth. It's a perfect situation. No voices of protest will fill the streets because it is well

59

known that "niggers" with criminal records are fair game for anybody, especially if one has a license to carry a weapon.

Much of the current Black studies have focused on either the Black family, Black women, Afrika, the Black homosexual community or Europe's and America's influence on the Black world. Few Black scholars or activists have given serious attention to the condition of Black men. There are many reasons for this: 1) much of the published scholarly work on Black people is by Black men and many of them do not see the importance of public self-analysis; 2) it is easier to get studies on Black women or the Black family published; 3) few Black male scholars wish to "wash dirty clothes" in public — and the other side of that is if the Black male situation is accurately assessed, it also means for the intelligent scholars and activists to "clean up their own acts;" 4) many of the scholars and activists are actually functioning in their personal lives contrary to the best interests of Black people (some outright traitors) and finally; 5) studies that bring clarity and direction to the Black male situation as an integral part of the Black family/community are unpopular, not easy to get publish and very dangerous. Too many Afrikan American scholars have looked at the Black situation in America from a European sociological framework, and in doing so, their work has been instrumental in distorting reality and exists as a body of "negative ammunition" to secure faculty positions and publishing contracts, and is ego grease for their warped worldview and sense of importance.

Not Allowed To Be Lovers

The root, as well as the quality, of Black life is in the relationship established between Black men and women in a white supremacist system. Black struggle, that is the liberation of our people, starts in the home. This is not to suggest that the dominant society does not affect what happens in the home, but to a significant degree individual members of the family — regardless of the political system they endure — are still able to define relationships among themselves and the society if they are able to *divest* themselves of *role models imposed from the outside*. Indeed, this is not easy and requires an almost complete negation of present values to those that put people in relationships first and prioritize the development of children. Sound and loving relationships are the core of a sane, happy and fruitful life. This is crucial because all too often our patterns of behavior have nothing to do with the real world but are sincere imitations of white European-Amercian madness.

Black life, especially interaction between Black men and women, is perceived from the outside as being fragmented, unstable, insecure, and woman-dominated. This image is solidified by white and Negro doctoral theses and mass media nonsense. If this view of the Black situation is "the" truth (and yes there are elements of truth here), we are indeed in trouble and possibly headed for complete destruction as a people. However, if our family construction, as I believe, was/is built upon a very positive man-woman relationship, one that has enabled us to weather the most severe form of human bondage, then and only then is there hope.

Yes, there is hope, but in the last twenty-seven years or so there has been serious cultural slippage in the Black community to the point that many Black men and women are becoming antagonists, and the liberating cooperation, respect and single-mindedness of spirit and purpose that existed are being replaced with the most gross forms of competition, decadent individualism and sexual exploitation.

Black men in the United States are virtually powerless, landless and moneyless in a land where white manhood is measured by such acquisitions. Most Afrikan Americans have been unable to look at their lives in a historical-racial-political-economic context. Thereby, without the proper tools to analyze, many Black men have defined their lives as Black duplicates of the white male ethos. The problem (and there are many) is that Black men in relationship to Black women cannot, a great majority of the time, deliver the "American dream." Therefore, the dream is often translated into a Black male/female nightmare where Black men, acting out of frustration and *ignorance*, adopt attitudes that are not productive or progressive in relationship to Black women, i.e., many Black men end up treating (or trying to treat) Black women like white men treat white women. The political and sexual games that exist in most cultures of the world that are largely demeaning and disrespectful to women become, due to a lack of *self definition*, Black men's games also.

That this quality of life exists in white America is not unexpected. Alvin Toffler in his persuasive books *Future Shock* and *The Third Wave* forecasted the dismantling of the American family, a concept he called the "end of permanency." To a greater and somewhat extreme degree, other social scientists and novelists (Huxley, 1953; Orwell, 1950) have concluded that the raising of children will be completely taken out of the

61

hands of the biological parents and replaced with state farms, institutions or schools, which will program the children from birth. This, indeed, may well be the wave of the future of child rearing in the west when in reality the development of a good many of the nation's children is currently left to daycare centers, the streets, pre-schools and the favorite standby — television.

The cultural *values* that are the stabilizing ingredients of the Afrikan American family quite often are not coming to the children in a progressive manner from the parents, extended family, cultural institutions or community, but from incompetent training centers, mass media nonsense and negative peer relationships. The cultural imperatives that direct and develop a people — in this case, Black people — are being replaced with chocolate city silliness and spiderman solutions.

Young Black boys are not taught the positive aspects of Black manhood and Afrikan responsibility. And young Black girls by the age of thirteen are more concerned with hair, clothes and how to be sexually active without getting pregnant rather than understanding the life process and their special place in it. Couple this with the failure of *most* educational institutions in the Black community, the oppressive nature of the political system, the non-responsiveness of the economic sector and the killing style of the legal apparatus, and it's truly a wonder that Black people are able to function sanely at any level. The fact that today's Black children are tomorrow's adults is not cause for much jubilation if we are serious about true liberation, true wholeness and bright tomorrows for all people.

There is hope. Black people have survived the middle passage, chattle enslavement, the buffalo and little men in white robes with black books. As dim as the sun's rays are, the *will* remains to conquer this oppressive and impersonal world. In our darkest moments, we must never forget that the United States, actually the West, is not a reflection of Black people, but we, in our sleeping hours (which is sometimes twenty-four hours a day), all too frequently duplicate the negative aspects of it.

Sleeping Hours and Confusion About Existence and White World Supremacy

Of all the species that populate the earth, *homo sapiens* (human beings) are the most unpredictable and complex. A complete and working knowledge of human behavior is still being pieced together by anthropologists, archaeologists, historians, Egyptologists, theologians, ethnologists, political scientists, philosophers, psychologists and socio-biologists (social-biology — the most recent "bioscience" — examines evolution, ecology and animal behavior, as well as takes into account the subject's complete sociological and biological history).

If we can appreciate the difficulty that scientists are having trying to bring meaning, reason, and understanding to the human race, it is no small wonder that the average man or woman is often confused and downright ignorant as to why people function as they do. In terms of analyzing and codifying human behavior, most of us cannot separate *fact* from *theory* or *wishful thinking*. If one is critical, this same judgement can be applied to the social sciences (anthropology, psychology and sociology) and one would not fall too short of detecting astronomical confusion and/or dis-agreement among the scholars as to *why* humans behave a particular way. One can easily spend a lifetime studying the theories and counter-theories of Herbert Spencer, Max Weber, Emile Durkheim, Sigmund Freud, Karl Marx, B.F. Skinner, Jean Piaget, Carl Jung, Alfred Adler, Herbert Mar-cuse and others and emerge totally bedeviled and misdirected. Most of the Western World's most eminent scientists of human behavior can't seem to agree or disagree on anything. The pitiful aspect of this is when a Black social scientist absorbs much of their nonsense, accepts it as undebatable and "god-given" fact, and tries to apply it to the Black situation without question. The "educated" elite of the Western World have made a rather comfortable living out of disagreeing and openly fighting each other over the reasons why people, for example, excrete waste in a sitting position rather than standing.

The major quality that separates men and women from the rest of the animal world is the use of *language* (speech) and the invention of/and adaptation to *culture*. David Barash, in his *The Whisperings Within*, states that human beings:

> form societies in which, for example, age and power are closely al-
> lied, in which relatives are distinguished from non-relatives, in
> which men and women do predictably different things, in which ex-
> change, barter and gambling occur, and in which there is some sort
> of formalized association between men and women. Some of these
> things show our similarity to other animals, others such as our use
> of language and our ability to carry out rapid culture change, show
> our uniqueness. But any way you slice it, human nature, diverse as

it is, looks narrow indeed in the wider context of the diversity of living things.

Thus the nature of humans, or what is best known as *human nature,* is now an accepted description of the actions of the most distinctive and flexible animal in the world — human beings. Many take the position that human behavior is acquired through two very complex (and not completely understood) developmental avenues: 1) Biological — which is an examination of the *homo sapien's* relationship to plant and animal life. This study also takes into account evolution, ecology and environment; genes and genetic make-up is of crucial importance. I will also take the liberty to add nutrition, keeping in mind that little scientific work has been done in this area by biological or social scientists; and 2) Culture — the act of developing intellectual and moral (ethical) faculties; integrated patterns of human behavior that include thought, language, action and invention. A culture, if it is to survive and develop, depends upon a people's capacity for learning and transmitting knowledge to succeeding generations. The development of family, institutions and governing bodies are examples of cultural entities. Ideologies, philosophies and political thought emanate from cultures working to perpetuate themselves (Mead, 1949; Tiger, 1969; Freedman, 1979).

For instance, the philosophy of White World Supremacy or white racism is both biological and cultural (Diop, 1959; Wobogo, 1976; Bradley, 1981; Welsing, 1989; Fuller, 1986). Europeans (the white race), upon discovering that other people and cultures existed and flourished independently of Europe and realizing that they (Europeans) were/are indeed a numerical minority, developed a system of thought and action that would help to guarantee white survival and development and at the same time put white people at the *center of the world, indeed the universe.* This system of thought essentially stated that white (Western-European) thought and action was right, necessary, best, the only way, correct, powerful, godly, clean, efficient, beautiful, etc. From the prehistory of the white race, all of their support systems began to confirm that white (European) is the past, present and future. The scholars, religious leaders, politicians, scientists, educators, military and business men of the white race took this message, in book and gun powder, to all parts of the earth and physically and mentally forced the "inferiors" to accept it (Bradley, 1981; Wright, 1986).

Therefore, this European frame of reference, which is diametrically opposed to most things not white (or European), spelled the near death of many non-white people and cultures worldwide (Fanon, 1967). White World Supremacy (white racism) emerged as an effective survival and defense mechanism for the development, perpetuation and maintenance of white political, philosophical, scientific and military thought on an international level. All the people who had the misfortune of being conquered and absorbed by the culture of Europeans (or their children, the Americans) have for thousands of years been reacting to white supremacy, the extreme survival expression of a people who are less than eleven percent of the world's population. The works of Chancellor Williams, John G. Jackson, Yosef ben-Jochannan, Frances Welsing, Neely Fuller, Cheikh A. Diop, John H. Clarke, Harold Cruse, Shawna Maglangbayam, James G. Spady, Anderson Thompson, Jacob Carruthers, Asa Hilliard, Na'im Akbar, Vivian Gordon, LeGrand Clegg II, Maulana Karenga, Molefi Asante, Michael Bradley and others have documented the most ancient as well as current racism. (Also see Madhubuti's *Enemies: The Clash of Races*, 1978.) Any meaningful discussion of the Black situation in the United States must not only understand this systematic pattern of thought and action, but must be sensitive to how it (white supremacy or racism) has been integrated into the entire life of Afrikan American people and has intimately affected Black peoples' interaction among themselves as well as with other cultures and races (Greer and Cobbs, 1968; Wright, 1986). Few state it better than Michael Bradley in his important book, *The Iceman Inheritance*:

> Racism itself is a predisposition of but one race of mankind — the white race...Nuclear war, environmental pollution, resource rape...all are primary threats to our survival and all are the result of peculiarly Caucasoid behavior, Caucasoid values, Caucasoid psychology... There is no way to avoid the truth. The problem with the world is white men. (Bradley, 1981)

Misinformation

That there are more televisions, radios, record players, tape recorders and VCR's in the average Black home than books* or computers has a great deal to do with where our information-gathering priorities are. It is now an accepted fact that the public school system, for the majority of Black people in most urban areas, is a dismal failure and will continue to be a failure. Not only cannot a great number of our young people read, write, compute or articulate their thoughts (Copperman, 1979; Shneour, 1974), there exists in many of them a severe dislike and fear of the written word, language (Madhubuti, 1984). And, since there are only a few places where large quantities of lifegiving and lifesaving information is available** to the majority of Black people, we now are finding that most Black people rely heavily and almost exclusively on mass media — television, radio, newspapers, magazines — and each other (Mander, 1978; Mankiewiez and Swerlow, 1978).

The fact that many Black people have bought into white America's gigantic melting pot lie is directly related to white seasoning, acculturation, the breakdown of the Black family, the weakness of Black social and business institutions and the sophisticated influence of other outside forces (i.e., integration has not worked). One cannot speak too loudly of the effects television and mass media have played in programming Black families for failure. If *Dallas* and *Dynasty* are the most successful white shows and *The Cosby Show* and *Amen* are their counterparts, one can easily understand why many Black families, as a unit, may have difficulty deciphering the real world. The traditional institutions that have held the Black community together, such as the church and the family, are current-

---

*I am mainly talking about books that provide information, knowledge, skills and inspiration that enable people to effectively deal with the real world.

**Information — that is, *working knowledge* that is current, accurate and functional can be found in computerized data banks which are controlled by the federal government, the military, private corporations and large universities. The other area that quantities of information can be found is in *written materials*, mainly *books*, scholarly, theoretical and professional journals, etc. Therefore, libraries, schools, universities and bookstores are a functional part of a community that is aware of its own intellectual needs.

ly not as effective as they should be in this highly racist, capitalist, scientific, technological and white male-centered world.

For example, rather than taking the lead in our struggle, a significant number of the Black churches have acted as interpreter and mediator with death; many church leaders have insulated themselves in medieval rhetoric and hidden behind black books that have little meaning to fourteen-year-old junkies or young men and women who seek answers to negative peer pressures and awsome world realities. Many churches practice outdated "traditions" and support outmoded practices of male chauvinism and unquestioned male dominance that have little to do with today's reality. It is important that we understand that many Black ministers in their pseudo-positions of power and influence are not necessarily the best examples of strong Black male leadership. This is especially sad in many Black churches where Black women, in terms of membership, far outnumber Black men. Indeed, the Black church would not exist as such a force if it were not for Black women who have, by and large, financed "modern" Black churches. This male leadership is, for the most part, patronizing and backwards (yet loving and considerate) in relationship to Black women, and is a profound statement on Black leadership. Indeed, if one seriously studies Judaism, Christianity and Islam (the so-called western religions), one will understand why in the actual world women are relegated to a position of polite tolerance. Religious symbolism for God in all three religions is masculine and very seldom do women share in decision-making or power-yielding positions in the sacred text or the hierachy of the church, synagogue or mosque. This sad state of affairs not only applies to the church, but sadly has filtered down throughout most of the world's religious, social and political structures.

War on Black Men

First, for the conscious observer, it should be quite obvious that this society is bent on destroying Black people, specifically Black men, as quietly and efficiently as possible (Obadele, 1968; Yette, 1971; Willhelm, 1971; Pinkney, 1984). What is not talked about is the ability *of great numbers of Black men to survive America's worst conditions, and their potential for revolutionary and progressive organization, which remains the greatest threat to white male rule.* This is why *most* of the Euro-American systems and sub-systems are structured to systematically keep *conscious*

67

Black men out. However, if Black men wish to become imitation white men, there exist within the political-industrial-military complex significant token positions (Gibson, 1978) — which are used to legitimize the system and to cloud its true relationship to Black people, a relationship of slavemaster to slave. In fact, the "slave" position is the major rank that Black men, regardless of title and income, are allowed to occupy.

The Kerner report, issued over twenty-one years ago, stated that the nation was moving toward two societies, one Black, one white — separate and unequal; and ten years later a major investigation by the *New York Times* (Herbers, 1978) confirms the accuracy of the report. In reference to the Kerner report, Robert Blauner, in his book *Racial Oppression in America*, states:

> Despite the Kerner Report, it is still difficult for most whites to accept the unpleasant fact that America remains a racist society. Such an awareness is further obscured by the fact that more sophisticated, subtle, and indirect forms, which might better be termed neo-racism, tend to replace the traditional, open forms that were most highly elaborated in the old South. The centrality of racism is manifest in two key characteristics of our social structure. First, the division based upon color is the single most important split within the society, the body politic, and the national psyche. Second, various processes and practices of exclusion, rejection, and subjection based on color are built into the major public institutions (labor market, education, politics, and law enforcement), with the effects of maintaining special privileges, power, and values for the benefit of the white majority.

Simply put, Black people in the United States are *powerless*. I define power in terms of the ability to make *life-giving and life-saving decisions*, as well as the ability (knowledge, resources and desire) to deliver on the decisions made. As a part of the political body, Black men do not have much, if any, power to speak of; as a cultural unit, Black men do not make important life-giving or life-saving decisions about Black life on a local, national or international level. Black men are not able on a national or mass level to protect Black women, educate Black children, employ Black youth, clothe Black families or house Black communities. Our input into a national Black domestic policy is laughable; our involvement in a "Black" foreign policy is minor. Our relationship to Black women is quickly approaching the point of disaster. Black economic-political clout on the world level is miniscule, and our understanding of the forces that regulate our lives is embarrasing — especially since we are supposed to be the most "educated" and the most "creative and talented" community of Black men in the world.

Black Men/White Men: White on Black Crime

For the 15.5 million Black men in the United States,* life expectancy is 62.9 years compared to 68.9 for white men; infant mortality is 27.6 per 1000 for Black people compared to 14.1 for whites; and Black male infant mortality exceeds that of Black females. Admission rates to mental clinics and hospitals is 998 per 100,000 for Black male in-patients (whites 642.1) and 873.4 per 100,000 for Black male out-patients (whites 599.4). The 1976 death figures for Black men are staggering: heart attacks 176.5 per 100,000; cancer 179.2 per 100,000; accidents, strokes and hemorrhages 79.3 per 100,000 and homicide 55.8 per 100,000 — bringing the total to 590.8 deaths per 100,000. These figures do not include drug related deaths or suicides, which are extremely high and far out of proportion for the Black male population. Other statistics in the areas of employment, education, under-employment, male heads of households are also discouraging.

Therefore, in the United States Black men are still involved in the establishment of significant firsts, such as: first jailed, first killed in the streets, first under-employed, first fired, first confined to mental institutions, first imprisoned, first lynched, first involved with drugs and alcohol, first mis-educated, first denied medical treatment, first in suicide, first to be divorced, first denied normal benefits of this country, first to be blamed for "Black" problems — indeed, Black men are the *first* victims (Boskin, 1976; Weisbord, 1975; Fedo, 1979; Ginzburg, 1969).

The concept of Black men being the first victims (Ginzburg, 1969) is not to set in motion the argument of who is oppressed the greatest, Black

---

*This data was compiled by Howard University Institute for Urban Affairs and published in their *Urban Research Review,* Vol. 6, No. 1, 1980. This entire issue of the *Urban Research Review* is devoted to the study of the Black male and is highly recommended. Much of the work was done by Dr. Leo Hendricks. In reviewing more current data, it is clear that these figures are, indeed, conservative.

men or Black women. Oppression is oppression, and to quibble over degrees of oppression, more often than not, is an accurate measure of the effectiveness of white oppression. However, there are some basic male dynamics that need to be understood: men run the world; this is not a sexist statement but one of fact. Also, men fight men (and women) to maintain control of "their" part of the world. There may be women in leadership positions (elected and appointed), but they are there because men see such concessions as politically wise and in their best interest. White men control most of the world — economically, politically, and miltarily — and undoubtedly control all of the Western /Northern World.

Other facts are: 1) White men *do not fear* white women; they are concerned, yes, but fearful, no; white men and women are partners, be it senior and junior partners; 2) White men do not fear Black women. The white man's relationship to Black women traditionally has been one of use, sexually and otherwise; the wide spread of color that exists among Black people proves this point — it was white men raping Black women that produced the mixed race Black person worldwide (Weisbord, 1975; Day, 1972; Stember, 1976; Hernton, 1965); 3) White men *do fear Black men*. This fear may not be spoken and obvious to many Black people, but if one understands the history of white male/Black male relationships, it is quite evident that it is a history of war, with the horrid and severe physical and psychological enslavement and elimination of Black men by white men (Ginzburg, 1969; Williams, 1974). Sterling Brown's classic words are instructive when he says of white men venturing into the Black community, "they don't come by ones, they don't come by twos, they come by tens."

The Black male/white male confrontation is not only racial and cultural, it is also a serious question of what group of men is going to "rule" the world. The concept of *shared* power has always been a major question within the white male ethos, especially if it involves the inclusion of men outside their racial or cultural grouping (Tiger, 1969). However, it must be understood that white men actually don't like or trust each other. Their cultural, religious and nationalist wars are legendary. Any serious study of European wars will validate this point. When one analyzes the war-like nature white men exhibit among each other, only the naive and severely mentally handicapped would expect white male attitudes towards Black males to be any different than they are. These attitudes are historical and cultural and, therefore, psychological (Bradley, 1981; Wright,

1986; Akbar, 1984; Welsing, 1989) and intimate. To change such negative and "natural" attitudes would require a revolution of the most profound kind. Michael Bradley in his important book *The Iceman Inheritance* carefully documents the white race's war on the non-western world, and clearly gives reasons for western man's racism, sexism, and killing aggression.

The Black male/white male dynamic can be best described as one of continued and unrelenting *war*, with Black males being consistently on the losing end of most battles (Williams, 1974; Martinez and Guinther, 1988). One of the major problems is that most Black men in the United States are fighting the wrong war — that is, many are fighting to get a "piece of the pie," therefore not understanding the "bio-social" nature of white males, which is that of conquest, domination and self-development, not one of sharing (Storr, 1972; Lorenz, 1962) power or decision-making with the vanquished (i.e., former slaves). The best that most Black men can hope and work for within this society is a "job" which, indeed, has been defined by many disillusioned Blacks as "a piece of the pie."

It is true that the future of any people can be measured by its cultural sophistication and the political, economic and military success of its male population in dealing with its natural and unnatural enemies. However, when that male population can't or doesn't *clearly* and *definitively* identify the *enemy*, it *cannot*, on a continuous basis, develop effective means and methods of neutralizing or eliminating said enemy. If this is the case, the future of that people can only be one of doubt and continued subjugation; and subtle, yet effective, elimination and/or subjugation is all but guaranteed in any white-American "multi-racial" situation, especially when the racial minority in that culture is economically obsolete (Willhelm, 1971; Yette, 1971) and Black. When a people does not have strong, resourceful, energetic, honest, serious, intelligent, committed, incorruptible, fearless, innovative and fighting men in a world ruled by the force of men, then that people is in serious trouble. When a people does not have men of integrity and vision, long term and lasting development is just about impossible.

The internal direction of Black people to a large degree is destructively influenced by the ongoing Black male/white male conflict. White men in the United States control everything of material value; this is true in all of the life-giving areas such as economics, entertainment, politics, science, sports, education, law, communication, real estate and the military.

71

If Black men want to be a part of the Euro-American structure in an "intimate and non-superficial" way, they will have to give up the most important aspect of their being, their Blackness. And in thought and actions they will have to become *white*; a transformation that is ultimately impossible but tempting enough to unconscious Black men that millions in this country on a daily basis unknowingly betray their people, themselves and the future of their children.

The history of Black/white racial interaction demonstrates that even if Blacks were allowed into the white infra-structure at important levels, they still would not have access to "ultimate and decisive" information or binding decision-making powers. The reason is quite obvious. Information is power (Brucker, 1973); and if it is translated and used in a self-protective manner, its value is of critical importance to those who have exclusive and first use of it. Generally, the information that the Black community organizes around is at best second-hand and is often of minimal value, having been filtered through the white screening systems before Blacks are able to see or use it. When any people (especially if it is *landless* and *defenseless*) loses its men in a world ruled by men, that people ceases to be a threat to anybody. The loss of Black men between the ages of thirteen and twenty-nine, which is the warrior class, represents a danger of genocidal proportions. To destroy or neutralize Black men creates a critical void in the Black family structure and forces Black women (without men) to assume the role of women (mothers) as well as men (fathers). About sixty percent of current "heads" of households in the Black community are women. This unusual condition has created some obvious readjustments, mostly negative:

1) The present generation of Afrikan American children is, by and large, being raised by Black women and their extended family network. The strain on single mothers is unduly harsh and often unreal. This condition influences the mothers' activities with their children as well as how they approach future relationships with Black men.

2) Black men have ceased to have a major influence on the development of their children, therefore leaving the "education" of the children to their mothers and other outside forces.

72

3) It is quite obvious now that single mothers without the proper male support are having serious difficulty raising sons. By the time most young boys reach the age of thirteen, the negative options that are available are overwhelming, especially from their peers.

4) The socialization of Black males without conscious and caring Black men around is, more often than not, replaced with gangs or other negative groups.

The U.S. white supremacy system works overtime to disrupt Black families and neutralize Black men. The most prevalent tactics used are these:

1) Create Black men who will *be* and *act white* in thought, actions and image (i.e., acculturation or seasoning). This produces Black men who consciously work in the best interest of their teachers. *Therefore, no serious definition of Black manhood is ever contemplated.* The call from white people is to always to rise above one's culture, tradition and history — if you are Afrikan American.

2) Drive Black men out of the economic sector, thereby making it impossible for them to take care of themselves and their families in "the American way." If fruitful work is not available, most men will seek other avenues of employment. A life of "crime" or the underground economy is the next step for many of them.

3) Use the prison system as a breeding ground for hard, non-political Black men who, for the most part, will return and prey on their own communities. (There are exceptions.)

4) Supply Black men with unlimited negative options (incorrectly defined as freedoms) such as drugs, night life, alcohol and unrestricted sex. The use of drugs and other stimulants has seriously affected the Black community in a destructive manner. The constant search for "fun," "pleasure," or the next "high" is the best example of an immature, enslaved mind.

5) Drive Afrikan American men *crazy* so that they turn against themselves and the Black community. Then the only recourse left will be a) mental hospitals or homelessness, b) suicide or c) Black on Black destruction.

6) Make them into so-called "women," in which case homosexual and bisexual activity becomes the norm rather than the exception. Men of other cultures do not fear the so-called "woman-like" men of any race.

7) Teach Black men to believe in a force(s) greater than their own people, their own culture, their own destiny. Afrikan American men's internal monitors (i.e., gut feelings and gut reactions, their spiritual connectors to reality and their sense of self) have been destroyed spiritually and culturally. Their moves toward self-determination and self-reliance are always questioned and put down as unimportant or meaningless.

8) Kill them — not just mentally, but physically, and do it in a way that strikes fear into the hearts of other Black men. This fear of death and/or imprisonment has been an important hindrance in keeping Black struggle "legal" and above ground. The killing of Martin L. King, Malcolm X, Fred Hampton, Mark Essex and others influenced the actions and non-actions of an entire generation of Black men.

Locking Black people (especially the men) into a legal process *that by definition doesn't work for them* has effectively set the Black struggle back years (Wright, 1988; Spence, 1989). *The freedom of Black people* cannot be won in the United States through legal means or *on a part time basis only*. The negative politization of Black men has effectively wiped out many serious *full-time* Black male freedom fighters. *Making it* in America to a great many Black men today means *how much money they can make in the shortest amount of time*, doing the least amount of work. Family Building, Nation Building, sincere deep Black male/female partnerships, are literary and academic verbage for the most part among Black men. The *vision* to see beyond the crippling mentality of sophisticated beggars is clearly on the decline among Black men.

74

Even though there exists much in-fighting among white male leadership, there does exist structured maximum and effective information flow. Contrary to popular belief, leadership in the United States is "shared" and decisions are "collective" (Green, Fallows & Zwick, 1972). However, within the Black community ultimate leadership is in the hands of one group, Black male ministers, and these men, by and large, are not "political" in a self-developing or self-protective manner for the Black majority. (See chart).

White Western Leadership	Black Western Leadership
(information is shared and decisions are collective)	(information is limited and decisions are inclusive)
1. Businessmen and industrialists; economic support systems	1. Male religious communities
	********************

2. Politicians and diplomats	2.
	  A. Politicians
	  B. Educators
	  C. Businessmen

3. Military: Armed Forces; CIA; FBI; state and local law enforcement	3. & 4. There is *no* working Black military or scientific community; if they exist, they are not effective
4. Scientific and technological community	
******************	******************
Support System	Support System
A. Educators B. Religion C. Entertainment D. Communication E. Sports	A. White people

Black male Christian ministers, whose theological training, for the most part, is based on a deep "moral and spiritual" commitment to a white Supreme Being, find it extremely difficult to separate that Supreme Being from the white male image (Welsing, 1979; Akbar, 1984). But to bring the argument back to earth, this male leadership, due to training, acculturation, seasoning and desire is not equipped intellectually or in any other way to deal effectively with white politicians, who will kiss Black babies at Sunday morning service and arrange the death of Black men and women who they are dissatisfied with at night. The Black leadership's understanding of and opposition to white international corporations and their concept of a one world economy made in their own image is, for the most part, nonexistent. The white military structure (U.S. Armed Forces, CIA, FBI and local, state and federal "law" agencies) spends a great deal of time laughing at Black impotence in the area of self-defense (Blackstock, 1975). The question of a Black defensive or offensive force has definitely taken a back seat in most areas of the Black community. Ever since the "set up" and total disruption of the Black Panther Party and Black Liberation Army, the Black Liberation movement has moved the question of a Black self-defense to the back burner. One must understand that the U.S. military apparatus is trained to *kill* and *not negotiate*, and the moral and spiritual values that Afrikan American leadership represents play no part in their worldview (Marchetti and Marks, 1974; Agee, 1975; Janowitz, 1971).

Finally, the key to continued Euro-American development and expansionism has been its ability to actively and "successfully" challenge and regulate not only the *known*, but also the *unknown* of the physical, material and spiritual world. This challenge, for the most part, has been overseen by the scientific and technological communities, whereas in our community no such apparatus exists — unless one includes the Black steps made in the area of hair style arrangement and disfiguration. However, the killing point of our leadership is that their worldview does not allow or encourage them to challenge the *known* or the *unknown*. If the information needed is not in the Bible, the Holy Koran or some other spiritual or holy book, then that information is generally considered of little value and is often disregarded and ridiculed. The position of Black male leadership is, at best, weak, unorganized and ineffectual (See "Greed..."). It is said that when a people has more religious leaders than business and military men in a world ruled by business and military men, that people is in *serious trouble.*

Black Men Need Family: Functional and Extended

As Black families in America are being effectively dismantled and destroyed, their male members often confusingly seek other alternatives — e.g., bacherlorhood, gangs (*Ebony*, 1980, Perkins, 1987). The white and negro destroyers of Afrikan American families know that deep in the heart and meaning of *any* people the one real barometer of a people's strength is loving, strong, productive, creative, and unified families, which when connected become communities.

The Black family, beyond the individual, represents the smallest unit of organization among Black people and is reponsible for the first line development of future generations. Properly functioning Black families will produce healthy male-female relationships; create sane, healthy and energetic youth; provide basic life-giving and life-saving support systems (economic, social, educational, health, military, etc.); and clearly define, in a programatically and progressive manner, the roles of men, women and children. Doctrines of right and wrong, concepts of love and caring are family-centered. Human values (spiritual and material) are first practiced and taught at a functional level by the family. The major social agency that any Black progressive movement (or Nation) cannot do without is *family.* Generally, when the family structure is seriously altered or ceases to function at a loving, political and cultural level, the effects of such a weakness will greatly determine the future development of that people.

There are within the Black community several family arrangements, but the two basic family types are 1) *monogamous* or nuclear — man, woman and children; and 2) *extended* — a) an extension of the nuclear, to include grandparents, aunts, uncles, and close neighbors and/or ; b) single- parent family (mainly women), to include children, male friends, brothers, sisters, aunts, uncles, grandparents and friends; c) poly-nuclear family, to include man, two or more mates, children, aunts, uncles, grandparents and friends. In the Western world, monogamy is the accepted and often the only legal form of male/female bonds. The much discussed nuclear family is monogamous-based and has the sanction of and is pushed by the state, church and other institutions. The extended

77

family in its various forms — mainly the single-parent (mother headed) household — is becoming the most prevalent alternative to monogamy. Traditional family structures (extended family) and knowledge of such quickly are fading from certain sections of our community, and the role of Black men is rapidly becoming "whatever it takes," regardless of how it affects Black life.

Many Black men and boys twelve years and older now realize that they are, indeed, marginal to this economy, and that as technology advances and job requirements become more technical, their chances of "good" employment are just about negligible. *Black young men are quickly becoming an illiterate, non-verbal, directionless, unattached, non-responsive, uncreative, jobless problem.* Those of you who don't believe this and wish to continue to color-coat our situation, come walk with me. White on Black crime has taken a disastrous toll on the warriors of our people. It has not always been this way.

In the tradition of our people the men were intimately involved in the raising of children, especially the male children. The Afrikan way was one where fathers passed their skills on to their sons. The arts of food gathering (hunting and agriculture), medicine, building (housing and public dwellings), military science and other skills were not skills that the sons of the nation acquired accidentally (Kenyatta, 1938). The young men were not only taught to be providers and protectors of their families and nations, they also were instructed in the art of healthy love-making, and knowledgeable sexual development was not relegated to the cult of the misinformed. Therefore, the elder men, whether they were biological fathers or not, played key roles in the development of the young Afrikan males into warriors, husbands, fathers, statesmen, artisans, leaders, etc. This carefully structured guide into Black manhood does not exist in the United States today at a mass level, and young Black male development is left to Black women, peer association, white men or *chance* (Perkins, 1975, 1987).

The models of Black manhood for most Black males today are very negative and anti-Black women. The mass media, again, has been instrumental in portraying Black men as studs, pimps, super-detectives or imitation white men (Bogle, 1973). Films such as *Superfly, The Mack, Shaft, Sweet Sweetback's Badass Song, The Great White Hope, Blackula, Legend of Nigger Charley, Slaughter, Watermelon Man, A Soldiers Story, The Color Purple, Native Son, Colors* and others represent a profound comment on the type of popular miseducation that a majority of Black youth continue to receive on a daily basis in the Black community. Without permanent and structured positive male education, young Afrikan American males have been left to themselves and the streets.

The most important example of young Black male/female relationships can be seen in the astronomical rate of Black babies born out of wedlock. In 1979, 62% of Black babies in Chicago were of unmarried Black women (DeVise, 1979); and in 1978, half of all Black children born in the United States were to single Black women (Feinberg, 1978). This high birth rate is mainly among Black teenagers between the ages of fourteen and sixteen (Scott, 1979). These fatherless homes lower the chances of the children developing into productive Black men or women, and the economic and social strain on the mothers will undoubtedly have an effect on their continued development. Hannibal Tirus Afrik has stated most forcefully in an analysis of the Black male problem:

> the glorification of the "phallic power," hustling, conning and strong-arm techniques against our own people is rewarded with materialistic trinkets and false ego-tripping. The best way to build a 'rep' in the neighborhood is through getting over on Black folks.

I might add that the impregnation of sisters adds "positively" to the "reputation" of young Black men. Of course, this has little to do with assuming responsibility for the children's development and well-being. Young Black males' attitude towards family and Black women today is such that familyhood is the lowest priority in their fight for survival. The most dominant characteristic of Black males' non-caring attitude toward their community is the recent epidemic of Black on Black rape (ya Salaam, 1978; Douglass, 1978). This forceful intrusion into the most intimate aspect of Black womanhood is without precedent in Black history and familyhood. However, its appearance in the Black community is cause for immediate action on the part of conscious Black men. Sexual assaults on Black women are probably double that which are reported, and in many cases rapes "involve close friends or acquaintances of the women involved" (Staples, 1973). Black women have come together to try to protect themselves, but unless Black men step forward and actively deal with each other, little will be done about this most serious of problems.

Indeed, it is now an accepted fact that when a society does not provide healthy releases for its male population's more aggressive, competitive, risk-taking and combative nature, that male population will release itself whenever it finds the opportune time, even if its negatives act against its own people. Black men's sexual aggression against Black women is an extension of a very serious cultural, economic, political and biological dilemma. Carol Jacklin and Eleanor Maccoby have documented important biological differences between the sexes:

1) Males are more aggressive than females in most human societies for which evidence is available.

2) The sex differences are realized early in life, at a time when there is no evidence that differential socialization pressures have been brought to bear by adults to "shape" aggression differently in the two sexes.

3) Similar sex differences are found in man and subhuman primates.

4) Aggression is related to levels of sex hormones and can be changed by experimental administration of these hormones (Gilder, 1979).

These findings have been confirmed by other behavioral scientists (Tiger, 1969; Freedman, 1979; and Lorenz, 1974). That Black men are obsolete as a labor force in this country ultimately means that the frustrations and energy within are denied normal releases; and when normal avenues are removed, self-destruction cannot be far away, especially in a society where the total livelihood of Black men is dependent on what white men do.

In Richard Gilder's *Naked Nomads: Unmarried Men in America,* he writes about the "naturalness" of male aggression and its intimate affect upon men:

> The denial of aggression or the attempt to abolish the impulse in men may well create a more threatening and exploitative society in which the Louies and other psychopaths, from high government offices to the streets, ride roughshod over everyone else...We are not

allowed to suppose that male aggression will inevitably lead to male dominance in most competitive activities. We assume instead that the successful man is a product of discrimination against women. We fail to recognize that the absence of arenas for aggressive male groups will lead to the eruptions of such aggressions against the society itself, or the festering of them in the mind of the men. And as in Victorian England, when suppression of sex led to an epidemic of perversity — all kinds of lurid flowers in the secret gardens of society, so the denial of male affirmation in modern life leads to pervasive distortions and perversions of healthy masculine aggression — to violence and pornograpy, to fear and exploitation of women, to the quest for potency through drugs and alcohol, to punch-drunk music and to fighting at sports events. Millions of reckless men feed on the masculinity of a few heroes — boxers, football players, politicians, rock stars...Male aggression and violence animate our movies, T.V. shows, magazines, newspapers, politics, culture. Our city streets are guiled by it. Our city schools are terrorized by it. "Liberated" women are obsessed by it — laboring through hours of karate, palavering endlessly through rap sessions on rape. It would be better to confront the reality and address the real problem, which is the lack of ways for men to achieve sexual identity and express aggression.

The killing point of Black life in America is that the racial and cultural aggression by whites has effectively moved Black people closer to *total* extinction in the United States. Konrad Lorenz in his important book *On Aggression* states:

> The balanced interaction between all the single norms of social behavior characteristic of a culture accounts for the fact that it usually proves highly dangerous to mix cultures. To kill a culture, it is often sufficient to bring it into contact with another, particularly if the latter is higher, or is at least regarded as higher, as the culture of a conquering nation usually is. The people of the subdued side then tend to look down upon everything they previously held sacred and to ape the customs which they regard as superior. As the system of social norms and rites characteristic of a culture is always adapted, in many particular ways, to the special conditions of its environment, this unquestioning acceptance of foreign custom almost invariably leads to maladaptation. Colonial history offers abundant examples of its causing the destrucion not only of cultures but also of peoples and races. Even in the less tragic case of rather closely

related and roughly equivalent cultures mixing, there usually are some undesirable results, because each finds it easier to imitate the most superficial, least valuable customs of the other.

Conscious Black men realize that they control insignificant amounts of land, produce few needed goods, and provide little independent lifegiving or lifesaving services for their communities; they also realize that they are *totally dependent* on the national socio-economic system for survival. Some would call this slavery, not freedom; the name has changed, but the game remains the same. Black men in America *do not make any earth-changing decisions about anything that concerns the well-being or future of Afrikan American people.*

Many Black men know this and have developed a comfortable compromise. Some feel that money and/or political clout within the system is the road to manhood. Others think that "education" or some special talent is the way out. However, most Black men by the age of thirty-five understand such powerlessness and establish a "working" existence. However, a significant number have said that enough is enough and have begun to struggle against what they see as certain death if there is not movement.

Many see that the first line of this struggle is a complete redefinition of Black male/female relationships. Maleness and femaleness are biological facts. That is, one's gender is generally an absolute (except in the West, where sex change operations are being considered and performed) and stay with one for life. The definitions of what a man or a woman is or should be are both cultural and biological. That is, there are many universal traits that men and women share worldwide, but so too are there differences that are culturally local and significant. The core of much of the Black male/female problem lies in incorrect definitions. In redefining Black men and women, several areas of study should be undertaken and understood first: 1) Afrikan and Afrikan American history; 2) European, Asian and Euro-American history; 3) White Supremacy (racism); 4) the dynamics of culture and biology; 5) the misuse of religions in defining male/female roles; 6) modern economic and political systems; and 7) psychology, especially the psychology of the oppressed as well as the psychology of the liberated. Actually, a cleansing of incorrect attitudes and actions is beginning to come about in parts of the Black community, and Black women continue to play a partnership role in the new definitions.

War on Black Women

That Black women have been a major and positive historical force in the Black struggle is undeniable. The works of Joyce Ladner (*Tomorrow's Tomorrow*), Robert Staples (*The Black Woman in America*), Inez Smith Reid (*Together Black Women*), Andrew Billingsley (*Black Families in White America*), Toni Cade Bambara (*The Black Woman*), Jeanne Noble (*Beautiful Also Are the Souls of My Black Sisters*), Paula Giddings (*When and Where I Enter*) and other writers — like Alice Walker, Gwendolyn Brooks, Toni Morrison, Vivian Gordon, Sonia Sanchez, June Jordan, Mari Evans and Assata Shakur — attest to this. The works of Gwendoloyn Brooks and Toni Morrison are must reading. The poetry of Mari Evans and Sonia Sanchez is direction for young women seeking their way. Black women sit on corporate boards and run their own companies. Black women head civil rights organizations and are invited to international conferences. Rosa Parks is credited for igniting the Civil Rights Movement of the sixties. In our women is the legacy of Queen Ann Nzinga, Harriet Tubman and Fannie Lou Hamer. Above all, Black women are visible. Yet, with all of this visibility and much, much more, Black women are considered in this society to be, in some minds, not quite as low as Black men in America but certainly in the running.

The struggle against white supremacy has been unrelentingly waged by Black women. Zora Neale Hurston's *Dust Tracks on a Road* and Angela Davis' *Women, Race and Class* speak eloquently of Black women fighting the real fight. From the works of Chancellor Williams (*The Destruction of Black Civilization*), Cheikh Anta Diop (*The Cultural Unity of Black Africa*), and Paula Giddings (*When and Where I Enter*), we see firsthand the role Black women have played in the liberation struggle. Assata Shakur's most recent autobiography *Assata* puts Black women in the front ranks of serious Black struggle in the world. Indeed, Black women have been the stabilizers of the race. Jorja Palmer confirms this in a strong rebuttal to narrow anti-man Black feminism when she suggested that Black women are...

...the transmitter of culture...the keeper of the cultural flame...the nourisher, comforter and anchor in all matters of life and death of that culture...It is not by chance, no accident, no false appeal to our senses when it is said, the world over, that the hand that rocks the cradle rules the world.

Sociologist Joyce Ladner seconds this when she states in *Tomorrow's Tomorrow*:

In many ways the Black woman is the "carrier of culture" because it has been she who has epitomized what it meant to be Black, oppressed, and yet given some small opportunity to negotiate the different demands which the society placed upon all Black people. Thus, she can be considered an amalgam of the diverse components which comprise Black culture: the pains and sorrows as well as the joys and successes. Most of all, it was she who survived in a country where survival was not always considered possible.

There is a saying in the Black community: "When you educate the woman, you the educate the race."

As white men have focused on keeping Black men in their "place," not allowing them to take care of their families or protect the most precious parts of them ("their women" and their children), Black women have *had* to be strong and resourceful in untold ways. In fact, Joyce Ladner feels that Black women are the only women in this society who have forged their own definition of womanhood:

By this I simply mean that much of the current focus on being liberated from the constraints and protectiveness of the society which is proposed by Women's Liberation groups has never applied to Black women, and in that sense, we have always been "free," and able to develop as individuals even under the most harsh circumstances. This freedom, as well as the tremendous hardships from which Black women suffered, allowed for the development of a female personality that is rarely described in the scholarly journals for its obstinate strength and ability to survive. Neither is its peculiar humanistic character and quiet courage viewed as the epitome of what the American model of feminity should be.

84

The sophisticated use of racism and capitalism has placed unconscious Black women in the positon of being a major competitor of Black men for jobs, education, housing and other services and necessary resources.

Black women did not place themselves in this delicate position; as wards of this system, they have been maneuvered and strategically used for the benefit of the white majority just as Black men have. Since there are so few jobs available, few openings for quality education and little housing that is habitable in the Black community, both Black men and women quite naturally try to acquire the best available for themselves and their families. Dr. Phyllis A. Wallace, a Black economist at the Massachusetts Institute of Technology (MIT), in an interview in *Black Enterprise* stated that 38% of all Black families are headed by women. Also, 44% of all Black children live in female-headed families and one in five of the mothers have never been married. Dr. Wallace also points out that the median income of Black female-headed families is $5,900. Black male median income is $9,420, whereas the median income of Black two-parent families is $15,700. Keep in mind that the poverty line is $6,700 for a family of four (Wallace, 1979). Therefore, the majority of the Black female-headed families live below the poverty level, and the majority of the never-married female family-heads are dependent upon the poverty-breeding welfare system. These are 1979 statistics and considered very conservative today.

The Black two-parent household is rapidly becoming a vanishing breed in the United States (U.S. Government Report on Black People in U.S. 1979). Many Black fathers who leave the family situation very seldom contribute to the upkeep of their children at the same level they would if they were there. Therefore, unskilled Black mothers, who comprise the the majority of heads of households, are unable to prepare their children for the highly scientific and technological labor market of the 21st century. When one sees that more than 40% of Black families headed by single Black women (Wallace, 1979) are responsible for almost half of the next generation of adult Black men and women, one can easily understand the frustration and downright anger many Black women expressed toward Black men. According to Dr. Wallace, these women are the least educated and the most lacking in marketable skills; they have children as dependents without child support, and they have little upward mobility.

The disruption of the Black family has come partially through the elimination, displacement, assimilition and/or co-opting of Black men.

The Black male on a day-to-day basis finds himself in an insecure and hostile world where his presence commands little, if any, respect; where his marketability as worker and provider is slowly eroded by unemployment, underemployment and hyper-inflation; and where his association with Black women and children is often frustrating and non-developmental. The entire Black community is jeopardized, and its survival and development at a healthly level is seriously threatened by this erosion.

It must be understood that biological and sexual roles within the human species are not interchangeable. The paralyzing damage done to many Black men, as a result of not having *positive Black male role models* to emulate and surpass, has been devastating. Black males' warped understanding of their roles as warriors, providers, husbands, fathers is superceded by the street pimp mentality (Hare, 1977, 1984). Long term sexual commitments are becoming increasingly rare, and Black women are left on their own to be both mother and father; a role that is just about impossible to perform. The sexual deficiencies and needs of men and women are, indeed, different and correlate along biological and cultural lines (Gilder, 1973; Stassinopoulus, 1973; Mead, 1949).

Developing in the Black community are short-term sexual patterns, where responsibility to sexual partners is shorter than the sex act itself. However, stable and developmental societies are based on long-term sex patterns and the birth of children represent committments made and kept (Gilder, 1973; Hare, 1984). Irresponsibility in regards to who a Black woman lets make love to her is recent. We must understand that generally women and many men have a sense of completion and value through the act of reproduction. The nine month carrying period, the delivery, the nursing all are uniquely feminine and not understood by the average man. Therefore, it is not unusual that women, on the whole, have been more discriminating in choosing their mates. Their investment in the birth process is much greater than the men's and, quite naturally, women are in a better position to seek and to bring into the world "superior" children who are both mentally and physically strong and able to cope.

The concept of hypergamy ("to marry upward") is widespread among many people but is especially a strategy of women (Barash, 1979). Very seldom today (this was not the case forty years ago) do we see a Black professional woman in a long-term relationship with a Black man not of her educational, economic or professional level. The reverse is more common — a Black professional man with a non-professional Black wife.

Black women teachers, doctors, lawyers, etc. are therefore placed in a very difficult position in terms of developing long-term relationships with Black men since more and more Black men are being forcefully excluded from "upward" mobility. Another side of this question is that it takes a Black man with an *exceptionally strong ego and enlightened worldview* to seriously, on a long-term basis, deal with a Black woman who is educationally, financially and professionally his superior. Few of these relationships work.

The idea of sex must again be put into the family context. Short-term sexual encounters or "conquests," especially in the age of AIDS, must be discouraged. This is not to suggest that *all or most* male/female sexual activity must lead to procreation, but if the family is to be the major entity for socialization, *children* must cease being accidents and again be seen as priority. When sex is easy, quick and involves many partners, its meaning is surely to diminish, developing a "get it while its hot" or "pussy is a penny a pound" mentality; and the proponents of this approach cannot possibly be serious about anything or anyone other than *themselves*. According to Gilder:

> ...the women's attitude, which devalues the procreative symbolism of intercourse, encourages the man to abandon the long-term sexual commitments that are the basis of his marriage and his role in civilized society. For if sex is not profoundly important—if the woman treats it as a perfunctory pleasure, a matter of tension and release like unsocialized male eroticism — then the structure of male socialization itself is imperiled. The man is subtly pushed towards the uncivilized patterns that come so naturally to him and that are insistently propogandized in the society.

The socialization of Black males is by no means an easy task. Too much of this socialization is left to forces that are unable to effectively direct the bio-sexual energies of young Black males. Most young Black men do not want to be seen as "Mama's boys" and therefore are left to their own and their peer group's inventiveness to prove that they are "men." The *rites of passage* that institutionalize a boy's movement from boyhood to manhood are now left to failed schools, pool halls, street gangs, armed forces and other negative influences (Perkins, 1987). It is now obvious that manhood and womanhood carry two separate but complimentary meanings. And it seems necessary that the "first" teachers of our people — Black mothers — be aware of the positives and negatives of both. Too many Black women consistently are associating their oppression with Black maleness. This is a difficult question because Black men *do* abuse Black women and children. Therefore, many Black women's fears, concerns and indictments of Black men are correct. However, Black women must understand that the positive masculine releases that white men have are not functioning within the Black community for Black men. White men in this world build cities, run countries, develop businesses, start political parties, maintain armies, develop technology, run universities, go to the moon and live in and on the ocean. Most Black men generally watch white men do these things, play a supporting role, or clean up after them. Normal outlets for Black aggression among many Black men do not exist, and Black men too often turn such aggression inward or towards those they "love" the most. The *quality* of the home life, where Black women have traditionally had a very secure and demanding voice, must return; and Black men must again assume a position of responsibility in the home. This is not going to be easy, but it is definitely necessary if we are to move into the 21st century with any hope of survival and development.

Misdirected Warriors

A profile of the average Black person that took part in the rebellions of the 1980s in Miami is a 27.8 year-old (warrior class) male, unmarried, high school dropout before completing his senior year. He is dissatisfied with his neighborhood and home, unemployed and of the opinion that the criminal justice system discriminates against Blacks. He is angry and bitter, and he "believes America is not worth fighting for" (Morin, 1980). There is more, but the key element here is that young, single Black men can either represent a positive progressive force or one that just continues to react to crisis after crisis.

It is also true that single Black males are committing most of the Black on Black rapes and crimes in our communities. These individuals represents a *real* danger, and their energies need to be channeled into functional work and struggle. There is very little that Black women can do for men in this state of mind other than organize into self-defense units, lock their doors, stay off unknown streets after dark and buy weapons. The *negative politicization* of Black men by this white supremacist society may be the final step in dismantling and destroying the Black world in the United States (i.e., let Black men destroy and disrupt their own communities).

For thousands of years men have been patriarchal and have sought male dominance and attainment (Goldberg, 1974). Thus, male dominance has been a practically universal law. This is *not to suggest that it is correct* but *only reality, a fact*. There are only a few societies where this has not been the case — up until today in America, where Black women, rather than Black men, are now the primary decision-makers in the family. Male dominance is on the decline in the Black community (due to white on Black crime), which places that community in jeopardy. *Unwarranted* competition between Black men and women for jobs, housing, health care, education, political positions, etc. only leads to further erosion of Black male/female relationships. Understand what I'm saying: under "normal" conditions this unusual competition may not exist, for there are *natural* ways to solve these problems when a people controls its *own* land, means of production and distribution, and support systems. White men have boxed Black men into a corner ("contained") with only one option — to come out fighting, regardless of who they destroy. Without question, those closest to them will be destroyed first — mates, sisters, daughters, sons, brothers and others of their community. This is a no-win situation for Black men, especially when most don't realize that they've been "set up" and that the biological/cultural and sexual differences and needs that normally exist between Black men and women are not being allowed to develop and express themselves in a healthy and productive manner.

Black male patriarchy, dominance and attainment are not being realized among most Black men, and many *incorrectly* feel that this is because Black women have written them off as serious providers, partners, lovers or protectors. This is not the whole truth. Often Black women understand Black men at a greater level than the men understand themselves. Many Afrikan American women realize that if Black men are going to rise to meet the real needs of the Black world, they have got to stop "mothering" them and really work for partnerships in struggle and life. Black men as a collective body have not been able to get our act together, and it is not accurate or in our best interest to blame Black women for our current condition. In this war situation that we are in, our women can not effectively deal with white men; they need us — *that's our job*.

89

We, Black men, have to stop and take a close look at ourselves and ask two important and penetrating questions:

1) Why are Black women, by and large, more responsible than we? (One reason is that many go through a birthing process. (However, there are exceptions.) Carrying a child for nine months, breastfeeding and actively rearing that child — 75% of the time, makes most Black women more responsible. Men, for many reasons, need to be a part of the whole birth and parenting process. It will give them a new understanding of life and a new sensitivity in understanding Black women and children, and will bring a much more functional definition to parenthood.

2) Is life worth living as wards of the state, wards of our women and without the ability to *actively* determine our own destiny?

It is now clear that politically conscious Black men can influence unconscious Black men under the right conditions. Black women who are conscious generally will not be listened to, and white men and white women who can influence Black men will do so only in the best interest of the white race. The best way to effectively influence other Afrikan American men is to 1) be an example of what a real Black man is and should be; 2) be able, in an organized manner, to offer a bright and practical future to Black men, even if that future is difficult and dangerous to obtain; and 3) provide brothers with a purpose and vision of life that is beyond the syndrome of "making it" in white America.

The family still represents the basic and best learning institution. Families give Black men purpose and reason to fight and build. Parenthood in the proper context (family) bestows on men a new urgency around life and future. It slows them down and dictates that they not only care about tomorrow, but that they also must prepare to take it because tomorrow will affect their offspring in crucial ways.

90

Male Patriarchy* and Misconceptions of Black Female Matriarchy**

The current American family pattern, which is patriarchal, is designed to maximize the influence of males over females and children. In fact, the status of women within such family arrangements can be directly traced to the "white constitution for the institution of marriage anywhere in Western civilization," and that constitution is the Bible (Baker, 1979). This well may be a misinterpretation of the Bible; however, few men, Black or white, have come forth to challenge such an interpretation. The family arrangement of the West, for the most part, is not working within the Black community and is experiencing serious difficulty in the white community (Metrus, 1979; Gardner, 1978) as well.

The biblical family structure is closely examined in David Dakan's *And They Took Themselves Wives*, where he states the common ideal of family that is associated with the Bible:

> Sexually, the norm is virginity prior to marriage, with all sexual relations limited to married heterosexual couples. Great significance is assigned to the female's virginity prior to marriage and to her fidelity after marriage. Fundamental authority within the family resides in the husband-father. Children are expected to be deferent to their parents, and the wife-mother is expected to be deferent to the husband-father. Social status and material inheritance from parents to children are usually transmitted patrilineally. Parents are obliged to provide maintenance, protection, and education for the children. The husband-father is primarily responsible for bringing outside resources into the household and to toil and sweat for food (Genesis 3:17-19). The wife-mother is responsible for production of in-house resources, and the appropriate use of resources in housekeeping and nursing. Physical nurturance and protection against everyday dangers rests primarily with the wife-mother. Protection against outside dangers, such as marauders and predators, is largely the responsibility of the husband-father. Early education of the children

---

*Social organization marked by the supremacy of the father in the clan or family, the legal dependence of wives and children, and the reckoning of descent and inheritance in the male line (Webster, 1979).

**A system of social organization in which descent and inheritance are traced through the female line.

rests with the wife-mother; while later education, particularly of the male children, is the obligation of the husband-father.

However, today this biological-social organization clearly works against the development of Black people in the United States. Why is this so? The authority of the husband-father role goes hand in hand with the ability of the husband-father to provide for his family's basic needs such as food, education, housing, clothing, a measurement of security and material well-being. Also, in today's consumer-oriented society, wives, husbands and children are looking for a certain amount of consumer goods and entertainment that may or may not be of any real value but are viewed as measurements of a family's success by family, friends and others.

Most secure employment opportunities in the white economic sector, for the most part, are closed to the average Black man. This precipitates a situation that forces many Black men to develop a *hustler-survival mentality* that eventually is manifested at the most destructive level, that of interpersonal relationships between Black men and women and Black men and children. It is obvious that when the Black man cannot effectively negotiate a life for himself and his family within the existing structure, he will *go outside* of it and do whatever is necessary to maintain himself and those he has assumed responsibility for. To many Black people, this type of action is viewed as *failure,* and very subtle spoken and unspoken attitudes develop within the family and community to accent such "failure." Black men react in a variety of ways:

1) Some become introverts, and their actions are only shared with a few male partners. They are loners in relationship to their families and the "legitimate" Black community.

2) Some move to lives of "crime," which definitely is psychologically damaging because their culture does not condone such actions, and neither do their families.

3) Most Black men in America have never been very communicative with their women, and when friction develops, it often becomes "easier" for the men just to leave home since a great deal of street education is grounded in avoiding social responsibility.

92

4) Many Black men find other women and develop relationships in keeping with current realities (difficulties). Therefore, explanations for why things are so bad will not have to be made in the future. However, this is not to suggest that intimate and sexual contact is not maintained with the first family.

5) Other Black men resort to *suicide* — that is, self-destruction through drugs (i.e., alcohol, cocaine or other stimulants that are openly available in the Black community) (Hendin, 1969).

6) Some become immersed in self-pity and the destruction of self-worth. A begging dependency on the welfare system which fosters in Black males a beggar mentality and the loss of self-esteem.

7) Others exploit their own people. Black on Black crime. This avenue is quite prevalent among former prisoners who when released cannot find adequate employment and turn to the streets again. The great equalizer has been misdirected violence. Many men engage in very serious wife/woman beating. Other than rape, the ultimate act of powerlessness and worthlessness is the rise of child molestation in the Black family; this is of critical concern.

8) A few Black men have been turned into revolutionaries, sought other men of like values, and begun to organize in many ways. These men have also redefined their relationships with their women and made new and more meaningful lives for themselves and their families. This group of men is small and can be considered the exception.

The Black family is in a serious period of disintegration. With fathers absent, Black women have had to assume dual roles that few, if any, have been prepared for. The impotence of the Black male population has forced Black women to be *strong* and resourceful in unusual ways. Many outside the Black community confuse this *strength* with *dominance* and, thus, conclude that the two-parent Black family is basically matriarchal, which is definitely not true (Staples, 1976).

Black female "matriarchal" actions have been complimentary, moving in concert with Black men. That Black women on many occasions have had to make and act upon their own decisions only points out the high level of non-involvement of Black men in the family structure and the independent nature that Black women have had to assume in the United States. We must keep in mind that more often than not the decisions made singly by Black women do not affect Black men but are generally directed towards making their lives and those of their children liveable. More often than not, when there is a man in the house he is the "head," and the Black woman recognizes this and negotiates her life so that conflicts are kept to a minimum. However, many of today's Black women, who currently are single family heads, refuse to enter relationships that do not give them a certain amount of mobility and decision-making power; this is correct. Afrikan American men and women must be partners.

Monogamy, Omnigamy, Illegany and Polygyny: Where Are We Going?

Where are we going as a people when we allow a great many Black families to become non-functional units or units composed of only single adults and children without support? It should be obvious that monogamy as the "only" way towards happiness and development has its limitations and hazards (Goldberg, 1976). It should also be obvious that as the sex ratio now stands, it is impossible for "every" Black woman to have a monogamous relationship with a Black man (Staples, 1978; Madhubuti, 1978; Scott, 1977). And, unless Black people boldly and consciously tighten up *their* family arrangements, their future will continue to be uncertain. As stated earlier, all social, political, economic and military movement against an enemy is deterred when a people's internal operation is weak and non-functional. If Black men and Black women can transcend Western cultural influences and openly and honestly face themselves, while continuously questioning the functionability and legitimacy of their family arrangements, without a doubt they can recapture their rightful place in this world.

As a start, let's critically but briefly look at some current Black male-female social arrangements and try to understand the positives and negatives of each.

94

As European Christians took the world, the one man/one woman form of male/female relationships became dominant (Awoonor, 1975; Leith-Ross, 1965; Beidelman, 1971). The Catholics were especially forceful in this regard, preaching that polygynous arrangements were pagan and tools of the devil (Beidelman, 1971). In fact, until the spread of Western ways, 70% to 75% of the world's people were polygynous (Wilson, 1978; Freedman, 1979; Barash, 1979). Monogamy as a social arrangement has not been able to meet the needs of a great many of those who believed in it; marriages fail because after the basic needs of food, shelter, and clothing are met partners are also looking for intellectual stimulation, shared values, "romantic love," continued sexual pleasure, high levels of intimacy, economic security, commonality of vision and moments of deep personal completion. To say that this is not working among many Black people is an understatement. However, in white America the traditional family — husband at work, wife at home and two children — now makes up only 7% to 10% (Selson,1979) of existing households.

According to Lionel Tiger (1978), the divorce rate has jumped 250% in the past twenty-one years. The number of single-person households is increasing within the society, especially in the Black community. From the most current information available (CPS,* 1978), over one-fifth of all American households in 1978 consisted of persons living alone, and 62% of these single-person households were maintained by women. The number of Black women maintaining single households since 1970 has just about doubled due to five factors: 1) Black women not getting married; 2) married men leaving home; 3) Black women widowed; 4) divorce; and 5) the non-availability of marriageable Black men. According to CPS data, there are approximately 2.5 million Black single female-headed households.

Monogamy in this country is certainly having its ups and downs; when you couple this with the mid-eighties mentality held by many Black men and women that "single is best," the future seems in trouble. However, it must be understood that not *everybody* needs to be married or is capable

---

*Current Population Survey (CPS) — Marital Status and Living Arrangements: 1978.

of marriage; yet, if a people are to develop and expand their positions in the world, it is absolutely certain that this cannot be done without procreation. This cult of the singles goes hand in hand with white Western education that pushed the ultra-individuality rather than community, and many Afrikan American men and women see no need for long or short term commitments of any kind that are not immediately financially and sexually rewarding. Another reason that many young Black professional men don't marry is that marriage would cut off their *sexual exploration and, thus, confine their sex drive to the pattern of one woman.*

Monogamy as an institution has, to a degree, been a stabilizing force in most societies. However, people must realize the inherent limitations of monogamy and make internal adjustments if it is to work on a developmental level. The larger question is, can one person (male or female) supply another with all his/her needs for life? These needs are not only sexual but material, emotional, social and intellectual. Men and women have allowed and encouraged *prostitution* (Winick and Kinsie, 1971) because most people recognize that monogamy, especially for men (and this is cultural), has not worked (Wilson, 1978); and many women will endure their men having brief sexual encounters as long as they do not threaten or impinge on the emotional, financial, etc. security of their relationships. However, many women have not accepted the fact that the sexual patterns of men and women are extremely different (Freedman, 1979; Wilson, 1978; Barash, 1979) and that monogamy as an institution has attempted to contain the male's "natural" behavior, binding his sexual urges to the one-woman pattern (Gilder, 1973, 1987). This has not been successful and more men and women are making their commitments to monogamy later in life, if at all (CPS, 1988).

Omnigamy (Serial Marriages)

Omnigamy, or serial marriages, has been the West's answer to polygyny (Tiger, 1978). Lionel Tiger has pointed out that this society, which was once based on the principle of solid monogamy "until death do we part," has shifted toward a pattern of serial marriages, in which people experience more than one spouse — if only one at a time. Tiger states that a "third to a half" of the marriages formed in this decade will end in divorce. This failure is astonishing when you consider that if anything else failed at such a rate it would be abolished or seriously altered.

96

Black participation in omnigamy is not as extensive as that of whites. The trend, it seems, is that if the first one doesn't work, be extremely careful about the second. And since Black professional women have entered the job market and are closer to surpassing Black men in terms of positions of responsibility and money (O'Connell, 1979), they have definitely become a part of the growing single-parent households in the country.

Omnigamy is statistically the most prevalent alternative white social arrangement because it is *legal*. However, there will continue to be some doubt on the parts of persons moving towards marriage again, as they ask themselves, "Will it work?"

Illegany (The Ball Game)

The male is on home plate and has women on first, second, and third. This is, in reality, nickle and dime pimping and whoring that lonely and insecure women allow into their lives. The male in this arrangement is busy running bases trying to service and control as many women as he can, and responsiblity to the "real" needs of these women and their children is not even a part of the equation.

Illegany, or the ball game, is what I feel is becoming the dominant Black male/female social arrangement in the country. This Afrikan American form of polygany is closer to pimpism than anything else, depending on the line that the male is running to the female(s) involved. Generally one will find a single, married, divorced or separated male dealing with two or more women. And the women more than likely have some knowledge of the other women but never discuss them due to deep patriarchal holds most men have on their mates. Here are some of the most prevalent elements of illegany:

1) It's underground. Knowledge of affairs is restricted to a few friends or running buddies.

2) Women are generally supporting themselves (jobs, welfare, etc.) and may be contributing to the males' support.

3) If children are involved, the male may act mainly as disciplinarian — especially if the children are not biologically his.

97

4) These relationships are short-term unless children are involved.

5) Children are considered illegitmate by the society, and the father does little to invalidate this nonsense.

6) Male has irregular visiting schedule, but shows up at least once a week. Mostly unexpected, this is to keep the women off guard.

7) Time male spends with female is basically sexual; there is little verbal communication.

8) The pressures on the female are very great, many of her friends (who may be involved in similar situations) think she is a fool to put up with his "shit."

9) Very seldom do females visit males without invitation.

10) Relationships are male-centered.

11) Women in all economic levels engage in this type of arrangement.

12) Males contribute little, if any, financial help to females.

13) There are few, if any, social pressures on males to become more responsible.

There is more to this. However, these are the most outstanding characteristics of illegany. This type of misuse of Black women needs to be cut into and cleaned up. However, this will not happen unless people are willing and able to openly and honestly make major adjustments in their lives and actively seek developmental alternatives. Audrey B. Chapman in her book *Man Sharing* has tackled this problem head on and has come up with some very practical and innovative solutions. And because of this, she has suffered much abuse and criticism from other Black women — much of it undeserved and highly insensitive to the larger problem of Afrikan American family life.

The question may arise as to whether or not there is ever a situation where Black women take advantage of Black men; the answer is yes. Scott and Stewart (1979) speak of the *Pimp-Whore Complex in everyday life* and illustrate how Black men and women play games with each other daily. However, in the final analysis, males have an upper hand in the category of *emotional and physical abuse*.

Polygyny (Many wives)

As mentioned earlier, up until the spread of Western culture, the great majority of the world was *polygynous*; multiple mating among males and females existed. *Polygyny* (many wives), the most prevalent form of multiple mating, covered much of Africa and the world before the intrusion of Christians or Muslims (Awooner, 1975). *Polyandry* (many husbands) also existed but to a much lesser degree. *Polygyny* for much of Afrika was/is patriarchal, and women were virtually the property of males. One other form of marriage called *levirate*, where a man inherits his brother's widow (Ayisi, 1979), also existed.

Western culture, particularly Christianity, to a large degree has altered traditional polygynous societies (Racliffe-Brown and Forde, 1970; Leith-Ross, 1965). But where these societies still exist, some things are very striking. All of the women are under the protection of the men. Prostitution is not as prevalent because *all* women must marry in their teens from fifteen to twenty (Kenyatta, 1938). In the Gikuyu culture, there is no term for "prostitution," "unmarried" or "old maids" (Kenyatta, 1938). However, this does not mean that "prostitution" does not exist.

Before European intervention in Afrika the female children were seen as "connecting links" between generations and from clan to clan. Through marriages the clans were bound and the communality of the females were accented. In fact, Kenyatta states:

> ...the tribal customary law recognized the freeedom and independence of every member of the tribe. At the same time all were bound up together socially, politically, economically, and religiously by a system of collective activities and mutual help, extending from the family group to the tribe. The Weltanschauung of Gikuyu people is: 'Kanya gatuune ne mwamokanero' ("Give and take").

This philosophy of "Give and Take" is in concert with Ayi Kwei Armah's description of the Afrikan Way (1979), a state of *reciprocity* or mutual exchange. Children in Afrikan society are seen as rewards and are also evidence of a woman's and man's well-being. Therefore, the more wives, the more children. In the Gikuyu tribe, the wife initiates the question of another wife after a year or so, especially if she is with child:

My husband, don't you think it is wise for you to get me a companion (moiru)? Look at our position now. I am sure you will realize how God has been good to us to give us a nice and healthy baby. For the first few days I must devote all my attention to nursing our baby. I am weak...I can't go to the river to bring water nor to the field to bring some food, nor to weed our gardens. You have no one to cook for you. When strangers come you have no one to entertain them. I have no doubt that you realize the seriousness of the matter. What do you think of the daughter of So-and-so? She is beautiful and industrious and people speak highly about her and her family. Do not fail me, my husband. Try and win her love. I have spoken to her and found that she is very interested in our homestead. In anything that I can do to help you I am at your service, my husband.

Even if we have not enough sheep and goats for the dowry our relatives and friends will help you so that you can get her into our family. You are young and healthy and this is the best time for us to have healthy children and to enlarge our family group, and thereby perpetuate our family name after you and I have gone. My husband please act quickly as you know the Gikuyu saying: 'Mae megotherera matietagerera mondo onyotie' ('The flowing water of the river does not wait for a thirsty man').

However, one doesn't want to leave the impression that polygyny was restricted to Afrika. One of the best examples of Euro-American polygany was the Mormons (O'Dea, 1957). Plural marriages, as they were called, were essential to the early development of the Mormons. In fact, due to their plural relationships, the Mormons literally were forced out of Illinois — only to eventually take up settlement in the Great Salt Lake (Utah) area. "Women were not allowed to remain single in Mormon land and virgins were presumed to be barred from heaven — therefore, no prostitutes and no spinsters. Every plural wife had or was supposed to have a house of her own and became a sister to the other wives of their single husband; they all felt much freer than single wives in that they were liberated from excessive male lust and free to raise smaller families" (de-

Riencourt, 1974). Due to an aroused public and severe problems with the federal government, the Mormons discarded polygyny in the 1890s.

Polygyny has survived in Afrika even though its forms may have altered to a degree due to the Christian and Muslim (who allowed up to four wives) onslaught. It has been noted that Islam had an "easier" time in Afrika because it did not disrupt the multi-wife tradition (Awoonor,1975). As young Afrikan men absorbed themselves in Western education, they too took on the culture of the West. Among the Western "educated" young Afrikan men and women monogymy is now the prevalent form (Sithole, 1972). However, we must not give the impression that polygyny was/is all peaches and cream. Women did and do have problems (Achebe, 1959), and there are avenues that they are able to take to get out of undesirable relationships. However, on the whole, monogamy (which has always existed in Afrika) and polygany seem to have found their mutual places in Afrika.

Black people in the United States, for the most part, have walked a thin line between monogamy and illegany, and the results have not always been healthy. Prevailing cultural moods restrict innovative and creative thinking or actions in regards to personal realtionships and most Black people continue to stay underground with relationships outside the traditionally accepted form. The inability of monogamy to accomodate the total needs of Black people is often spoken to, but little has been done to suggest other alternatives that might accomodate Black people's needs. The exceptions are most notably men (Semaj, 1980; Obadele, 1975; Scott, 1976; and Madhubuti, 1978). Whatever is ultimately decided upon, Black women will have to play a *paramount role in its design and execution*. I think that Audrey B. Chapman has taken a big step in this direction.

New Lives

Research over the last twenty years has confirmed a fact of which few people were in doubt: men and women are uniquely and complimentarily different in the ways their brains function — i.e., their thinking patterns (Restak, 1979; Goleman, 1978); in their actions (Mead, 1949; Hall, 1979; Harris, 1975); and in their genetic and biological make-up (Wilson, 1978; Farb, 1978; Tiger, 1971; and Freedman, 1979). These differences are complimentary, positive and functional when a people realize and carry out their "proper" roles within that society. Our capacity for change is unlimited if we recognize the importance of change. My contention is that in the United States Black people are on a collision course with certain death. And, the only way we can avert it is by shifting gears and *totally redefining, from our own experiences and world realities, what is best for us at all levels of human involvement.* The redefinition most immediately needed is one for the family because we are losing our children.

Children

A people's offspring are priority. When a people does not place the development of its children as foremost on its list of priorities, that people is killing itself internally. All serious nation-builders think in *generations* and often in *centuries* and therefore the children are *automatically an integral part of the future.* Currently, Black children are in serious trouble due to the disintegration of the Black family, where we have an abundance of single-parents, working mothers, unsupportive fathers and insensitive people in day-care and home-centers as our children's first-line teachers. My focus is on the children because the children's development is key to the success of any social arrangement ultimately adopted by Black people. Congruently, if Black adults develop, the children will develop. If the quality of adult relationships are loving, productive and secure, the chances increase that the children's will be also.

Extended Families, Functional Communities

Margaret Mead noted as early as 1949 that "In modern societies where polygany is no longer sanctioned and women are no longer cloistered, there is now a new problem to be met, the competition of females for males" (Mead, 1949). Attempts at solving this problem in the Black community through illegany or other variations of it has made conditions much worse.

Extended families are biological and/or social groupings of men, women and children that have banded together to share resources, ideas, politics and love. An extended family is *not* meant to replace monogamy but supplement it. However, the extended family is meant to replace *illegany*. Yet, it must be noted that *no* family arrangement will succeed if the partners involved are not mature and willing to compromise and make adjustments in their own lives. The extended family could be either sexual or non-sexual. A person's sexual needs should *not* be the major deciding factor for such an arrangement.

The central question should not be, *"Does a man need more than one woman or a woman more than one man?"* Rather, it should be, *"Can a mature single Black man or woman fulfill the emotional, economic, sexual, intellectual, spiritual and security needs of more than one partner?"* These questions would have to be answered on an individual basis, but let's generally look at a few absolutes that brothers should consider:

1) A Black man who has not exhibited responsibility in monogymous relationships probably will have difficulty maintaing relationships with two or more Black women.

2) A Black man who has not achieved a "responsible" level of economic stability probably will have trouble handling more than one relationship.

3) A Black man who has not developed himself intellectually and culturally probably will not be able to satisfy such needs in two or more Black women.

4) A Black man who has had difficulty relating to and developing long-term relationships (friendships, work relations, social relations, etc.) with one woman probably will not be able to meet the emotional needs of two or more Black women.

5) A Black man who has exhibited sexual insecurity and spiritual vacantness undoubtedly will experience these same problems with one or more Black women.

6) A Black man who does not or has not related to children (his or others) on a high level definitely will have to prepare himself, and monogamy is the best start.

This is my way of stating that for the vast majority of Black men in the United States the extended family that includes more than one mate is *not* the solution. However, for the others, such a family structure *may* be a serious option, and consideration of it should be undertaken. However, it

103

must be understood that it is much easier to *collect* sisters and have babies than to build businesses, schools, institutions and nurture children to adulthood. It is said that white men collect nations, while brothers collect sisters.

Young Women for Young Men

The suggestion to study and consider the extended family is not a subtle or sociological maneuver to provide Black men with many women or vice versa. In fact, I feel that this type of family arrangement should only be for mature adults; and mainly for single, divorced or widowed women with children. The ideal age — in terms of experience and maturity — should be thirty-five and over. For men, the suggested age is forty and older.

Also, rather than men seeking to add to their families, the best situation would be a wife inviting a "single," divorced or widowed "sisterfriend" into her family. In the age of liberated women, one can also imagine two or three women (friends-sisters) coming together and approaching a brother with the idea of an extended family, making him an offer. Again, I must stress that the man be forty or older because most serious men should have defined themselves intellectually and financially by that age. Obviously, men without serious means of support cannot hope to develop and sustain one-on-one relationships and, therefore, the extended formation would not be a serious option.

Another important point is that *young women should be left for young men*. Young Black men have enough to deal with without worrying about losing their mates to older, more "experienced," financially secure Black men. It is extremely difficult and nearly impossible for a young, inexperienced (sexually and otherwise), poor Black man to compete with a more "worldly" older brother who has resources.

Sex — The 10% Solution

Throughout history, males have been more sexually active than women; this is both in frequency and number of partners (Wallace, 1979; Gilder, 1973; Tiger, 1969; Freedman, 1979). This was by design and is cultural. In the West, male and female sexuality has been suppressed by Christian thought. Sexual pleasure in the past has been condemned as a sin, and its suppression has aided men and women in developing new forms of perversion and neurosis. The emergence of rape, pornography and incest (Butler, 1979) is closely related to psycho-sexual problems. The most sought after experience by humans, after eating, is sex, and to continuously keep it in the closet will undoubtedly cause serious problems for future generations.

The key to healthy, enjoyable sex is to understand that a person should study ways to sexually satisfy a partner — and communication (which is crucial to good sex) is primary. The first reason for sex is reproduction, and this must never be forgotten. Most sexual encounters are for pleasure and not reproduction, but that is not an adequate reason to lose sight of the primary purpose of sexual activity. According to Donald Symms in the *Evolution of Human Sexuality*, the male and female have two different sexual strategies. Whereas the male strives toward multiple sexual partners, the female — who can only bring a limited number of children into the world (while the male's capacity for reproduction is almost unlimited) — seeks a permanent relationship with a good provider to help guarantee the survival of her children. However, *the proliferation of birth control in the United States has dramatically altered the strategies of both males and females.* The use of birth control has had a liberating as well as destructive effect on relationships. A significant book that brings clarity to this important subject is *Crisis in Black Sexual Politics*, edited by Nathan and Julia Hare.

It is clear that sex is integral to any loving relationship. The individual sex drive among women and men — according to Dr. Samuel Okpaku — is a "powerful force that permeates consciously and subconsciously every phase of her or his activities and interactions with others." (Okpaku, 1984). However, it is also clear that in most serious relationships sex takes up less than 10% of a couple's quality time — *be it an important 10%*. Yet, the crucial point is that 90% of a couple's time is used in other family and related activities. The emphasis in enlightened relationships will revolve around those activities that happen outside of the bedroom. Those activities — work, study, entertainment, spiritual development, eating, institution building, etc., will take up about 60% of a couple's quality time with the remaining 30% used for sleeping.

As important as sex is, much more is needed for couples to build and sustain a relationship. A new relationship that is highly sexual will not grow or develop if it cannot move beyond the bedroom to the mind-room.

105

Traditional Black families have always been extended, where members represented two and sometimes three generations. In fact, it was not uncommon in the south to see father, mother, children, grandparents and a great grandparent under one roof. The value of this type of living arrangement is that the art of familihood is experienced and learned simultaneously. All the rites of passage from birth to death are expressed in an atmosphere of respect.

The extended families also included same sex communal households. This is where grandmother, mother and daughter lived and shared experiences and life together. The call is to build family networks that work. Same sex male and female households are generally temporary but can be a fruitful starting point. This arrangement is most often seen when two women or two men share an apartment and expenses until they decide to marry or live alone.

Cultural Change is Not Easy, but it is Necessary

If most Afrikan American people were financially secure, educated, lived in clean neighborhoods, had good jobs, controlled their communities and felt protected, both physically and mentally, from harm's way, there would still be problems. No community, no matter how well off materially or spiritually, is insulated from *white world supremacy* (racism). Also, Black people are not perfect, even under ideal conditions. However, one must remember that the *seasoning* that Black people underwent during the long period of enslavement has left negative physical and psychological scars. Therefore, transformation will be difficult and will require a commitment of the most profound kind. Throughout this book I make suggestions; here are a few with which to start:

1) *Accurate Definitions are Needed.* In the chapter "Were Corners Made for Black Men to Stand On?" I give a beginning definition of Black manhood. This definition is only a starting point, but I think it should be incorporated in all early learning situations for Black boys. What it means to be a Black man starts with understanding the transition from boy to man. Those *rites of passage* that define us, such as birth, naming, birthdays, formal schooling, graduations, age groupings, sexual activity, high school education, military and/or college, marriage and other cultural forces,

106

are *crucial* in stabilizing and giving direction to young Black boys and girls.

2) *Examples* of what is right and what is workable. Black boys, like others need possibilities. They need to know that there is a beneficial tomorrow for them. This means that they need to be around "successful" and "caring" men — men who are not caught up into themselves, but Black men who have made an impact in the world and will not lie to young men about the sacrifices necessary for "success." Young men and women need examples of successful Afrikan Americans in all of the lifegiving and lifesaving areas. These examples are not to be paraded out as showcases once or twice a year, but must somehow be "programmed" into the lives of our children. Examples of right and wrong, good and bad, positive and negative are value-based and often involve moral decisions. Knowing what is best under many different situations requires critical thinking and a great deal of knowledge and self-confidence. This is why child-rearing or parenting should be taught and not left to the whims of the misinformed.

3) *Study* (individual, family and group) — Serious study should be like eating. Our homes should be mini-learning institutions. A people "may" achieve liberation through sheer physical force, but they cannot maintain that liberty without intelligent and wise men and women. If our children see us studying everyday, they will too. *Turn the television off* — and if you watch it, do so with discretion. One of the reasons that our analysis is faulty is because our information is faulty. Study should be both practical and theoretical. However, the greater focus must be in that area that you plan to be most active. We must become "specialists" as well as men and women who possess a good "general knowledge" about the forces that move the world. However, it is imperative that all Afrikan American people have more than a working knowledge of their own people's contribution to civilization. I am not talking about a "slave" history but a history that accurately states the Afrikans' contributions to science, religion, health, art, humanities, mathematics, etc.

4) *Love* of self and people is one of our highest principles. Rather than "falling in love" — *learn to love*. Grow into love. Sometimes it is an easy process; often it's difficult. The *Afrikan* way is to give as well as receive. Caring beyond the normal is normal for our new direction. Be willing to share self and material possessions beyond the expected.

5) *Family Development*. First-line struggle. If you and your partner cannot communicate, check yourself out first. Make sure that you are aware of her needs and your "shortcomings" before "jumping" into her chest. The key to family is shared values and communication. *Family-making* is a teaching and "being taught" proposition. The key is always "progressive compromise" around principles and values that work for us rather than against us. Open up to your woman; let her share your pain and joy; do not hide special weaknesses or strengths. Remember, being strong is not a macho character or expensive makeup. Strength is positive decision-making and living up to responsibilities, whatever they may be.
   A. Every serious Black man should be relating positively to a Black woman.
   B. Relationships should be nonviolent and proactive.
   C. Try not to send children to be taught by people who do not care for them.

6) *Activist for life*. Progressive activity in an organized manner in all areas of human activity. This is important because of this system of corporate capitalism where money or profits are valued over people. Therefore, people have to organize and be prepared to do battle in many areas at any given time to combat evil corporations and any other entities. Also, organized struggle will generally move people past pure theory. Struggle is not impressing others with your ability to quote revolutionaries. Struggle, in the first analysis, is *work* and the ability to function productively with other Black people in an organized manner. The building of institutions, parties and nations depends first on effective building of Black individuals and families.

108

A. Each family needs to start a defense fund. The money will be used to acquire "materials" that will aid in the defense of the family in times of emergency.

7) *Afrikan American Cultural Boot Camps.* Fathers *must* become involved in parenting. Men must form men's groups to aid in the development of conscious young people. Due to the lack of functioning families, we must, in the meantime, develop alternatives. Year-round "boys and girls" camps or clubs functioning out of churches or other Afrikan American cultural institutions are needed. An experience that I'll never forget is my U.S. Army boot camp training. I think that such a concept is now needed in most Black communities. The Afrikan American Cultural Boot Camps would be an educational system that would immerse young people in a total cultural, physical and academic learning experience away from their homes. They would operate on a "boot camp" philosophy but out of an Afrikan American philosophical frame of reference.

These camps would be operated by Afrikan American people and would solicit the services of retired and active high school and college coaches, retired and active military drill sergeants, university professors and parents interested in a complete and radical change in the education of their children. Such cultural camps should ideally be located in rural areas. They would be run during the summer from one to four weeks and on the weekends year-round. "Support camps" would be set up in most Black urban communities. The type of losses we experience each day only means one thing — *we are at war.* Our young people must learn this before we lose them. Each sizable community would develop "100 Black men" groups to give financial, emotional and ideological guidance to the Afrikan American Cultural Boot Camps.

8) *National Afrikan American Think Tank and Leadership Council.* A national group of Black men and women who have proven beyond a doubt their commitment to Black people. Their charge is to think about the future and to begin charting a course of direc-

tion for Afrikan American people. This think tank/leadership council would include: parents, public and private school teachers, university professors, business leaders, religious leaders and representatives from major national organizations, such as National Council of Black Studies, National Association of Black Psychologists, African Heritage Association, NAACP, Operation PUSH, National Urban League, National Black United Front, Nation of Islam, etc. This group must not be made up of the same tired old guard.

9) *Become responsible men and stand up.* Stop crying on wives/ lovers breasts about how the "man" treats you on the job, in the streets, at school and elsewhere. It is not that we need to present a false picture of our lives, but sisters are under enough weight themselves and do not need their men's false tears. That is how our women lose respect for us. They are actually waiting on us to do something about the "man" if we are going to continue to call ourselves men. If Black women can't occasionally lean on the shoulders of Afrikan American men, who can they lean on? We are incomplete without each other.

10) Develop a *work* attitude about the world. Nobody is giving anything of value away, and if someone does, you can be sure that he or she can take it back. We must become *business-oriented.* The real economic base of the United States is small and medium size businesses. We must teach our children early the *necessity* of starting *their* own businesses, and I'm not talking about franchising McDonald's or Wendy's. Living in a multi-cultural and multi-racial world controlled by white people is not easy. When Afrikan Americans begin to take control of their own lives, then they will become a serious threat to white control. The two best ways to relate to white people during this time of war are...
   A. Business only. Work with them, study with and under them, but do not allow them into your institutions at a decision-making level.
   B. *Never* let them into your heart or mind. *Stop* confessing inner secrets to them.

110

11) *The search for truth* should always be our guiding force. Times and situations change. Just because something was correct in the sixties, seventies and eighties doesn't mean that it can be used in the 21st century. Always be willing to question past actions as well as accept constructive criticism. Advocating an Afrikan American cultural movement doesn't mean being dogmatic and insensitive to other positions. Good is good, no matter where it comes from.

Struggle in the United States is extremely dangerous. However, our very lives depend on an ongoing conscious movement for liberation. The goal is development and bright tomorrows for all people.

We All Hurt But Most of Us Can Be Healed

People involved in serious day to day struggle of survival are not about to get involved in cultural nonsense that they feel is going nowhere. It is enough just to be able to clothe, house and feed ourselves. The *personal* side of struggle is often overlooked, but mothers and fathers who maintain their families, raise their children into productive adults are to be congratulated and supported. It is clear that we cannot build and sustain a "nation" if we cannot develop families that are culturally stable, physically strong, creative and ready to defend their people.

People endure through the power of their minds and the strength of their vision. A people's culture, if it is functioning properly, will supply the vision. Our supreme capacity to adapt has allowed Black people worldwide, but especially in America, to continue to change and grow. Whether our adaptability is in our best interest will be answered, most certainly, in the next decade. However, it is evident to those who wish to notice it that Black people are reshaping their lives according to what they think is best and, in the long run, beneficial to them and their loved ones.

As some Black women join white men and Negro men as part of the occupying force, we must certainly realize that people — all of us — *do what we have been taught to do.* Black women and men, just as most people, move out of self-interest and self-protection; that some of them are being positioned as legal killers against their people speaks to the weakness of Black people and their misunderstanding of Afrikan American political, racial and economic status. If the men do not step forward to

111

take control and /or give leadership, the women have only one option — to do it themselves. Black women are doing the best that they can do. Black men need to come forward in force.

As mentioned earlier, it is no accident that our leadership largely comes from the ministry. When a people has more preachers than military men in leadership positions in a world ruled by scientists, politicians, industrialists, and military men, without a doubt that people is in trouble. Contrary to popular belief, *we are not our own worst enemy.* Our national Black male leadership has not exhibited any semblance of consistent and noncontradictory examples of Black manhood. This must be corrected, for in this world it is us (Black men and women) and them (white men and women), and we must make sure our backs are covered.

It is time for Black people to retake the responsibility of Afrikan American cultural design. We have the capacity and the resources (mental and economic) to do what we want to do. We need to rearrange our lives around values and principles that are best for Black people. The *family* and close communities remain the foundation of all nations, and the protection and intimacy that they provide for their members is irreplaceable. The family is, without a doubt, the best institution in which to raise our children, and when it wavers so does everything else. If we are truly working for a collective and sharing society, the quality of the persons involved in that society depends on the quality of the families. And the ultimate quality of the family depends upon the beauty of interpersonal relationships:

> There is no beauty but in relationships. Nothing cut off by itself is beautiful. Never can things in destructive relationships be beautiful. All beauty is in the creative purpose of our relationships; all ugliness is in the destructive aims of the destroyers' arrangements. The mind that knows this, the destroyers will set traps for it, but the destroyers' traps will never hold that mind. The group itself is a work of beauty, creation's work. Against such a group the destroyers will set traps for the body, traps for the heart, traps to destroy the mind. Such a group none of the destroyers' traps can hold (Armah, 1979).

If we are to move toward maximum development, Black men and women are the key elements in such movement. Many Black people in the United States, for better or worse, move on the solutions to their

112

problems and needs without discussion. That is real. The starting point is already over when comunication begins.

Black men and women must move toward a more meaningful partnership where their complimentary elements become the defining rather than the negative aspects of each. Consciously try to make each other happy. Communicate at the highest level possible on all subjects, no matter how small or large. Recognize each others' weaknesses and strengths, and forever reach into the soul of the other. Compliment the good, correct the bad and draw strength from the positive. Question the world and be ready to implement the answers. Create a life-style of seriousness and you can be sure that the world will look at us differently. Our vision is clear, and our children demand that we reach for the best. Again, meet as lovers and do not be afraid to say, "*I care.*"

REFERENCES

Achebe, Chinua. *Things Fall Apart*. New York: Astor-Honor, 1959.

Akbar, Na'im, *Chains and Images of Psychological Slavery*. Jersey City: Mind Productions, 1984.

Armah, Ayi Kwei. *Two Thousand Seasons*. Chicago: Third World Press, 1979.

_____. *The Healers*. London: Heinemann International, 1989.

Awooner, Kofi. *The Breast of the Earth*. New York: Doubleday, 1975.

Ayisi, Eric O. *An Introduction to the Study of African Culture*. London: Heinemann, 1979.

Bambara, Toni Cade. *The Black Woman*. New York: Signet, 1970.

Beidelman, T.O. *The Kaguru: A Matrilineal People of East Africa*. New York: Holt, Rinehart & Winston, Inc., 1971.

Billingsley, Andrew. *Black Families in White America.* Englewood Cliffs: Prentice-Hall, Inc., 1968.

Blackwell, James E. *The Black Community: Diversity and Unity.* New York: Harper & Row, 1985.

Blauner, Robert. *Racial Oppression in America.* New York: Harper & Row, 1972.

Bogle, Donald. *Toms, Coons, Mulattoes, Mammies and Bucks.* New York: The Viking Press, Inc., 1973.

Boskin, Joseph, ed. *Urban Racial Violence.* Beverly Hills: Glencoe Press, 1976.

Bradley, Michael. *The Iceman Inheritance.* New York: Warner Books, 1981.

Bronfenbrenner, Urie. *The Ecology of Human Development.* Cambridge: Harvard, 1979.

Brucker, Herbert. *Communication is Power.* New York: Oxford University Press, 1973.

Butler, Sandra. *Conspiracy of Silence: The Trauma of Incest.* New York: Bantam, 1979.

Chapman, Audrey B. *Man Sharing.* New York: Morrow, 1986.

Cress-Welsing, Frances. *The Cress Theory of Color-Confrontation and Racism (White Supremacy).* Washington, D.C.: published by author, 1970.

_____. *The Isis Papers: The Keys to the Colors.* Chicago: Third World Press, 1990.

Day, Beth. *Sexual Life Between Blacks and Whites.* New York: World Publishing, 1972.

Davis, Angela Y. *Women, Race and Class.* New York: Vintage, 1983.

de Riencount, Amaury. *Sex and Power in History.* New York: David McKay Co., Inc., 1974.

Diop, Cheikh Anta. *The Cultural Unity of Black Africa.* Chicago: Third World Press, 1978.

Douglas, Grace. *Rape: Taking by Force.* Rumble, 1978.

Edelman, Marian Wright. *Families in Peril.* Cambridge: Harvard, 1987.

Esfandiary, F.M. *Optimism One.* New York: W.W. Norton & Col., Inc., 1970.

_____. *Up-wingers.* New York: The John Day Co., 1973.

Fanon, Frantz. *Black Skin, White Masks.* New York: Grove Press, 1967.

Farb, Peter. *Humankind.* Boston: Houghton Miffln, 1978.

Fedo, Michael. *They Was Just Niggers.* Ontario: Brasch and Brasch, Publishers, 1979.

Feinberg, Lawrence. "Half of Black Children Born to Unmarried Women." *Washington Post.* (5-4-78).

Gardner, John W. *Morale.* New York: W.W. Norton & Co., Inc., 1978.

Gibson, D. Drake. *70 Billion in the Black.* New York: Macmillan Publishing Co., Inc., 1978.

Giddings, Paula. *When and Where I Enter: The Impact of Black Women on Race & Sex in America.* New York: Bantam, 1985.

Gilder, George. *Sexual Suicide.* New York: Quadrangle, 1973.

_____. "Can Women Fight?" *Chicago Tribune,* (2-18-79).

Ginzburg, Ralph. *100 Years of Lynchings.* New York: Lancer Books, Inc., 1969.

Goleman, Daniel. Special Abilities of the Sexes: "Do They Begin in the Brain?" *Psychology Today.* November, 1978.

Green, Mark J., Fallows, John M. and Zwek, David R. *Who Runs Congress?* New York: Bantam, 1972.

Grier, William H. and Cobbs, Price M. *Black Rage.* New York: Basic Books, Inc., 1968.

Guinther, Jon and Thomas Martinez. *Brotherhood of Murder.* New York: McGraw-Hill, 1988.

Guttentag, Marcia and Secord, Paul F. *Too Many Women?* Beverly Hills: Sage, 1983.

Hall, Edward T. *Beyond Culture.* New York: Doubleday, 1976.

Hare, Nathan. "Street Pimp," *First World.* Vol. 1 Nol. 4. 1977.

Hare, Nathan and Julia. *Bringing the Black Boy to Manhood: The Passage.* San Francisco: The Black Think Tank, 1985.

_____,eds. *Crisis in Black Sexual Politics.* San Francisco: The Black Think Tank, 1989.

_____. *The Endangered Black Family.* San Francisco: The Black Think Tank, 1984.

Harvey, Aminifu R. *The Black Family: An Afro-Centric Perspective.* New York:UCCRJ, 1984.

Hendin, Herbert. *Black Suicide.* New York: Basic Books, Inc., 1969.

Herbers, John. "Two Societies: America Since the Kerner Report." *New York Times.* (three part series), 1978.

Hernton, Calvin. *Sex and Racism.* New York: Doubleday, 1965.

Hilts, Philip. *Behavior Modification.* New York: Harper's Magazine Press, 1974.

Hurston, Zora Neale. *Dust Tracks on a Road.* 2nd Ed. Urbana: Universtiy of Illinois, 1984.

Huxley, Aldous. *Brave New World.* New York: Bantam Books, Inc., 1953.

Kenyatta, Jomo. *Facing Mt. Kenya.* London: Secker & Warburg, 1938.

Ladner, Joyce. *Tomorrow's Tomorrow.* New York: Doubleday, 1971.

Leith-Ross. *African Women.* New York: Praeger, 1965.

Lorenz, Konrad. *On Aggression.* New York: Bantam, 1967.

McAdoo, Harriette Pipes, ed. *Black Families.* Beverly Hills: Sage, 1988.

Madhubuti, Haki. *Enemies: The Clash of Races.* Chicago: Third World Press, 1978.

_____. "Black Writers and Critics: Developing a Critical Process Without Leaders," *The Black Scholar,* 1978.

_____. *From Plan to Planet: Life Studies: The Need for Afrikan Minds and Institutions.* Chicago: Third World Press, 1983.

_____. *Earthquakes and Sunrise Missions.* Chicago: Third World Press, 1984.

Mander, Jerry. *Four Arguments for the Elimination of Television.* New York: William Morrow and Co., Inc., 1978.

Mankiewics, Frank and Swerdlow, Joel. *Remote Control.* New York: New York Times Books, 1978.

Marvin, Harris. *Cows, Pigs, Wars and Witches.* New York: Vintage Books, 1975.

Mead, Margaret. *Male and Female.* New York: Morrow, 1949.

Metraux, Rhoda. *Margaret Mead: Some Personal Views.* New York: Wallace and Co., 1979.

Noble, Jeanne. *Beautiful Also Are the Souls of My Black Sisters.* Englewood Cliffs: Prentice-Hall, Inc., 1978.

Obadele, Imari A. *War in America: The Malcolm X Doctrine.* Chicago: Ujamaa Distributors, 1968.

_____. *Foundation of the Black Nation.* Detroit: Home of Songhay, 1975.

O'Connell, Brian J. *Blacks in White-Collar Jobs.* New York: Universe Books, 1979.

O'Dea, Thomas F. *The Mormons.* Chicago: University of Chicago Press, 1957.

Okpaku, Samuel O. *Sex, Orgasm and Depression.* Chrisolith Books, 1984.

Orwell, George. *1984.* New York: The New American Library, 1950.

Perkins, Useni Eugene. *Home is a Dirty Street: The Social Oppression of Black Children.* Chicago: Third World Press, 1975.

Pinkney, Alphonso. *The Myth of Black Progress.* New York: Cambridge University Press, 1984.

Radcliffe-Brower, A.R. and Forde, Daryll, eds. *African Systems of Kinship and Marriage.* Chicago: Third World Press, 1975.

Restak, Richard M. *The Last Frontier.* New York: Doubleday, 1979.

Robinson, Lovie. "The Case For Staying Single," *Ebony,* 1979.

Scott, Joseph. "School Age Mothers," *Black Books Bulletin,* 1979.

_____. "Polygyny: A Futuristic Family Arrangement for African-Americans," *Black Books Bulletin,* Summer 1976.

Semaj, Leahcim Tufani. *Black Books Bulletin.* 1980.

Shakur, Assata. *Assata: An Autobiography.* Westport: Lawrence Hill, 1987.

Sithole, Ndabaningi. *The Polygamist.* New York: The Third Press, 1972.

Slesin, Suzanne. "Changing Housing as Families Change," *New York Times,* (11-22-79).

Spence, Gerry. *With Justice for None.* New York: New York Times Books, 1989.

Staples, Robert. *The Black Woman in America.* Chicago: Nelson Hall, 1973.

_____, ed. *The Black Family: Essay and Studies.* Belmont: Wadsworth Publishing Co., 1986.

_____. *Introduction to Black Sociology.* New York: McGraw-Hill Book Co., 1976.

_____. "The Myth of Black Sexual Superiority: A Reexamination," *The Black Scholar,* April, 1978.

Stassinopoulos, Arianna. *The Female Woman.* New York: Random House, 1973.

Stember, Charles Herbert. *Sexual Racism.* New York: Harper Colophon Books, 1976.

Stewart, James and Scott, Joseph. "The Pimp-Whore Complex in Everyday Life," *Black Male/Female Relationships,* Vol. 1, No. 2. 1979.

Storr, Anthony. *Human Destructiveness.* New York: Basic Books, 1972.

Symons, Donald. *The Evolution of Human Sexuality.* London: Oxford University Press, 1979.

Tiger, Lionel. *Men in Groups.* New York: Random House, 1969.

_____. "Omnigamy: The New Kinship System," *Psychology Today.* 1978.

Wallace, Robert A. *The Genesis Factor.* New York: Morrow, 1979.

Weisbord, Robert G. *Genocide?* New York: Greenwood Press and the Two Continents Publishing Group, 1975.

"Where Are the Eligible Men?" *Ebony,* 1980.

Willhelm, Sidney M. *Who Needs the Negro?* New York: Anchor Books, 1971.

Williams, Chancellor. *The Destruction of Black Civilization.* Chicago: Third World Press, 1974.

Wilson, Edward O. *On Human Nature.* Cambridge: Harvard University Press, 1978.

Wilson, William J. *The Truly Disadvantaged*. Chicago: University of Chicago Press, 1987.

Winick, Charles and Kinsie, Paul M. *The Lively Commerce: Prostitution in the United States*. Chicago: Quadrangle.

Wobogo, Vulindlela. "Diop's Two Cradle Theory and the Origin of White Racism," *Black Books Bulletin,* Vol. 4, No. 4. 1976.

Wright, Bobby. *The Psychopathic Racial Personality*. Chicago: Third World Press, 1986.

Wright, Bruce. Black Robes, White Justice. New Jersey: Lyle Stuart, Inc., 1988.

ya Salaam, Kalamu. "Rape: A Racial Analysis," *Black Books Bulletin*, 1980.

Yette, Samuel F. *The Choice: The Issue of Black Survival in America*. New York: G.P. Putnam's Sons, 1971.

II. Missions and Visions

"You watch. I will be labeled as, at best, an 'irresponsible' black man. I have always felt about this accusation that the black 'leader' whom white men consider to be 'responsible' is invariably the black 'leader' who never gets any results. You only get action as a black man if you are regarded by the white man as 'irresponsible.' In fact, this much I had learned when I was just a little boy. And since I have been some kind of a 'leader' of black people here in the racist society of America, I have been more reassured each time the white man resisted me, or attacked me harder — because each time made me more certain that I was on the right track in the American black man's best interests. The racist white man's opposition automatically made me know that I did offer the black man something worthwhile."

Malcolm X
The Autobiography of Malcolm X

The Question

Question: What is the greatest challenge you face as a Black man?

Answer: My continued quest is to be a responsible, loving and effective Black man, husband, father, writer, educator and publisher in this ocean of *white world supremacy* (racism), and not to allow *white supremacy* to alter or destroy my memory, spirit, drive, integrity, worldview, convictions and values, which are the results of twenty-five years of work, excruciating pain, serious study, critical thinking, actions and organized struggle.

Also, with my wife, my challenge is to pass on to our children positive Afrikan (Black) values, which demand the maintenance and development of our family, extended family, community and people, by highlighting and pushing progressive ideas as well as historical examples of Harriet Tubman, Nat Turner, Martin R. Delaney, Marcus Garvey, Mary McLeod Bethune, Fannie Lou Hamer, Martin Luther King, Malcolm X and others.

My fight is to be an inspired example of a caring, healthy, intelligent and hard-working brother who understands this *war* and works daily for the development of our brothers into multi-talented, family-based, conscientious Black men who will not settle for anything less than self-determination and beauty for all people.

Never Without A Book:

Educating the poor and rich:
Two hundred plus books every
conscious Afrikan American should study

I

From the age of thirteen, after my mother introduced me to *Black Boy* by Richard Wright, seldom has there been a day that I've been without a book. For a poor boy coming from the lower east side of Detroit by way of Little Rock, Arkansas, books at such a *late* age represented *revelation* and *intellectual liberation.*

I grew up in the Black church (Baptist) and the unforgiving urban streets. The three "skills" I learned very early were how to pray, rap and lie to white people; without them one could not survive in Black Town, U.S.A. Books revealed to me other *possibilities*, introduced me to poverty greater than my own and wealth that was unimaginable. In books I discovered that Black women and men could not only write and publish, but that words — combined in a certain way, somewhat like a musician combines notes into music — *could make a difference.* I learned that, if used wisely, language (written and spoken) distinguished and freed a person, if only temporarily, from the awesome weight of race, gender, class and poverty in America.

Books taught me a new language, a new music. I had been exposed to the melodic lines of Black song writers. Growing up in Detroit in the late fifties, one could not escape the profound influence of the Motown sound. Little Stevie Wonder was approaching genius, while the Four Tops and the Miracles filled the streets with love songs. The tempting Temptations and the Supremes had not gone crazy yet. And writing poetry was something that was *just not done* by "real men." The creative atmosphere was different. So, if I was caught writing poetry, I generally said that I was writing lyrics for Little Anthony and the Imperials.

I became aware of the liberating force of literature very early. Like most young Black men, as a teenager I met each day with a certain amount of fear. This fear was both physical and intellectual. Being tall, thin, light-skinned and about the size and weight of a 6'1" skeleton didn't help my stature among the local brothers. Also, going to a high school out of my neighborhood was a daily exercise in avoiding a beating and/or intellectual embarrassment. Learning how to fight, run and rap at the earliest sign of danger got me through school with only a small razor cut and a mind that was not beyond repair. Conquering the written word made high school something to look forward to each day. I knew how brothers fought in the streets, but I had no idea of the extent to which we were being annihilated intellectually in the class room and elsewhere where language and cultural knowledge were the weapons of power and destruction.

Among the Black writers that I read during this period (1955-1959) was Chester Himes — *Cast the First Stone, The Lonely Crusade, Third Generation*, and *If He Hollers, Let Him Go*; these four novels exposed me to the complexity of Black involvement within the problem of white supremacy (racism). I continued with Richard Wright and consumed *Native Son, Lawd Today, Uncle Tom's Children, Black Power, Eight Men, White Men, Listen, The Color Curtain, 12 Million Black Voices* and *The Outsider*. Through Richard Wright and Chester Himes, I received a beginning in literary and political education. Frederick Douglass' *My Bondage and My Freedom* incited me to think, at a new and more questioning level, about the issue of slavery and Black people in the United States. However, it was Booker T. Washington's *Up From Slavery* that signaled in me other possibilities for Black people who had functional skills. None of these books were assigned in school; nor was there *ever* an Afrikan American writer discussed or even mentioned during my early formal education. The Detroit Public Library became my second home, and along with Black music, I began collecting Black literature.

My mother was killed in 1959; my sister was fifteen, unmarried and with her first child. I had become a disillusioned firebrand with a basketball court full of unanswered questions, trying to understand Carter G. Woodson's *The Miseducation of the Negro*. After my mother's death, I Greyhounded it to Chicago, lived with an aunt for a while, and ended up with a room at the YMCA. I completed high school and, in between the few "boy" jobs that existed at that time, continued my adventure into books. Margaret Walker, Sterling Brown and Claude McKay were the poets I was reading. Also, I had become aware of the "negro" political struggle and began seeking materials that would shed light on it. I was

128

glad to leave the fifties but did not realize how the sixties would change me, my people and America.

II

By 1960, the paperback revolution was changing the *entire publishing industry*, and books written by Blacks were becoming the "in" thing. By this time, I had discovered the "Chicago" writers Frank London Brown (*Trumbull Park*), Lerone Bennett, Jr. (*Before the Mayflower*) and Gwendolyn Brooks (*A Street in Bronzeville, Annie Allen* and *Maud Martha*). The works of Langston Hughes entered my world with his *The Langston Hughes Reader*. The "boy" jobs were unstable and didn't pay enough to meet my major expenses of food and housing, so I decided to leave Chicago.

The year 1960 was to be a pivotal one for a number of reasons. I discovered that the needs and problems of what little family I had were so great that they could not help me. I also learned that life's options for a young Black man ranged from few to almost none. The only value a high school diploma had was that, for one who could read, it would facilitate entrance into the armed forces. However, due to a minor heart problem, I couldn't pass the physical and was rejected by the Air Force.

After being rejected by the military (the poor boy's answer to the future and full employment) I did not see too much of a bright tomorrow. I joined a Black magazine selling caravan that traveled throughout downstate Illinois. We stopped in small towns — going from door to door — hawking the popular magazines of the day. There was little money or enjoyment in this work, but it was a way to get out of Chicago. I traveled with an all Black group of young women and men in a caravan of four cars. My second "skill" came into use because the selling pitch was "We are working our way through college." The interesting thing about this slice of life is that this was the first time college *ever entered my mind at a serious level*. I did not think that a university education was possible for poor Black people in America.

Anyway, my travels with these young "entrepreneurs" ended in St. Louis where they left me in a two-dollar-a-day hotel with a serious virus that would not allow food or liquid to remain in my body. Upon recovery, I did "boy" work to survive and spent my evenings in the public library of St. Louis. By that time I had discovered Carter G. Woodson's *The Negro in Our History*; W.E.B. Du Bois' *Souls of Black Folks, Black Reconstruction in America, Dust of Dawn, The Suppression of the African Slave-Trade to the United States*; and *Crisis* magazine. However, the work that was to cause me much conflict and inner searching was the *Philosophy and Opinions of Marcus Garvey*. I was becoming more and more aware of the issue of *color*, and these books gave me the historical and political foundation that would lead me to a realistic and deadly understanding of *white world supremacy*.

In October of 1960, without funds or the possibility of a job in a city that was less friendly than Detroit or Chicago, I tried to join the military again. This time it was to be the U.S. Army. Because of my "heart" condition, I knew that the physical exam could be a repeat of my Air Force experience. Therefore, when I walked into the examining room, which was a large, wide open area, I looked for the youngest doctor. They were all white males. During my examination, he caught an irregular heartbeat and asked if I had a heart problem. I promply said, "No. This is the first time that I've been away from home. I've never been around this many white people before, and I'm a bit nervous." I got in and was shipped to Fort Leonard Wood, Missouri for basic training.

On the bus to basic training, I was reading Paul Robeson's *Here I Stand*. The book, according to the drill sergeant that welcomed us to the camp, was written by a Black communist (the word "Black" was just as negative as "communist" in 1960) and would only confuse and corrupt my negro mind. He took the book, held it high above his head as an example of "forbidden fruit," and — in between gutter room invectives — tore the pages from the book, distributing them to the new male recruits and instructing the "ladies" to use the pages as toilet paper. I will not go into this in any more depth except to say that, for me, the military was a blessing in disguise, even though it was there that I had put my life in the hands of men less intelligent than I.

By this time, I was reading E. Franklin Frazier's *Black Bourgeoisie* and Drake's and Clayton's *Black Metropolis*. Race-politics in the United States was heating up, and upon completion of basic training, I was shipped south to Fort Bliss, Texas for advanced training in military mediocrity. In Texas, partially because there was little to do, I made a decision that would change my life. I took a speed reading course that enabled me to increase my reading speed greatly. I decided that I would become as knowledgeable as possible about Afrikan and Afrikan American people. I was nineteen, and I consciously stopped apologizing for being Black and went on the offense.

III

My study regiment for the next five years (1961-1966) was to read *a book a day* and write a 150 to 200-word review of the book. The reading went close to schedule, but the review writing revealed another inadequacy— that of my putting words on paper to convey critical meaning. Also, the task of critically analyzing what I read presented a problem. I was not prepared to do either well. But, I was in the military; I had learned discipline, and I had plenty of time. In fact, at that time the U.S. Army's unofficial motto was "hurry up and wait."

John O. Killens' *And Then We Heard The Thunder* gave me insight on Black men fighting in a racist military. It also gave me the confidence I needed to take the balance of my military time and use it to my advantage. I learned from Killens to get good yardage out of a bad situation. I realized the full range and scope of Black writing by reading anthologies and the collected works of authors. Books like James Weldon Johnson's *The Book of American Negro Poetry*; Sterling Brown's, Arthur P. Davis' and Ulysses Lee's *Negro Caravan*; and Arna Bontemps' and Langston Hughes' *The Poetry of the Negro* made it clear to me that writing as a profession was not only possible but necessary. The ignorance that Black people lived with spoke directly to their station in life. However, the lack of self-knowledge displayed among many Black people convinced me that, if nothing else, I must never put myself in the position where my ignorance would embarrass me. The study of Black people became as important to me as love-making. Therefore, reading was not only developmental, it was pleasurable; it was food and new life.

My favorite spots for acquiring Afrikan American literature — at that time it was still "negro literature" — were the Salvation Army used clothing stores and used book stores. I remember the ultimate joy of finding a mint condition, first edition copy of Richard Wright's *Native Son* for 25¢. From that day on, I was in first gear about books. Since 1961, every trip I've taken has included visits to local book stores. I found copies of Alain Locke's *The New Negro* and *The Negro in American Culture* — completed after his death by Margaret Just Butcher. Julian Mayfield's *The Hit*,

Wright's *Color Curtain*, and Saunders Redding's *The Lonesome Road* were all found in mint condition at used book stores.

The first time I encountered the term "Afro-American" was in the title of an anthology of short stories edited by Nick Aaron Ford and H.L. Faggett, *Best Short Stories by Afro-American Writers*. Up until that point (1962), the term "Negro" — capitalized due to the Garvey movement — was the "correct and accepted" designation for people of Afrikan descent in America. Ford and Faggett's title forced me to reassess what we called ourselves. Lights began to click in my mind. In contemplating this question, the crucial issue of self-definition and self-reliance took on a larger meaning. The key to any people's liberation quite logically starts with that people defining itself. As long as a people accepts the conqueror's definitions, it will be *impossible* to imagine other worlds.

Two other points need to be made about my reading. Most of the authors who influenced me were Black men, and in much of their literature they displayed the sexist attitudes and beliefs of the culture. By this time, I was reading James Baldwin's *Go Tell It On the Mountain* and *Notes of a Native Son*; Ralph Ellison's *Invisible Man*; William Gardner Smith's *Last of the Conquerors*; Ann Petry's *The Street*; Claude McKay's *Selected Poems*; Paule Marshall's *Brown Girl, Brownstones*; LeRoi Jones' *Preface to a 20 Volume Suicide Note*; John A. Williams' *Night Song*; William Melvin Kelly's *A Different Drummer;* and Lewis Lomax's *The Negro Revolt*.

The two writers who signaled to me the possibilities of poetry were Margaret Walker and Gwendolyn Brooks. Walker's *For My People* gave me fighting poetry in free and unclustered form. However, it was Gwendolyn Brooks who gave me the greatest gift — the gift of *time, caring* and *example*. This woman is as close as anybody can be to existing without *hypocrisy*.

It was the serious examples of Gwendolyn Brooks, Dudley Randall and Margaret Burroughs that pushed me to start Third World Press, the Institute of Positive Education, *Black Books Bulletin* and the African American Book Center. Because of the influence of Gwendolyn Brooks, Margaret Burroughs, Hoyt W. Fuller, Dudley Randall and Malcolm X, I am the man that I am today. I learned from them that one must *never give up in the right fight*. Yet, one must always be prepared to carry the battle to a more effective level. I may be one of the few writers of Afrikan descent who do not have to give credit or thanks to white people for our development or "success" as writers or publishers. My books have sold a million plus copies not because of white publishers, but due to the fact that Dudley Randall's Broadside Press, Chicago's Third World Press and our readers never gave up on us. That is truly progressive and revolutionary.

I left the military in September of 1963, just as four little girls were being bombed in Birmingham, Alabama. To a young man with a warrior's attitude, this state of affairs was unacceptable. I also left the military with an unofficial Ph.D. in Afrikan American literature and the words of Robert Hayden ringing in my ears, "Mean, mean, mean to be free."

IV

There are literally thousands of books that should be read by people who are truly trying to bring beauty into this world. In the United States in 1988, over 56,000 books were published. Therefore, a reader needs to be selective in her or his reading. Readers need to understand that the *introduction* to knowledge does not mean the acceptance of knowledge. There is a wealth of armchair intellectuals in the West, and the damage they do — as far as I know — has never been accurately calculated. Knowledge, if it is indeed useful, must lead one to an active consciousness; a creative and productive mind-set; a *doing* and problem-solving life-style; an environmentally conservative approach to nature; a sharing and loving presence among children and others; and the *will* to find and be an example of an enlightened person who is seeking wisdom.

The books listed here are not all-encompassing. I chose the books that I think provide a good starting point for a person seeking wholeness. I tried to divide the selection evenly between women and men. I *strongly* support the position that reading *must* become like eating — done daily and consuming the best.

Libraries are the one true gift for poor people in America. However, most poor people don't take full advantage of public libraries. We pay for libraries through our tax dollars. A well-stocked and well-staffed library is a blessing. I would not have gotten hooked on books if it wasn't for the Detroit Public Library. The free library system in this country is still an undiscovered secret.

Finally, a few tips: 1) if parents read, chances are children will read; 2) develop reading time for the home — a time when television and radio are off and books are on; 3) try to visit the library weekly as a family; 4) take children to bookstores (new and used) and encourage them to spend their own money on the books they want; 5) each home should have a library (i.e., a collection of best-loved books to be read often and shared with others); 6) parents should read to young children; 7) self-discipline is the key to a life of reading pleasure — read for information and fun; and 8) remember, books are like good fruit — rare and precious and healthy.

The first list of books is comprised of writers of Afrikan descent: Afrikan, Afrikan American, Afrikan Caribbean, etc. The second list is of non-Afrikan writers; books that I feel will bring another, yet important, perspective to international understanding. Finally, those persons who have first use of knowledge and use it in a way that advances world development are to be congratulated and rewarded. Look for them, and join their ranks; they are truly in the minority and know something the rest of us don't.

Black Writers

Achebe, Chinua
Things Fall Apart
Anthills of the Savannah
The Trouble with Nigeria

Akbar, Na'im
Chains and Images of Psychological Slavery
From Miseducation to Education

Alexander, Margaret Walker
Jubilee
Richard Wright: Daemonic Genius
This is my Century: New and Collected Poems

Angelou, Maya
I Know Why the Caged Bird Sings

Armah, Ayi Kwei
Two Thousand Seasons
The Healers
The Beautiful Ones Are Not Yet Born.
Fragments

Asante, Molefi Kete
Afrocentricity
The Afrocentric Idea

Baldwin, James
The Fire Next Time
The Evidence of Things Not Seen
Another Country
Price of the Ticket

Bambara, Toni Cade
The Sea Birds Are Still Alive

The Salt Eaters
The Black Woman (ed.)

Baraka, Amiri
Black Magic Poetry 1961-1967
Home: Social Essays
In Our Terribleness (With Billy Abernathy)
Black Music
Blues People

Beason, Jake Patton
Why We Lose

Bell, Derrick
And We Are Not Saved: The Elusive Quest for Racial Reform

Ben-Jochannan, Yosef
Black Man of Nile
African Origins of the Major "Western Religions"

Bennett, Jr., Lerone
Before The Mayflower
The Shaping of Black America

Biko, Steve
I Write What I Like

Blackwell, James E.
The Black Community: Diversity and Unity

Bontemps, Arna
Black Thunder

Brathwaite, Edward Kamau
Islands
Masks
Rights of Passage
Sun Poems

Brooks, Gwendolyn
    Blacks: Collected Works
    Report From Part One
    To Disembark
    Winnie
    Primer for Blacks

Browder, Anthony T.
    From the Browder File

Brown, Claude
    Manchild in the Promised Land

Brown, Sterling
    Collected Poems of Sterling Brown

Carruthers, Jacob
    The Irritated Genie
    Science and Oppression
    Essays In Ancient Egyptian Studies

Cesaire, Aime
    Discourse on Colonialism
    Collected Poems

Chinweizu
    Decolonizing The African Mind
    The West and the Rest of Us

Cliff, Michelle
    The Land of Look Behind

Clifton, Lucille
    Good Woman: Poems and a Memoir 1969-1980
    Next: New Poems

Cortez, Jayne
    Coagulations: New and Selected Poems

Cress-Welsing, Frances
The Isis Papers: The Keys to the Colors

Cruse, Harold
The Crisis of the Negro Intellectual
Plural But Equal

Davis, George and Clegg Watson
Black Life in Corporate America

Diop, Cheikh Anta
The African Origin of Civilization
Pre-Colonial Africa
Black Africa: The Economic and Cultural Basis for a
Federated State
The Cultural Unity of Black Africa

Douglass, Frederick
Narrative of the Life of Frederick Douglass

Drake, St. Clair
Black Folk Here and There: An Essay in History
and Anthropology
The Redemption of Africa and Black Religion

Du Bois, W.E.B.
The World and Africa
The Souls of Black Folk
Black Reconstruction in America
The Autobiography of W.E.B. Du Bois
Dusk of Dawn
(Anything by Du Bois)

Dunbar, Paul Laurence
Collected Poems

Dumas, Henry
Rope of Wind

138

Ark of Bones
Goodbye, Sweetwater

Ellison, Ralph
Invisible Man

Evans, Mari
Black Women Writers — 1950-1980
I Am a Black Woman: Poetry
Nightstar: Poetry

Fanon, Frantz
The Wretched of the Earth
Black Skin, White Masks
A Dying Colonialism

Fields, Julia
East of Moonlight

Frazier, E. Franklin
Black Bourgeoisie
The Negro Family in the United States

Fuller, Hoyt W.
Journey to Africa

Fuller, Neely
The United Independent Compensatory Code/System/Concept

Gaines, Ernest J.
In My Father's House
A Gathering of Old Men
The Autobiography of Miss Jane Pittman

Gary, Lawrence E. (ed.)
Black Men

Gayle, Jr., Addison
   The Black Aesthetic (ed.)
   Richard Wright
   The Way of the New World
   Wayward Child: An Autobiography

Giddings, Paula
   When and Where I Enter: The Impact of Black Women on
                              Race and Sex in America

Gilbert, Herman
   The Negotiations

Gordon, Vivian
   Black Women, Feminism, and Black Liberation: Which Way?

Greenlee, Sam
   The Spook Who Sat by the Door

Hale, Janice E.
   Black Children: Their Roots, Culture, and Learning Styles

Harding, Vincent
   There is a River

Hare, Nathan & Julia
   The Endangered Black Family
   Bringing the Black Boy to Manhood
   The Black Anglo-Saxons (Nathan Hare)
   Crisis in Black Sexual Politics (eds.)

Hayden, Robert
   Collected Poems

Head, Bessie
   A Question of Power

Himes, Chester
Third Generation
If He Hollers Let Him Go

Hooks, Bell
Ain't I A Woman

Hurston, Zora Neale
Mules and Men
Their Eyes Were Watching God
Tell My Horse
Moses, Man of the Mountain
Dust Tracks on a Road

Jackson, John G.
Man, God and Civilization
Christianity Before Christ
Introduction to African Civilization

Jackson, George L.
Blood in My Eye

James, George G. M.
Stolen Legacy

Johnson, James Weldon
Autobiography of An Ex-Colored Man

Jones, Reginald L. (ed.)
Black Psychology

Jordan, June
Civil Wars

Karenga, Maulana
Introduction to Black Studies
The Husia

Kawaida Theory: An Introductory Outline
Kwanzaa: Origins, Concepts, Practice

Kelly, William Melvin
    A Different Drummer
    A Drop of Patience
    Dancers on the Shore

Kenyatta, Jomo
    Facing Mount Kenya

King, Jr., Woodie (ed.)
    New Plays for the Black Theatre

Ladner, Joyce A.
    Tomorrow's Tomorrow: The Black Woman
    The Death of White Sociology

Landry, Bart
    The New Black Middle Class

Madhubuti, Haki R.
    Don't Cry, Scream
    Book of Life
    From Plan to Planet
    Enemies: the Clash of Races
    Earthquakes and Sunrise Missions
    Killing Memory, Seeking Ancestors
    Black Men: Obsolete, Single and Dangerous?

Mandela, Nelson
    The Struggle is My Life

Mandela, Winnie
    Part of My Soul Went With Him

Marable, Manning
    How Capitalism Underdeveloped Black America

Marshall, Paule
Brown Girl, Brownstones

Martin, Tony
Race First

McAdoo, Harriette Pipes (ed.)
Black Families (2nd edition)
Black Children (with John Lewis McAdoo)

McKay, Claude
Selected Poems
A Long Way From Home
Banana Bottom

Monroe, Sylvester
Brothers: Black and Poor — A True Story of Courage and
Survival

Moore, Mafori and others
Transformations: A Rites of Passage Manual for
African-American Girls

Morrison, Toni
Song of Solomon
Tar Baby
Beloved

National Urban League
The State of Black America 1989 (annual report)

Neal, Larry
Hoodoo Hollerin Bebop Ghosts
Visions of a Liberated Future

Nettleford, Rex M.
Identity Race and Protest in Jamaica

Ngugi, Wa Thiong'o
Petals of Blood
Devil on the Cross

Nkrumah, Kwame
Ghana: The Autobiography of Kwame Nkrumah
Neo-Colonialism: The Last Stage of Imperialism

Nobles, Wade
Africanity and the Black Family
*Understanding the Black Family: A Guide for Scholarship
and Research* (with Lawford C. Goddard)
African-American Families: Issues, Insights and Directions
(with Goddard, Cavil and George)

Obadele, Imari
Free the Land!
Reparations Yes! (with Lumumba and Taifa)

Padmore, George
Pan-Africanism or Communism

Parks, Carole (ed.)
Nommo: A Literary Legacy of Black Chicago 1967-1987

Perkins, Useni Eugene
Home is a Dirty Street
Harvesting New Generations
The Explosion of Black Chicago Street Gangs

Pinkney, Alphonso
The Myth of Black Progress
The American Way of Violence
Red, Black and Green: Black Nationalism in the United States

Randall, Dudley
The Black Poets
Homage to Hoyt Fuller

Reed, Ishmael
Reckless Eyeballing
Flight to Canada
The Last Days of Louisiana Kid
Writin' is Fightin': Thirty-Seven Years of Boxing on Paper

Robeson, Paul
Here I Stand

Rodney, Walter
How Europe Underdeveloped Africa

Rogers, J. A.
Sex and Race Vol. 1-3
Great Men of Color, Vol. 1 & 2

Sanchez, Sonia
I've Been a Woman
Love Poems
Under a Soprano Sky
Homegirls and Handgrenades

Shakur, Assata
Assata

Smith, Barbara A.
Home Girls

Southern, Eileen
The Music of Black Americans

Soyinka, Wole
The Man Died
Ake
Season of Anomy

Staples, Robert
    Black Masculinity: The Black Male's Role in American
                  Society
    The Black Family: Essays and Studies
    The World of Black Singles

Steady, Filomina Chioma (ed.)
    The Black Woman Cross-Culturally

Terry, Wallace
    Bloods

Toomer, Jean
    Cane

Travis, Dempsey
    Real Estate is the Gold in Your Future

Van Sertima, Ivan
    They Came Before Columbus
    Journal of African Civilizations (ed.)
        Blacks in Science: Ancient & Modern
        Black Women in Antiquity
        Nile Valley Civilizations
        African Presence in Early Asia
        African Presence in Early Europe
        Great African Thinkers (Cheikh Anta Diop)
        African Presence in Early America
        Great Black Leaders Ancient and Modern
        African Presence in World Cultures

Walker, Alice
    The Color Purple
    In Search of Our Mothers' Gardens
    Living By the Word
    Horses Make A Landscape Look More Beautiful
    The Temple of My Familiar

Wallace, Phyllis
Black Women in the Labor Force

Walters, Ronald W.
Black Presidential Politics in America: A Strategic Approach

Walton, Hanes
Invisible Politics: Black Political Behavior

Washington, Booker T.
Up From Slavery

White, Evelyn C.
Chain, Chain, Change: For Black Women Dealing with
Physical and Emotional Abuse

Williams, Chancellor
The Destruction of Black Civilization
The Rebirth of African Civilization

Williams, John A.
The Man Who Cried I Am
Sons of Darkness, Sons of Light
Jacob's Ladder

Williams, Richard
They Stole It But You Must Return It

Williams, Terry
The Cocaine Kids

Wilson, Amos
The Developmental Psychology of the Black Child

Wilson, Julius
The Truly Disadvantaged

Woodson, Carter G.
   The Mis-education of the Negro
   (anything by Woodson)

Wright, Bobby E.
   The Psychopathic Racial Personality and other Essays

Wright, Bruce
   *Black Robes, White Justice: Why Our Justice System
                            Doesn't Work for Blacks*

Wright, Richard
   Black Boy
   Native Son
   Uncle Tom's Children
   The Outsider
   White Man, Listen!
   Black Power

X, Malcolm
   The Autobiography of Malcolm X

Salaam, Kalamu ya
   Our Women Keep Our Skies From Falling
   Revolutionary Poems
   What is Life

Yette, Sam
   The Choice

Non-Black Writers

Agee, Philip
   Inside the Company: CIA Diary on the Run

Amnesty International 1988 Report (a yearly report)

Barraclough, Geoffery
Turning Points in World History

Batra, Ravi
The Great Depression of 1990

Beit-Hallahmi, Benjamin
The Israeli Connection: Who Israel Arms and Why

Berry, Wendell
The Hidden Wound

Boyd, Billy Ray
For the Vegetarian in You

Bradley, Michael
The Iceman Inheritance

Brown, Dee
Bury My Heart at Wounded Knee

Brown, Lester R. and others
State of the World 1988 (a yearly report)

Carnoy, Martin
Education or Cultural Imperialism

Chomsky, Noam
The Culture of Terrorism
*Pirates and Emperors: International Terrorism in the
Real World*
The Chomsky Reader (ed. by James Peck)
On Power and Ideology (The Managua Lectures)
The Fateful Triangle: The United States, Israel & the Palestinians

Chorover, Stephan L.
*From Genesis to Genocide: The Meaning of Human Nature
and the Power of Behavior Control*

Coates, James
Armed and Dangerous: The Rise of the Survivalist Right

Cockburn, Alexander
Corruptions of Empire

Deloria, Jr., Vine
We Talk, You Listen
Custer Died for Your Sins
Behind the Trail of Broken Treaties

Domhoff, G. William
Who Owns America Now?

Flynn, Kevin and Gerhardt, Gary
The Silent Brotherhood: Inside America's Racist Underground

Frederickson, George
White Supremacy

Gabler, Neal
An Empire of Their Own: How the Jews Invented Hollywood

Galbrath, John Kenneth
The Nature of Mass Poverty

Gilder, George
Men and Marriage
Naked Nomads
Wealth and Poverty

Ginzburg, Ralph
100 Years of Lynchings

Gould, Stephen Jay
The Mismeasure of Man

Hapgood, Fred
Why Males Exist

Harrington, Michael
The Other American
The Vast Majority
The New American Poverty
Taking Sides

Harris, Marvin
Cows, Pigs, Wars and Witches: The Riddles of Culture
America Now: The Anthropology of a Changing Culture
Cannibals and Kings: The Origins of Culture
Our Kind

Herman, Edward S.
The Real Terror Network: Terrorism in Fact and Propaganda

Josephy, Jr., Alvin M.
Now That the Buffalo's Gone

Kennedy, Paul
The Rise and Fall of the Great Powers

Kiernan, V.G.
America: The New Imperialism
From White Settlement to World Hegemony

Kozol, Jonathan
Illiterate America
Death at An Early Age
Rachel and Her Children: Homeless Families in America

Lappe, Frances Moore
Food First
World Hunger Twelve Myths (with Joseph Collins)

Lerner, Gerda
The Creation of Patriarchy

Lessing, Doris
Prisons We Choose to Live Inside

Lewis, Norman
The Missionaries: God Against the Indians

Macdonald, Andrew
Turner Diaries

Machiavelli, Niccolo
The Prince

Malefijt, Annamarie de Wal
Religion and Culture: An Introduction to Anthropology of Religion

Martinez, Thomas and John Guinther
Brotherhood of Murder

Matthiessen, Peter
In the Spirit of Crazy Horse
Indian Country

Mead, Margaret
Male and Female
Keep Your Powder Dry

Mendelism, Kurt
The Secret of White Domination

Momaday, N. Scott
House Made of Dawn
The Names

Montagu, Ashley
The Natural Superiority of Women

Nader, Ralph
Big Boys: Power and Position in American Business

Omang, Joanne and Neier, Aryeh
Psychological Operations in Guerrilla Warfare: The CIA's Nicaragua Manual

O'Reilly, Kennedy
"Racial Matters": The FBI's Secret File on Black America, 1960-1972

Puzo, Mario
The Godfather

Raspail, Jean
The Camp of the Saints

Robbins, John
Diet for a New America

Russell, Bertrand
Unpopular Essays
The Basic Writings of Bertrand Russell

Schaef, Ann Wilson
Women's Reality: An Emerging Female System in a White Male Society

Schur, Edwin M.
Our Criminal Society

Seager, Joni and Ann Olson
Women in the World (An International Atlas)

Skinner, B.F.
Beyond Freedom and Dignity
Science and Human Behavior

Sklar, Holly
Trilateralism (ed.)
Reagan, Trilateralism and the Neoliberals

Spence, Gerry
With Justice for None

Stokes, Bruce
Helping Ourselves: Local Solutions to Global Problems

Tivnan, Edward
The Lobby: Jewish Political Power and American Foreign Policy

Toffler, Alvin
Future Shock
The Third Wave

Tucker, Frank H.
*The White Conscience: An Analysis of the White Man's
Mind and Conduct*

Turnbull, Colin M.
The Human Cycle

Tzu, Lao
The Way of Life

Tzu, Sun
The Art of War

Ward, Churchill and James V. Wall
Agents of Repression

Weyler, Rex
*Blood of the Land: The Government and Corporate War
Against the American Indian Movement*

Wilhelm, Sidney M.
Who Needs the Negro?

Williams, William Appleman
Empire as a Way of Life

Zwitny, Jonathan
*The Crimes of Patriots: A True Tale of Dope, Dirty Money
and the CIA*
Vicious Circles: The Mafia in the Market Place
Endless Enemies: The Making of an Unfriendly World

Twelve Secrets of Life

There are people in this world who live their entire lives without knowing anything about themselves, culturally or biologically. Many of these people run from any identification with their origins, especially if their origins are outside of mainstream America. Most of these people have little accurate knowledge about their bodies and generally depend upon the so-called "experts" for information about their health.

Learning to take hold of one's life is very difficult in a culture that values property over life. This is the same culture that developed the concept of "planned obsolescence" and throw-away underwear. Most Black people in this country are wards of the state. This dependency has rendered many of them neutral in the fight for Black liberation. Therefore, it is mandatory that Afrikan Americans develop "survival and development strategies." We must be able to disconnect from the oppression around us, whether it's political, economic or of a more personal form coming from friends, family members or co-workers. Negative people always will want to involve others in their defeated lives.

Beware of people trying to make their history, culture and traditions yours. Beware of people trying to put their troubles and fears onto you. The road to a life full of *stress* surely is paved with one's inability to say *no* to destructive behavior or activity in the home, on the job, in the streets or in singles bars at happy hour. Knowing one's capacity to deal with the damaged lives of others, as well as one's own "developing" life, can be the difference between *life* and *death*. The road to curing stress, anxiety and frustration is understanding the source of stress, anxiety and frustration. This is not easy because most of us live too close to the surface of life and seldom investigate underlying meanings or reasons for actions. The only messages most of us hear are the ones announcing the arrival of money or pleasure.

We are all prisoners of bad habits. People in the West generally do not "die" natural deaths. We kill ourselves in any number of ways: bad nutritional practices, lack of exercise, unchecked stress, obesity, alcohol and drug addiction, smoking, suicide, poverty, etc. Learning to say goodbye to negative people and situations is extremely difficult if one has grown up with such. Destructive behavior is learned from one's environment, (i.e., culture). Bad habits are acquired, and the habitual mind is very dangerous to the developing self.

This brings me to the bone of change: the ability to look at one's self honestly and design a personalized program for change. This program must include inner exploration, inner investigation, contemplative solitude, professional consultation and inner transformation. In order to effectively deal with a weakness, the weakness needs to be acknowledged. All people have inner selves. However, most do not discover their inner power until it's too late. Most people are transfixed in the past, hypnotized by past defeats or failures, and often they do not understand the sources of denial at a personal or professional level. We don't know where we want to go because we don't know where we've been; nor do we know where we are now. I am not talking about a geopolitical definition but one that connects us to each other regardless of the "systems" endured around the world.

Most people have experienced *rejection* and, therefore, many people build their lives around *not being* accepted. This terrible burden is a frequent reaction to being Black in a white-controlled world where one is rejected even before one is able to see the rejector. Learning what not to do can lead one to *what to do*. However, that is like going through the back door to open the front door. The inner self determines the outer self. Walking away from destruction, saying *no* to foolishness and silliness, refusing handouts and ridding one's self of debilitating habits is the road to wholeness.

Yet, there remains an inner emptiness in most of us. We live in a culture that respects, protects, praises and rewards people with power. And, this power is generally defined as the domination of people, things, ideas, resources and property. Therefore, we find ourselves dominated by the people who are able to play the power game the best.

The fight or quest for power, *as* the norm and ultimate definer, dehumanizes the seeker of truth. A culture built upon the ownership of people and things works against harmonious relationships and pits people against one another for the control of each other. Returning to the "self" becomes even more difficult, especially if one has never been there. And, in a wasteful and property-oriented culture, there ceases to be a "self;" there are just "things" and "others." Therefore, the inner or autonomous self is back-seated to the life of "acquisition" and misdefined "good life."

158

Chattel enslavement in the United States has been replaced with "material" and "mental" enslavement.

The secrets of a good and productive life are not really secrets. They are mainly common sense activities/actions that have been lost in modern Western life. Most people, due to their struggle for economic survival and misdirection, are too busy trying to keep up with people who have lost their way. *We must return to our source.* Start today by giving *yourself* an hour each day to reach for a *new you*. Start with finding and defining your own *space*. This can be in your home, at a library, under a tree, in a museum or along the path that you walk on each day. Seek a new *solitude* with yourself. Inner reflection requires an understanding of the meditative tradition. Study is in order. Slow down. Quiet your insides, and bring your *outer self* to a slow walk. Start today. If you don't, you may not be able to say no when the order is given to kill your own people. Remember, strengthen the insides and the outer will come.

1. *Self-knowledge*

The Ethiopians have a saying, "A cat may go to a monastery, but she still remains a cat!" Afrikans brought to America are still Afrikans. *Yes,* we have been changed. But, knowing one's self is key to knowing and understanding others. If a person hides from self-understanding or self-knowledge, his or her life will be built upon a bed of quicksand that promises slow but certain confusion, pain, self-doubt and lonely death.

All people need to take charge of their lives. The more a person understands her or his mind and body, the less she or he will destroy it. Ignorance breeds weakness and fear. One's history and culture are as important to good life as food and water. If you don't know who you are, you will be forever fighting other people's wars.

All people, if they are to develop, must ask the simple and correct questions that define life. Why are we here? Where did we come from? What is our purpose in life? Are we here to serve others or ourselves? Self-knowledge leads to self-understanding, which is the path to becoming a whole person. Remember the Afrikan proverb, "Wood may remain ten years in the water, but it will never become a crocodile." First, find the reasons for your own existence and condition. Respect learning. Seek to be *world class* in everything that you do. The best way to do this is through study, work and more study and work.

2. Family

People are shaped by other people and culture. All people have/had mothers and fathers. However, not all mothers and fathers are responsible. Therefore, Black families are undergoing a transition. If one is asked to list the five most important ingredients for the development of a good and productive person, family would be at the top of the list, far ahead of money, cars, clothes and fame.

Working families provide serious love. Members learn self-love and self-worth in functional families. Most importantly, a person's self-esteem is heightened in a family that is goal-oriented with members who are about the business of making life better. Families do fruitful things together, thereby giving their members a sense of oneness and collective doing. Families represent a lifeline among skyscrapers, clear water in sewage.

Families live in houses or apartments that they *make into homes*. A family's home is a refuge from a hostile world. When a person returns home, it is expected that he or she will find peace, welcome, warmth, food for body and mind, protection, love, support and rejuvenation. It is said in Afrika that "living is worthless for one without a home."

Children learn values and morals first in a family context. Integrity, truthfulness, responsibility, honor and shame should be taught first in a family situation. Therefore, one's philosophy of life is taught first at the family level. The one institution that a "developing" or "oppressed" people *cannot* do without is family. Nonfunctioning families will produce nonfunctioning people.

3. Community

There is an Ethiopian proverb that states, "To one who does not know, a small garden is a forest." That's what a family is in relationship to a community. A working community is the closest ecosystem that feeds, stimulates, supports and nurtures families. Communities are impossible without families, and families are strengthened and directly influenced by community-based institutions like houses of worship, schools, universities, businesses, cultural centers, etc. However, the major function of a working community is to make the lives of all its residents livable and enjoyable. This is why ethnic groups form communities. Communities

160

provide not only historical and cultural connections but also *familiarity*. Working communities are like self-contained units that fight the powers that be in order to maintain their existence. The leadership that emerges from a community is one whose allegiance is to that community and the families living in it. When a community fails, its residents are in trouble. When a community's institutions are dying or nonexistent, there is no community. The families are the trees, and the community is the forest. If the forest is alive and well, the family will receive the oxygen needed for life.

4. *Avoiding Stress*

Most people worry too much about things they can't change or control. This is why strong families and strong communities are necessary. They help insulate individuals and define the world in more realistic terms. Families put the world into context, thereby rendering meaning. Part of the stress problem in the United States is related to incomplete definitions, a misunderstanding of the purpose of life, an inability to cope, the necessity to keep up with the neighbors and living with *lies*.

To avoid stress one must examine one's self truthfully and without shortcuts. A Senegalese proverb states, "A healthy ear can stand hearing sick words." Thus, the road to health and a stress-free life is the acceptance of the sickness that revolves around one's own life. This requires a fresh start, a new spirit and the ability to attack each day while searching for happiness that is not defined by the ownership of people or things. Therefore, one must:

1) Seek truth and base one's life on it.
2) Understand one's own culture, history and traditions.
3) Be family-oriented — biological family or social family.
   Every individual needs loving people in her/his life.
4) *Change*: Remove bad habits from one's activities.
5) Seek life-giving and life-saving ideas.
6) Not fear failure as one works for "success."
7) Redefine success out of one's own needs and realities.
8) Realize that to be wrong is not failure, just a detour in the
   path to "success."
9) Value the simple things in life.
10) Seek interdependency rather than dependency.

11) Be productive. Avoid too much television. Be creative. Learn a craft. Take up exercising. Keep the body and mind active.
12) Slow down one's life.
13) Be more selective about the food one eats.
14) Be more selective about the people with whom one forms friendships.
15) Seek quality rather than quantity.
16) Cease the use of alcohol, drugs and cigarettes.
17) Learn to say *no* to destruction.
18) Attack one's own fears.
19) Try to see her/himself as others see her/him.
20) Never blame others for one's mistakes.
21) Not let anger cloud one's mind.
22) Avoid harming others unless they seek to harm her/him.
23) Let nothing stop one's search! Always consciously move from unawareness to awareness. Gravitate toward people who are doing good work. Seek inner harmony. Other people cannot provide one with ultimate happiness; they can only make one dependent upon them. Dependency brings on stress. Do not avoid problems. Learn to relax. Cultivate interests that will force a change in actions and attitude. Share love.

Life is, indeed, a path. The knower knows the right one to take. A stressless life is available to those who are willing to study and seek joy in less costly and destructive ways.

5. Critical Thinking

Very seldom are people taught thinking skills. Early in childhood we are told to use our minds, but how to use them is generally left to the individual. Answers to the stresses of modern life, for the average person, have been condensed to thirty-minute sitcoms and one-hour dramas. Solutions to most minor illnesses can be found in thirty-second commercials, and most psychological problems are now handled by radio talk show hosts.

Thinking for one's self is not easy, especially if it's been done by somebody else all of one's life. The mind is often captive by the insignificant. We generally have been taught to listen, do and believe without question.

162

It has become much *easier to believe than think.* Thinking requires intro-spection, investigation, silence, definitions, contemplation, challenges, competition, instruction and study. Thinking also demands that a person be curious about the world, its people, its animals, its vegetation, its ex-istence.

Most people who think critically about the world are doers. They are problem-solvers. Thinkers become teachers, doctors, judges, professors, poets, writers, artists, musicians and designers. They are thoughtful people who are always looking for better answers. They go beneath the surface of problems. They do not settle for the easy questions or answers about life.

6. Discipline/Motivation

Very little that is worthwhile is accomplished without discipline. Dis-cipline is a learned process; we are not born knowing it. Parents are children's first teachers of discipline. However, if a child is to move into adulthood with any chance of doing well (i.e., being productive and living a stressless life), he or she will have to learn self-discipline.

Part of the discipline process is the ability to separate desires from needs and prioritize one's life. In a highly material culture, it is easy to lose one's way. The unimportant becomes important, and fruit exists as some-thing to be eaten out of cans. Knowing when to say *no* and knowing one's own limitations is critical to self-discipline. Being able to attack the dif-ficult methodically and not allow the easier temptations of life to inter-fere with self-development is self-discipline.

Motivation is another important aspect of discipline. There must be something to drive us to move beyond the limiting expectations of losers; that something is *motivation.* Often motivation is the result of wanting something material, like a car. If this is the case, a person arranges his/her life in a way that his/her work, play, creativity, etc. is in line with acquir-ing that car. However, the type of self-motivation I am thinking of is that which inspires people to be better than they believe they can be. Self-dis-cipline and motivation are the fruits and vegetables of which superior gar-dens are made.

163

Most people in urban centers over-eat and, as a consequence, are over-weight and in bad health. People are popping pills for everything: pills to get up with, pills to force bowel movements, pills to lower blood pressure, pills to lose weight, pills to gain weight, pills to put one to sleep and pills (drugs) to cure everything from pot bellies to appetites. The West's answer to illness and disease is to develop another pill.

Over-eating is bad enough, but add to that the consumption of non-food (junk and processed garbage) and you have a crisis. The saying "You are what you eat" is not just a slogan, it's the *truth*. It is only logical that we develop physically and mentally from what we take into our bodies. It defies logic to think that we will have a healthy nation when the great majority of restaurants in the country are "fast food" outlets. Health is greatly curtailed when a person's primary diet consists of double cheeseburgers, sodas, potato chips, french fries, more soda, tomato catsup, milk shakes and desserts made from plastics.

Develop a diet that is in keeping with the natural flow of nature. Try moving toward a diet based on live foods, such as fruits, vegetables, grains, seeds, beans and plenty of *clean* water. In Nigeria, there is a saying that states, "Meat does not eat meat." The eating of meat has been a major contribution to poor health in America. (See "What's Food Got To Do With It?") Study the preventative health aspects of proper nutrition. Move toward 50% raw food and 50% cooked foods. Learn how to combine foods properly for eating. Investigate *fasting* and *colonic irrigation* as components of *preventative health.*

Why do young people look so old in the United States? Why are so many bellies hanging over the belts of young people and senior citizens? Even though "health" is a growth industry, it is mainly touching the affluent few who can afford $400+ a year health club memberships. To maintain a healthy mind, a youthful disposition, an eagerness about life, an active sex life and the strength to do productive work, one *must* exercise. Mind and body are connected; each person must find (design) an exercise program that will keep him or her healthy. Here are a few suggestions:

A) *Walking.* Most people walk, but do they know that by increasing their speed and using a little more arm motion, walking becomes one of the best exercises known? When done properly, walking is an excellent overall workout. Jogging in moderation can be added for those who are in good health and need a little more stimulation.

B) *Cycling.* Bike riding is not just for children; it is one of the best exercises available.

C) *Swimming.* The best way to exercise every muscle in the body is by swimming.

D) *Tennis, volleyball and other low contact sports.*

E) *Yoga.* The best way to stretch is to practice yoga. Yoga is part of a particular philosophy of life that stresses peace and good health. For many people in the world it is a way of life.

F) *Breathing.* Deep breathing three or four times a day is rejuvenating. Breathe in through the nose, pulling oxygen to the stomach; breathe out slowly through the mouth.

Most health consultants recommend that you consult your doctor before starting any new physical development program . I also encourage this because for any program to work, the participants must exercise at least forty minutes four times a week.

8. *Spiritual Search/Reciprocity:*

Always seek answers to the reasons for life. The religion one practices is not as important as the practice itself. Most "world" religions are based upon *doing good* in this world. Beware of cults. Beware of any philosophy of life that makes human beings into deities and places man or woman at the center of the universe. Seek a *way of life* that is non-conflictual but is self-protective. Study all spiritual paths. Study all religions. Pay particular attention to Afrikan spiritual knowledge. Learn to meditate, and try to bring quietness into your life. Study the works of the great spiritual thinkers. Bring more contemplation into your life. Beware also of the misuses of patriarchy in *all* world philosophies.

Reciprocity is a common Afrikan value. The giving is just as important as the receiving. When one smiles at a person, a smile is expected in return. Life's expectations are built around doing good for those you love. If doing good is *the way* in one's life, and if there is any justice in this universe, good should return to one. Only give what you can, and always receive in the spirit of the giving.

9. *Cultural Interaction:*

In most urban areas, visible and active Afrikan American cultural institutions have developed. These institutions generally have low budgets and, therefore, need to be sought out by interested individuals. Of course, the major cultural and spiritual institution in the Black community is the church. However, most Black churches still operate out of a white Christian-Judaic tradition, and that must be understood. Yet, due to the Black liberation struggle of the last thirty years, many ministers have reevaluated their teachings and have begun to preach from a more Afrikan-centered perspective.

We should be aware of the national professional organizations that are working in the best interests of Black people. For example: National Council of Black Studies, African Heritage Association, National Association of Black Social Workers, Association for the Study of Classical African Civilizations, National Black United Front and others.

Involvement in local Black men's and women's groups will give immediate support to persons looking for another way. Become more involved in cultural celebrations: Juneteenth; Black Liberation/History Month (February); Kwanzaa (Dec. 26-Jan. 1); Martin Luther King, Marcus Garvey and Malcolm X birthday observations; etc. The major point is that all people, especially children, need cultural interaction frequently. If one is to be one's self, one must be surrounded by and submersed in one's culture.

10. *Self-Reliance/Ambition:*

America was built on the backs of Afrikan people who were enslaved by whites. The "greatness" of this country was made possible by the "free" or slave labor provided by Afrikan people for over 300 years.

The education that most Black people have received in this country has prepared them to work for others. Most of our people are workers who produce wealth for others. America was also built on small and medium-size businesses. This move toward multinational and world capitalism has been very detrimental to the worker, both Black and white.

We must become more self-reliant in economics, politics and education. We cannot continuously depend on former slave masters and their allies to aid Black people. We must prepare our children to start, operate and succeed in their own businesses. We must move into the business cycle of this country and the world as entrepreneurs and owners.

11. *Creative Production:*

Enjoy life. Do things that bring you happiness. Life is too short to spend it in front of a television set, lost in the lives of others. If you do not have a hobby or art in which you now partake, think about learning something new. The world is too large and complex for a person to be confined to the southside of Chicago. Explore life. Travel, even if it's to neighboring states. However, if possible, travel abroad; nothing expands the mind like experiencing other cultures.

We often are able to find ourselves through our creativity. Whether one writes, paints, dances, acts or plays music, the more one practices these and other arts, the less stressful he or she will be. Become multi-talented; a person who can do many things well will be in greater demand. Remember, you do have a choice. A Cameroon proverb states, "Knowledge is better than riches." We Afrikan Americans say, "Knowledge leads one to riches."

12. *Adapting to Change:*

The world is a far different place than it was one hundred, fifty or even thirty years ago. The economy has changed drastically. The politics of the country are less exclusive. The production of food, by and large, has been taken over by large agri-business companies. Most urban water is polluted, and the education that a child receives in an urban school system is sub-par.

A person need not only be adaptable to change, he or she must be able to see change coming and initiate change. I'm not asking the reader to go into the business of forecasting the future, but it is important that one understands where the world is going in the areas of race, economics, politics, environment, food production, education, arts, etc.

Finally, a people (as well as an individual) needs to be able and ready to take its destiny into its own hands. As we liberate our minds, our bodies must follow. We must be prepared to run institutions, organizations, cities, states, nations (i.e., the world) — not as lone gun-slingers among hostile cultures but as participants who understand the necessity of *interdependence* and *sharing*.

We must not come as beggars or buyers but as men and women who understand that the value and worth of most people are tied to their indigenous and creative production. Poverty is slavery, and it *is* criminal that the world's wealth is controlled by a *very* small group of men. We cannot depend on rich people to share their wealth. Everything has an end, and as the Nigerians say, "The bird flies high, but always returns to earth." Those who control the world's wealth and resources are being pulled back to the earth every day.

REFERENCES

Gardner, David C. & Beatty, Grace J. *Stop Stress and Aging Now: The Methuselah Manual*. ATRA, 1985.

Null, Gary. *The Vegetarian Handbook: Eating Right for Total Health.* St. Martin, 1987.

Robbins, John. *Diet for a New America: How Your Food Choices Affect Your Health, Happiness & the Future of Life on Earth*. Stillpoint, 1987.

Samskrti & Veda. *Hatha Yoga Manual I*. Himalayan Publishers.

Samskrti & Franks, Judith. *Hatha Yoga Manual II*. Himalayan Publishers, 1982.

Sher Barbara & Gottlieb, Annie. *Wishcraft: How to Get What You Really Want*. Ballantine, 1987.

Five Most Often Used Excuses
Black Men Give Black Women

It takes more than *love* to make a marriage or relationship work. Love between partners is a glorious start, and for young people it may represent the answer to all questions. However, for more mature and experienced partners, there are other values just as important as love.

Following one's heart *only* may lead a person to a life of unhappiness and confusion. Serious relationships are built and sustained not only on heartfelt feelings but also on the degree to which partners are willing to "give up" a part of their lives to each other. The *sharing* component often is lost in the "new view" of relationships. However, a successful relationship — whether it leads to marriage or not — requires trust; responsibility; communication; productive partners; realistic worldviews; cultural knowledge and compatibility; discipline; clear definitions of fathering, mothering and parenting; and a supportive extended family. Most young people are floating in the upper stratosphere during their "first" love, and listening to their extended family is not one of their criteria for success or happiness. Therefore, two of the values they *must* learn are *patience* and *listening*, especially where elders and family are concerned.

The essence of this short essay is to call Black men on the games that most of us have been taught to play. Pulling the covers off of this "mean-spirited" and often unknown habit of *lying* and *running from relationship to relationship* only shows how Black men and women are shadows of each other. Once the shadow fades, neither of them can develop. We must face each other when we smile.

As I see it, after much consultation with Afrikan American men and women, these are the five excuses Black men use most often to avoid commitment and responsibility:

1) *You don't understand me!* Anytime a Black woman arrives at the crucial point of truly understanding the brother she is with, he says she doesn't understand him. Somebody is wrong; generally, it is the brother. Most Black men fear analysis of their actions from anybody, especially

the sisters with whom they are living or relating. This denial of reality is not uncommon among Black men. Generally, the woman a brother is with knows him better than anyone, with the possible exception of his parents and siblings. The Ashanti proverb states, "It is the wife who knows her husband." Until Black men can honestly face themselves and communicate with themselves, they will not be able to relate meaningfully to Black women. Understanding one's self starts with an admission of not understanding.

2) *Yes, you are right, but...!* Few Black men are willing to admit to errors or mistakes. Even though the sister may have read the brother to the bone, he cannot allow her the last word. This inability to be honest and accept responsibility when one is clearly at fault is a problem among many Black men. The truth and/or evidence may be staring him in the eye, but he can't bring himself to acknowledge it. This reminds me of the Afrikan proverb that states, "He who cannot dance will say: 'The drum is bad.'" Facing reality is difficult enough, but lying to one's self about reality can be tragic. Listening to one's partner, rather than challenging her every utterance, is maturity. However, in a patriarchal culture, seldom are men able to mature to the point where women are regarded as equals. Therefore, the *"but"* will always remain in the conversation.

3) *You are too good for me!* This excuse is probably the closest to the truth. Clearly, there are many women who are not internally ready for relationships, but by and large it is the brothers who plead unworthiness, which is an admission of failure — whether they mean it to be or not. By downplaying and questioning his own qualities, he is attempting to put the woman on the defense and solicit sorrow and understanding. If the sister has "been around the block," she will see through this immediately. She will understand that this man is not willing to make a long-term commitment and is not strong or honest enough to face the woman with the truth. Many Black men avoid the truth like it is a drug that will keep their penises soft. This excuse is given mainly to women who are educationally, professionally and/or financially superior to the men. Due to the nature of the patriarchal society, most men are unable to accept this type of relationship on a long-term basis. The exception is men who are secure and productive in their lives.

170

4) *I need my space!* Generally, this comes from brothers who couldn't define space if their lives depended on it. Often, they don't have a pot to pee in, but they are ready to call it quits and run. There may be another sister or the current relationship has moved to the point where a "higher" commitment needs to be made, articulated and practiced. These space-based brothers are generally men who have children and who have not developed/matured to the point of being fathers. Somehow in their early mis-education, they were taught that parenting is women's work, that house work is women's work, that diaper changing is women's work and that being involved in such interferes with one's manhood. Too many Black men are destroyed because of this. All space is what one makes of it. However, when space is shared, obviously couples have to talk about its usage. All people, especially in a highly competitive culture, need a place to "cool out," relax and be themselves. That's part of the definition of a home.

5) *I don't have any money and I don't have the time!* The *man* is on my back. This is the brother who is working on a job that demands a lot of time. Generally, his mate knows little about his finances, and he is always crying "broke." When the relationship started, nothing was too good or cost too much. However, as the months and years rolled by, the lack of communications around resources, enlargement of responsibility and probably undisciplined spending have led to financial problems. Rather than sit down like a mature adult and come up with a plan to *save* and pay bills, he just cries "poverty." The *time* question is very important. Most Black men do not have enough money. However, they do have time. If one's time (quality time) is not given to the relationship, where is it going? If relationships are to mature, if couples are to develop, time is more important than money because maturity, wisdom and wealth do not come overnight.

I am sure that many readers will argue against these five excuses. There are many others, but I've tried to condense them to those excuses that cut across class or economic lines. It must be clear that most Afrikan American men in this culture have not been taught to communicate with their mates, children, family, friends or themselves. This inability to face one's self, one's critics and one's actions is the basis for self-deception. A man has to be intimately in touch with himself in order to touch others.

The value of being able to touch and be touched is fundamental to quality relationships. The Tanzanian people have a saying: "Do not mend your neighbor's fence before looking to your own." Men in America have not been taught to be introspective or honest with themselves. Patriarchy not only demands that men be the providers, protectors and law givers, but it also suggests that men are *always right*. One cannot grow within such a definition. To avoid questions, dodge responsibility, accept false reality and hide from the music that Black men need in their lives can only bring regression. Remember, "a healthy ear can stand hearing sick words." We should try to live our lives without excuses, alibis and self-promoting lies. Most of us are disconnected from the security of family permanence. We are the people of concrete, and concrete cracks when it gets too hot. A returning to the earth is in order.

Before Sorry: Listening to and
Feeling the Flow of Black Women

The Vietnamese people could not have won their war against the French or the United States if the Vietnamese women had not particpated as first-line combatants and support troops. Female fighters were also instrumental in Nicaragua, Mozambique, Zimbabwe and many other nations in their wars for liberation. Front-line combat for women is not universal, but as valuable and functional support personnel, women have made a contribution which is beyond question. Many nations are learning from firsthand experience that a nation which restricts the equal participation of its women in all things political, economic and social *will remain second rate.*

In the opening procession at the 1988 Olympics in Seoul, South Korea, the picture that again confirmed the unequal status of women in the world was the sight of delegation after delegation marching past the review stand with few, if any, women among them. The countries that had the fewest female athletes and support staff are located in Afrika, Asia and Central America. The ruling pattern of most cultures, and most certainly Western culture, is the dominance of the patriarchy. In the United States, white males control everything of value and, therefore, wield awesome power over Black women and men in all of the life-saving and life-giving areas of society: law, economics, education, politics, military, religion, entertainment, sports, language, mass media and culture.

The Misdirection of Men

Most men in this country have been socialized to treat women like children. In fact, in many cases, children may have it better; they are not expected to be perfect. To imply that women are equal in America is like saying that deer don't have predators. A friend of mine, a minister who is considered rather progressive, confessed to me in a moment of weakness that he opens and closes his prayers thanking his male God that he's not a woman. Also, there was a recent photograph in *The New York Times* (12-1-88) of fifty Jewish feminists praying at the Wailing Wall in Jerusa-

173

lem. They were carrying the sacred text of Judaism, the *Torah*, and were dressed in prayer shawls and yarmulkes. The orthodox rabbis were furious. According to the *Times*, Rabbi Meir Yehuda Getz, who is in charge of the site, said, "A woman carrying a *Torah* is like a pig at the Wailing Wall." The point of these two stories is that male chauvinism (or sexism) is culturally based, and most, if not all, cultures practice it. Few men or women are exempt from its deadly hold.

The place and status of women in the world is dispicable. Women comprise over one half of the world's population, yet male children are still preferred in most cultures. Women's power most certainly is not commensurate with their numbers. In the case of women, large populations have not translated into clout. Joni Seager and Ann Olson reported in their eye-opening *Women in the World Atlas*, "For women, there are no developed countries. Although some places are clearly better for them to live in than others, it is not always true that the relatively rich countries of the world provide better circumstances for them as women than do poorer countries." Other facts documented by Seager and Olson include:

- In Afghanistan, 4% of eligible girls are enrolled in secondary school; in Australia, 88%.

- In Angola, fewer than 1% of adult women have access to contraceptives; in Belgium, 76%.

- Women in Ghana bear an average of over six children; women in West Germany, fewer than two.

- In Jamaica, the maternal mortality rate stands at 106 mothers' deaths for every 100,000 births; in Norway, there are fewer than eight deaths per 100,000 births.

Most women world over, but especially those in misdeveloped countries, find themselves in a state of powerlessness, dependency and inequality at all levels of society. There are profound differences in the status of Black women and white women in the world. The statistics presented in *Women in the World Atlas* make this clear. It is also evident that all women have been locked out of history-making, science-making and art-making. The only clear area of creativity on which they have a monopoly is baby-making.

One of the few studies that attempts to capture the status of Black women internationally is *The Black Woman Cross-Culturally*, edited by Filomina Chioma Steady. The significance of this book cannot be overstated. Dr. Steady and her contributors focused on the roles of women of Afrikan descent in the United States, Afrika, Caribbean and South America. The picture that emerges from this anthology reveals that: 1) Afrikan women are truly world women; 2) the problems Black women face worldwide are complex, and cross-cultural solutions do not necessarily work; 3) racism (white world supremacy), sexism, inequalities in wealth and lack of opportunities keep Black women dependent; 4) women are not the "weaker sex;" and 5) Afrikan women world over are fighting for enlightened partnerships with their men while actively resisting the domination of Black and white men.

I do not believe that the lives or futures of Afrikan American women should revolve around the thoughts, actions, wishes, demands or strategies of men. Men, mainly white men in our lifetime, have controlled, ordered and reordered the cultures of this planet to our detriment. Hundreds of millions of people, mainly children, go to sleep each night begging for food, shelter, clothing and small happiness. Most of the wealth on this earth is directly or indirectly concentrated in the hands of a few men. Out of a world population of 4.5 billion plus people, less than 5% control the world's wealth, and that percentage is getting smaller each year. If such a state of affairs is not *criminal*, I don't know the meaning of the word. In the United States, power is in the hands of a small white "power elite that is the leadership group of a property-based ruling class," according to William Domhoff's *Who Rules America Now?* This ruling class is 95% white men, and generally the 5% white women who are part of this elite are there by nature of their inheritance.

The White Male System and Its Partners

Ann Wilson Schoff in her book *Women's Reality* clearly understands the white male rulership in this country. She calls it the "white male system" and makes clear distinctions between the white male system and individual white males. The following is her definition of the white male system:

It is the system in which we live, and in it, the power and influence are held by white males. This system did not happen overnight, nor was it the result of the machinations of only a few individuals; we all not only let it occur but participated in its development...it controls almost every aspect of our culture. It makes our laws, runs our economy, sets our salaries, and decides when and if we will go to war or remain at home. It decides what *is* knowledge and how it is to be taught.

This definition is important in part because she simultaneously defines the white world supremacist system. It is obvious that white men are the main benefactors, but the system could not survive or prosper without white women. Yes, white men and white women fight; yes, white men control and manipulate white women; yes, white men define white women's place in the white male culture. However, the bottom line is this: *white people could not exist without white men and white women working overtime to reproduce themselves.*

The only way white people are created in this world, other than from gene pools or some other abberation, is by whites mating with whites. If a white person mates with any other person of color, the offsprings will not be white. Period. Therefore, it is clear that what really exists between white men and white women is a family battle that takes on different forms — depending on the country, politics, economics, education and white peoples' proximity to other races, especially Black people.

Vivian Gordon in her book *Black Women, Feminism and Black Liberation: Which Way?* clearly delineates the difference between white women's struggle and Black women's struggle. In her discussion on civil rights and women's studies, she makes a very telling point:

> The perspective of most women's studies programs is that Black and White women have suffered a common experience of oppression which is gender-specific. There is a pervasive unwillingness to acknowledge the distinctintly different nature of oppression for White and non-White women. Seldom is attention given to the extent to which White women have benefited from the oppression of Black women and/or have been active participants in racism.

Dr. Gordon's insight on the triple oppression all Black women face (racism, sexism and economic oppression) makes her book must reading for serious men and women. Her main position, however, is that Black women and white women do *not* share a common history, especially when it comes to oppression; that "white economic exploitation varies drastically for Black and White women;" and that "White women benefited from and participated in the oppression of Black women." Her clear analysis throws water on white women/Black women coalition triangles and shows how historically they have hurt mainly Black women. Dr. Gordon's book is an impassioned yet studied call for renewed cooperation between Black women and men as partners in this most difficult of world struggles.

Back Home

Where does this brief and incomplete discussion leave us? If I've been clear, it is certain that the first line struggle for Black liberation is solidly rooted in the relationship developed between Black men and women. Our buying into other people's systems, struggles, worldviews and values has all but destroyed us. Our rush to become "integrated" Americans has brought us much pain and misery and has had a debilitating effect on Black family life.

The smiles that used to be reserved for each other can be bought on street corners in strange cities. Our love for each other has gone the way of the 45 rpm records. Too many Black lives have been reduced to a killing *purposelessness*. Due to the inability of a significant number of Black people to analyze large social forces, they continuously blame other victims and themselves for our condition. This state of affairs must be rejected and replaced with a value-based culture that stresses enlightened partnerships.

In his very powerful essay, *Beyond Connections: Liberation in Love and Struggle*, Maulana Karenga outlines four basic "alienated arrangements" around which many Blacks build their lives. His analysis is so apropos that it is necessary to share it with you. These arrangements, all based on and reinforced by Western society, are 1) the cash connection; 2) the flesh connection; 3) the force connection; and 4) the dependency connection.

According to Karenga, the cash connection is the most basic and pervasive relation, stems from situations in which the power of money

...becomes, not only a means to control, define and deform, but also a *means of existence.* As a means of existence, money becomes a key social relation, a key social power, the power to satisfy human needs. And such a power is critical and highly sought after possession, *for those who control the means to satisfy human needs at the same time control those humans with those needs.*

Men control the money and other key resources of the world. The flesh connection, as an outgrowth of the cash connection, occurs when

...women and men...become commodities themselves — objects to buy and sell, own and dispose of at will. The natural form and context of sexual desire and practice between women and men, then, are distorted and deformed in a commodity society...And thus, human erotic impulse and need are transformed into a flesh connection, an exchange mediated by money and other economic arrangements. Joined to this process and practice is the obsessive emphasis on sex which pervades this society and blocks our minds through the mass media. This combination in turn gives rise and spreads to the *sexual commodity form* — the systematic commercial appeal to sensuousness through the packaging and selling of the human body — mainly, woman.

Dr. Karenga expands the theory of the flesh connection to the question of pornography and sees its proliferation, "rooted in and reflective of social and sexual pathology."

This society's emphasis on force and violence manifests itself not only in the media but also in White America's historical and current treatment of Blacks and other people of color. The force connection results when society's views and tendencies are internalized and practiced in Black male/female relationships.

Karenga defines the final arrangement, the dependency connection, as

...a logical and inevitable outgrowth of the others. To be seduced to trading sex and self for economic and physical security, to be defined in terms of your organs rather than in terms of your wholeness and to be threatened and beaten into submissive silence and compliant cooperation in your own defamation as a full human, can only imply and impose an unhealthy and anti-human dependence. Women are

178

locked into various forms of reciprocal sexual deference and dependency which always demonstrates male dominance.

Dr. Karenga is quite profound in his message and one can't do it justice with just a few quotes. His compass is a sharp one.

White men have put the burden of the racial and economic problem on the victims. This is like forcing the former enslaved who had been locked down for four hundred years suddenly to run a race against seasoned white marathoners. And, when the Black victims lose the race, they are blamed without examination or explanation for being lazy, unprepared, genetically inferior, uneducated and any number of other debilitating adjectives. As non-thinking victims (i.e., white property), most Blacks have accepted white definitions and worldviews. The damage that has been done to our families is catastrophic.

Mass Media: Loud Noise

Most people do not realize the extent to which outside forces affect their lives. The culture we live in is such a powerful force in shaping and guiding our lives that it seems natural to follow its directives even to our own detriment. One of the major transmitters of ideas, images, attitudes, futures, etc. to the average person, is mass media — mainly television. I've heard women talk about the characters in the soap operas as if they were family. Television is the ever present communicator that reminds us our dream falls short of the American ideal.

Jerry Mander in his *Four Arguments for the Elimination of Television* effectively illustrates how television has aided in completely altering life in America over the last forty years. By the age of seventeen, the average young person will have spent over 15,000 hours in front of the television, compared to 11,000 hours in the classroom. Thus, a technological, commercial and uncontrollable medium that appeals to the lowest common denominator has a monopoly on the socialization of most people. Couple such power with all the other problems facing young people and young couples, and it is truly a wonder that any relationships work.

The world is such a complex place, but television is able to solve most problems in thirty minutes (actually twenty-one minutes in between commercials) or an hour. Its message is simplistic and appeals too often to the easy way out. Popular culture (of which television is a part) more often than not pushes an escapest philosophy, whereas the difficult task of confronting and solving problems is seldom taught. People find themselves locked into easy negative answers like running away, taking drugs, overeating, having excessive sex, drinking alcohol, acquiring material possessions, etc.

This image of Black people was reinforced in the highly acclaimed prime-time two-hour CBS Special Report, *The Vanishing Black Family — Crisis in Black America.* In his authoritative "official" manner, Bill Moyers, the Texan "liberal," gave us the final word on the Black family in America: a smooth, well-scripted victim's viewpoint that was ahistorical, short-sighted, stereotypical, racist and destructive. Much of the destructiveness in Black life is the result of racist, economic and political decisions about Black life of which *most* people are unaware. This is very evident in the socialization of young people, and the *Vanishing Black Family* very smoothly used Black people to blame Black people for the mess we are in.

New Moves: Enlightened Partnerships/Loveships

The key to responsible, respectable and long-lasting relationships/loveships is an understanding of societal forces, unfiltered communication and effective follow-up by couples. The ability to talk about problems before the fighting starts is the sign of mature people who have some understanding of the complexity of life. Black couples must understand that "Black love" in the United States is much more than a commitment between two people; it is also the realization that there are political, economic, historical, racial, familial and emotional forces impacting upon that loveship.

Most Black men in America are afraid of strong, intelligent, independent and self-reliant Afrikan American women. If a Black woman has such attributions and is "beautiful" too, her problems with men will double. So-called "plain" women, or women who dress "down," are more acceptable under certain circumstances because they are viewed as less of a threat than the more "physically endowed" women with whom most men would probably want to sleep. In short, men are frightened by the intelligence of these women but highly tempted by their beauty.

The "fear" of women that exists among many Black men runs deep and often goes unspoken. This fear is cultural. Most men are introduced to members of the opposite sex in a superficial manner, and seldom do we seek a more indepth or informed understanding of them. Man's first view of women is as mother and maybe later as sister, aunt, grandmother and, finally, as lover. In 98% of a young man's life, he sees women as babysitters, cooks, house cleaners, day workers, nurses, waitresses, sales women, pre-school and elementary teachers and any number of other "care-giving" occupations defined as women's work. It is not necessarily the *service* that these occupations offer that restricts women; rather, it is the *value* that *society* attaches to the occupations that is demoralizing and restrictive. Generally, men in comparable occupations, like long-distance truck drivers or garbage collectors, make almost twice the salary of pre-school or elementary teachers. Which jobs are more important? Women have it rough all over the world. Men must become informed listeners. The hope and future of Afrikan American family life rides on the strength of Black loveships.

There are two books that Black men and women need to be aware of as they work to improve their lives: *Strategies for Resolving Conflict in Black Male and Female Relationships* by La Francis Rodgers-Rose and James T. Rodgers and *Focusing: Black Male/Female Relationships* by Delores Aldridge. These are two information-packed but easy-to-read books that discuss the racial myths, game-playing, stereotypes, economic inequalities and cultural dynamics that influence Black life. Just as important, both books give down-to-earth suggestions to aid couples in finding their own answers. Both books are must reading.

Finally, if we know what our problems are and we are intelligent, we must act. Black men must become proponents, perpetuators, actualizers and cheerleaders for solid Black loveships, or enlightened partnerships. Here are a few suggestions:

1) Always listen to your partner. Often this listening needs to be done at the times when you feel least up to it. But, try to put yourself into her *space* and open your ears and mind to the destruction or beauty in her day.

2) Reciprocity: Be on the giving side. Even though it is natural to expect kind actions, don't measure your love-moves solely on hers. Never forget important days: birthdays, anniversary, the

days she gave birth to your children, etc. Develop a sharing mode of life with your loved ones.

3) Always make her feel special. Never take your relationship/ loveship for granted. Never tire of saying "Thank you," "I love you," and "I'm really lucky to be with you." Think of original ways of displaying your love for her.

4) Involve yourself in all aspects of housework. Especially if both partners are working, they need to sit down and split up the cleaning and maintenance of the apartment or house. Housework is not women's work; it's just dirty work that men evaded and "redefined" as women's work.

5) Be involved in the birth of your children. Study the birthing process. Once the child is born, be involved in parenting beyond picking the baby up and kissing him or her.

6) Involve your partner in all important and not-so-important decisions. Even if she doesn't seem to be interested — involve her. To build a life together requires few secrets and input from all. Most women are socialized to leave all important decisions to daddy.

7) Encourage your lovemate to improve herself. Help make time for her to pursue her interests outside of the home. Create an atmosphere in the home that will encourage her to reach for her dreams.

8) Try to keep some excitement in her life. Do special things for her, especially when they are least expected — trips, gifts, letters and poetry written to her, etc.

9) Make sure she has her own space and time. Her life need not be built around yours. The two of you must move as a family that is still aware of individual needs. Encourage her to excel in whatever areas that are important to her. For the family to have meaning, there must be meaning beyond family.

10) Accept the blame for your own imperfections and try to change for the better. This can be done through study and renewed practice.

Remember, the deepest hurt is the hurt inflicted by lovers. To remain lovers is hard work; it is not natural. Everything grows old; the key to beautiful tomorrows is involvement in a loveship that ages gracefully. We are bound to make mistakes in our loveships; the key is to learn from them.

If Black women do not love, there is no love. As the women go, so go the people. Stopping the women stops the future. If Black women do not love, strength disconnects, families sicken, growth is questionable and there are few reasons to conquer ideas or foe. If Black women love, so come flowers from sun, rainbows at dusk. As Black women connect, the earth expands, minds open and our yeses become natural as we seek

quality in the searching
quality in the responses
quality in the giving and loving
quality in the receiving
beginning anew
fresh.

REFERENCES

Aldridge, Delores. *Focusing: Black Male/Female Relationships.* Chicago: Third World Press, 1990.

Domhoff, William G. *Who Rules America Now?* Englewood Cliffs: Prentice-Hall, Inc., 1983.

Gordon, Vivian V. *Black Women, Feminism, and Black Liberation: Which Way?* Chicago: Third World Press, 1987.

Karenga, Maulana. *Beyond Connections: Liberation in Love and Struggle.* New Orleans: Ahidiana, 1978.

Mander, Jerry. *Four Arguments for the Elimination of Television.* New York: Quill, 1978.

Rodgers-Rose, La Francis and Rodgers, James T. *Strategies for Resolving Conflict in Black Male and Female Relationships*. Newark: Traces Institute Publications, 1985.

Schaef, Ann Wilson. *Women's Reality*. San Francisco: Harper & Row, 1985.

Seager, Joni and Olson, Ann. *Women in the World Atlas*. New York: A Touchstone Book, 1986.

Steady, Filomina Chioma. Ed. *The Black Woman Cross-Culturally*. Cambridge: Schenkman, 1981.

A BONDING

For Susan and Khephra, August 20, 1989

we were forest people.
landrooted. vegetable strong.
feet fastened to soil with earth strengthened toes.
determined fruit,
anchored
where music soared,
where dancers circled,
where writers sang,
where griots gave memory,
where smiles were not bought.

you have come to eachother in wilderness,
in this time of cracked concrete, diminished vision, wounded rain.

at the center of flowers your craft is on fire.
only ask for what you can give.

do not forget bright mornings, hands touching under moonlight, filtered
water for your plants, healing laughter, renewing futures. caring.

your search has been rewarded, marriage is not logical, it's necessary.
we have a way of running yellow lights, it is now that we must claim
the
sun in our hearts. your joining is a mending, a quilt.

as determined fruit
you have come late to this music,
only ask for what you can give.
you have asked for eachother.

What's a Daddy? Marriage and Fathering

I

One need not go back over the statistics detailing the decline of Black children born into two-parent households. The figures do not speak well of the Black community. Marriage, whether "legal" (sanctioned by the courts), or common law (people deciding to live together without legal documents), is on the decline. However, the babies do not stop coming, and the *music* and *love* so badly needed in the rearing of children are disappearing quickly in the Afrikan American community.

We know that children will come. The circumstances in which they mature is where much of the problem lies. Leon Dash, in his important book *When Children Want Children,* clarifies for the uninformed and misinformed the reasons why single Black teenage girls have babies. His study notes the lack of self-esteem, self-love and self-confidence in most of these young women. However, the revelations that are the highlights of Mr. Dash's work are 1) culture plays a unique and important role in understanding the differences between Black life and white middle class life; and 2) many, if not most, Black teenage pregnancies are not accidental. The misunderstanding of the Black cultural models among white decision-makers is not new. However, the evidence that most teenage pregnancies represent a *survival strategy* is not openly discussed in the Afrikan American community and is of critical importance.

Stable families and communities are absolutely necessary if we are to have productive and loving individuals. Marriage represents the foundation of family. Without marriage (that is, some bonding tradition that sanctions and forces "partners" into commitments beyond the bedroom), families would soon die; or other types of families would form. Families are the foundation for community. Like a family, a functional community provides security, caring, wealth, resources, cultural institutions, education, employment, a spiritual force, shelter and a challenging atmosphere. Families and community shape the individual into a productive or nonproductive person. Without family, without community, individuals are left to "everything is everything."

Male/female bonding (marriage) is necessary if we are to rebuild viable and serious families and communities. Ideally, children should be born into a family where mother and father have made an emotional as well as a legal commitment to each other. Too often in the Black community, many of its members, mainly men, don't want to go the legal route to marriage. Many brothers disrespect the "white man's laws" and will not acquire marriage licenses. They would rather just jump over a broom. This is a delicate problem; I have little respect for most of such laws. However, *we are in the United States.* When I drive, I carry a driver's licence I got from white people because it is the law; if I drive without it and get caught, I will go to jail — without passing go. For the emotional and economic protection of the children and mothers, I strongly suggest all marriages in the Afrikan American community be legalized according to the "laws" of this land. These are a few reasons:

1) The license provides emotional security for women and children; if a father decides that it's over, the mother will have an easier time obtaining child support.

2) The license represents a government sanction. Therefore, it's the legal community's OK for such an event. The license adds an importance to the act that goes beyond the two people involved.

3) The legalization of marriage forces partners to struggle with each other at a higher level when times are hard. Without a license, brothers and sisters can "walk" at the slightest problem or provocation.

4) In cases where separation is necessary, brothers too will have legal claim on their children.

Marriage is not a vacation or a prolonged holiday. Eighty percent of marriage is work, compromise, adaptation, changes, intimate communication, laughter, confusion, joy, smiles, crying, pain, crises, reeducation, apologies, mistakes, more mistakes, new knowledge and love. If children are involved, include parenting and repeat everything above twice for each year of the marriage. If the marriage lasts for more than fifteen years, the couple probably should add *wisdom.* Of course, one may ask, "What about the other twenty percent?" I presume that even in a successful marriage the couple will sleep.

II

Fathers are the missing links in the lives of many young Afrikan Americans. In an increasingly dangerous and unpredictable world, absent fathers add tremendously to the insecurity of children. It is common knowledge that children function best in an atmosphere where both parents combine and compliment their energies and talents in the rearing of children. Even if pregnancy is an accident, it is clear that once a decision is made to bring a child to term, the rearing of that child cannot be accidental. Most children are born at the top of their game, *genius level*. It is the socialization process that turns most creative, talented and normal children into dependent and helpless adults. There are many aspects to child-rearing, but I would like to stress six:

1) Children need love and need to love. Provide a safe, secure home that is full of warmth, love and challenges. Parents should be complimentary in their parenting and not take anything for granted. Involve extended family in your parenting, especially grandparents and aunts and uncles.

2) Teach by example. Spend quality time with children. Provide options. Give children an open book on growth. Listen to them. When possible, give full answers to their questions, but encourage them to find answers on their own. Be slow to criticize, quick to congratulate.

3) Be conscious of building self-love and self-esteem in your children. Provide a cultural home where self-images are positive and warm, where Afrikan American culture is lived and taught in a natural and non-dogmatic manner.

4) Introduce your children to the unlimited possibilities of life. However, explain to them the necessity of work, discipline, study and patience.

189

5) Homes should be nonviolent. Parents should be slow to criticize each other in front of children. Arguments should be kept to a minimum. In single-parent homes, criticism of the missing parent in front of the child should be infrequent and/or tempered with understanding.

6) Housework is not women's work and should be shared equally by all, especially if both parents work outside the home.

III

In a patriarchal society, Black men must be able to offer their families a measurement of protection and, at a minimum, basic life-giving needs, such as clothing, shelter, food, education and security. The West and most of the world define manhood as the ability to protect and provide for one's family. If a man doesn't do that, according to most cultures, he is incomplete (i.e., not a man). A good many Black men are not able to deliver in these two areas. Here are some of the reasons:

1) White world supremacy (racism) — Black men are the major threat to white male rule.
2) Failure of integration — Many Black men believe(d) America's big lie of the melting pot theory.
3) Failure of national and local welfare system — the development of a beggar's mentality among many Black people.
4) Failure of public education.
5) Changing economic system — increased dependency on the state.
6) Our replacement in the market place by white women and teenagers.
7) Loss of self-respect, self-esteem and self-love.
8) Ignorance of one's own history and accomplishments.
9) Unawareness of changing world realities.
10) Lack of skills — especially business skills.
11) Fear.

For conscious men, none of this should be new. However, in this *war* situation that we live in, the circumstances demand that Black men rise to the *challenge*. And, a great part of that challenge is to be responsible husbands and fathers. Without both, a bright future is doubtful. Being a good and fruitful husband and father may be the most *difficult task facing Afri-kan American men.*

We now live in a time, a first in our history, when there are millions of Afrikan American children with absent fathers. Other than the period of chattel slavery, there has never been a time when the absence of Black fathers has been so grim. This tide of absent, unavailable, nonfunctioning fathers must be reversed. There are *no easy solutions.*

Fathering for most Black men is learned on the job. Generally, by that time, for many fathers it is too late. There are few classes in fathering. However, fathering *is* taught; it's a learned process. Most Black men give very little thought to the lifelong commitment that fathers *must* make to their children.

Children learn to do most things by watching and imitating their parents or care-givers. Formal education starts generally at the age of five for most children, and at two and a half for the blessed few who are able to benefit from Headstart or private schools. Children learn to be mothers or fathers by observing and studying their mothers, fathers, grandparents, aunts, uncles and television.

These days most Black boys learn to be fathers by watching the wind (i.e., spaces reserved for missing fathers). Many of them also receive instruction in fathering from their mothers' discussions about absent "dads" or whatever names these men are given. If there is anything clear about the Afrikan American community, it is that women are having serious difficulty teaching Black boys to be men and, by extension, to be fathers.

However, this not a condemnation of Black women who are trying, against great odds, to raise their sons into responsible and recognizable Black men. The facts suggest that many of them are not succeeding, and the facts also suggest that it is *ignorant, stupid* and *insensitive* to blame Black women for not *raising strong Black men.* The music in these women's lives is little, and to be left *alone* to raise the children may be an impossible task for many of them. However, we do know that millions of Afrikan American women do rise to the challenge and are responsible for millions of Black men who have made "successful" transitions from boyhood to manhood.

Again, it is not easy. There is a difference between raising children and rearing them. Mari Evans, in a very important paper, "The Relationship of Child-Rearing Practices to Chaos and Change in the African American Family," states:

191

...raising (children) is "providing for," while rearing is "responding to." Raising can be satisfied by providing the essentials: food, shelter, clothing and reasonable care. "Rearing" is a carefully thought out process. Rearing begins with a goal and is supported by a clear view of what are facts and what is truth (and the two are not necessarily synonymous). Rearing is complex and requires sacrifice and dedication. It is an ongoing process of "preparation." Joe Kennedy reared presidents; the British royal family rears heirs to the English throne; and when a young African doctor, born in the continent and presently in self-exile in a neighboring country because of her ANC (African National Congress) commitment was interviewed on the news recently and was asked if she was not afraid for her four-year-old son, given her political activism, said, "He has a duty to lay down his life for his people. He is my son, but he is also the son of an oppressed people," she announced the rearing of a "race man."...Obviously something different, some carefully thought out process, some long-range political view is present when one has a clear sense of one's own reality and therefore intends to rear presidents, rulers, or free men and women.

I think that Mari Evans, in her own unique and poetic manner, has set forth the challenge for Afrikan American people, the rearing of "race men and women."

If fathers give some thought to this, it should become clear that fathering (i.e., parenting) is also a political act. As a colonized people fighting for survival and development, Afrikan Americans must see our children as future "warriors" in this struggle for liberation. Mari Evans defined colonization as "suppression and exploitation designed to keep a people powerless, dependent, subordinate, and mystified." Again, we are at war for the minds, bodies, souls, spirits and futures of our children. Ms. Evans states it this way: "Child-rearing should be the primary concern of an oppressed people, and although the rearing of race men and women is obviously a stressful, complex and tedious process, it should be entered into at birth."

I want to make it clear that Black men cannot depend on others to do our job. Fathering must be as important to us as love-making (sex). It is easy to make babies but difficult to rear them. Below is the Afrikan American Father's Pledge that all Black men should consider:

Afrikan American Father's Pledge

1. I will work to be the best father I can be. Fathering is a daily mission, and there are no substitutes for good fathers. Since I have not been taught to be a father, in order to make my "on the job" training easier, I will study, listen, observe and learn from my mistakes.

2. I will openly display love and caring for my wife and children. I will listen to my wife and children. I will hug and kiss my children often. I will be supportive of the mother of my children and spend quality time with my children.

3. I will teach by example. I will try to introduce myself and my family to something new and developmental each week. I will help my children with their homework and encourage them to be involved in extracurricular activities.

4. I will read to or with my children as often as possible. I will provide opportunities for my children to develop creatively in the arts: music, dance, drama, literature and visual arts. I will challenge my children to do their best.

5. I will encourage and organize frequent family activities for the home and away from home. I will try to make life a positive adventure and make my children aware of their extended family.

6. I will never be intoxicated or "high" in the presence of my children, nor will I use language unbecoming for an intelligent and serious father.

7. I will be nonviolent in my relationships with my wife and children. As a father, my role will be to stimulate and encourage my children rather than carry the "big stick."

8. I will maintain a home that is culturally in tune with the best of Afrikan American history, struggle and future. This will be done, in part, by developing a library, record/disc, video and visual art

collections that reflect the developmental aspects of Afrikan people worldwide. There will be *order* and *predictability* in our home.

9. I will teach my children to be responsible, disciplined, fair and honest. I will teach them the value of hard work and fruitful production. I will teach them the importance of family, community, politics and economics. I will teach them the importance of the Nguzo Saba (Black value system) and the role that ownership of property and businesses plays in our struggle.

10. As a father, I will attempt to provide my family with an atmosphere of love and security to aid them in their development into sane, loving, productive, spiritual, hard-working, creative Afrikan Americans who realize they have a responsibility to do well and help the less fortunate of this world. I will teach my children to be *activists* and to *think* for themselves.

Along with the Afrikan American Father's Pledge, I would like to share with you Madhubuti's Home Rules:

Madhubuti's Home Rules (for children)

1. Don't lie, don't steal, don't cheat.
2. Don't embarrass your family; listen to your parents and other responsible adults.
3. Always do your best and improve on yesterday's work; develop a work attitude.
4. Learn as much as you can; always expand your knowledge-base.
5 Seek quality in all things rather than weakening quantity.
6. Always be creative; do not settle for easy answers or conclusions. Think for yourself and learn to be responsible for your decisions.
7. Learn from mistakes and always oppose that which is not good.
8. Do homework and housework each day.
9. Avoid alcohol, drugs and cigarettes.
10. Respect elders.

11. Be a self-starter, self-motivator; do not wait on others to set high goals/standards for you. Always seek the best and avoid the "crowd" mentality.
12. Never forget who you are and always speak up if you feel that you have been wronged.

We have to keep our children active, and it is never too early to prepare them for the outside world. Listed below are required skills for Black children. This list was compiled with the help of the brothers of the National Black Wholistic Retreat Society:

1. *Community and Family Service* — Volunteer once a week at a church or community center, working with young people or senior citizens

2. *Domestic Chores* — Cooking; gardening; ironing clothes; storing food; sewing; cleaning house; washing clothes; shopping for food

3. *Repairs*
   Car: Change oil; change tire; fix flat; check fluid levels
   Home: Plumbing — understand and repair water and sewer lines
            Electrical — replace outlets and light switches; make a
                   lamp
   Bike: change flats

4. *Academic Challenges* — Read at least one new book a month; develop computer skills; learn to play chess/checkers; practice math; learn at least one foreign language

5. *Religion* — Understand Christianity, Judaism, Islam, Maat, Confucious, Hinduism, Taoism, Buddhism, etc.

6. *Physical Fitness* — Swim one mile; run five miles; bike fifty miles; walk ten miles

7. *Interpersonal/Family Relations* — Male-female; male-male; female-female; parenting; problem-solving skills; sex/healthy love-making; reciprocity; family history

8. *Outdoor Skills* — Camping; fire building; compass and map-reading; knowing the city in which one lives

9. *Communications*
   Ham Radio — Novice license

10. *Transportation* — Riding a bike; driving a car; taking public transportation

11. *Defense* — Learn some form of martial arts; become competent with firearms

12. *Finance* — Banking (savings, checking, mortgages); stocks and bonds; insurance; wills and estates; credit unions

13. *Travel* — Local; national; international

14. *Health and Nutrition* — First aid; CPR; stress management; proper diet (vegetarian or low-fat); meditation

Finally, Black life in the United States is full of stress. If a "plan" for child-rearing has not been developed individually, parents should consult the "literature," professionals and grandparents for support and direction. Again, life is not easy, but we do have a choice: live or die. If we are men, we must make the decision to live and develop.

Afrikan American men must have a *greater* commitment to family and community. Families should probably be started later, after one has accomplished other tasks. It is clear that once two people decide to join hands as a family and, most certainly, once children arrive, those parents *must* dig in for the long haul. The parents' lives are not *just theirs anymore*. Their lives also must be shared with their children. More importantly, parents must understand that *often* their own "enjoyment," "adventure," "play time," and, yes, "happiness" may have to be sacrificed for the "joy, adventure and happiness" of their children. This is part of what it means to be a parent.

Our first responsibility with children is to give them opportunities, to provide them with options that most of us *never had*. That's what development and Black struggle are all about. This means, in very plain language,

196

that where one used to party or "go" every weekend, such activity must be reduced to once a month or every six weeks. The point is that our *time* and *resources* must go to rearing strong, creative, intelligent, culture-conscious Afrikan American children who will work for a better world. This also means partners may have to endure some unpleasantness in relationships that they wouldn't if children were not involved. What else is new? That's life — if one makes a bed, one has to sleep in it. Rearing successful children will make us better people, be our insurance in old age and protect us from having to repair broken adults.

What's Food Got to do With It?

Personal Energy, Economics, National Resources and Vegetarianism

As a young man, seldom could I go an entire hour without blowing my nose. It seemed as though I had a perpetual cold. During the spring, summer and fall of each year, my life was complete misery if I didn't take all kinds of antihistamines (i.e., drugs) to temporarily arrest my sneezing, running nose and watery eyes. I visited doctor after doctor with the same results, a prescription for a new and more powerful drug. At the age of twenty-six, I decided to take my health into my own hands.

At that time, the late sixties, health was not the "in" thing. Health food stores and restaurants were not as plentiful as they are today. In fact, the Black community of Chicago had only one of each. Today, Chicago has six stores and two restaurants owned by Afrikan Americans. However, during that period, with the exceptions of Dr. Alvenia Fulton and Dr. Roland Sydney, the proximity of Chicago's Black community to "natural" health was extremely limited. Both Dr. Fulton and Dr. Sydney have been untiring in their advocacy of a natural, drug-free way of life. Their example and commitment have been sources of inspiration to me. And, of course, one must also include the extraordinary efforts of Dick Gregory.

However, I first encountered an alternative way of eating by reading Elijah Muhammad's *How to Eat to Live.* By that time (1967), I had excluded pork from my diet. The Nation of Islam had created two foods that were popular in the Black community — bean soup and bean pies. Mr. Muhammad's basic message to me was 1) people eat too much food in this country, 2) people are eating the wrong "foods," and 3) there is a need for self-discipline. Around the same time, the slogan "You are what you eat" began to appear, especially at outdoor concerts and events where "natural" foods were being served. This saying makes a great deal of sense to me because it reflects the fact that one's actions can make or break her or his physical well-being. Once food enters one's body, the body, in all of its unique complexity, has to deal with it. For example, if a person consumes junk food, even if the body regurgitates the food, the food still will have negative effects on the body.

By 1970, Johari Amini-Hudson (the poet/scholar, now a chiropractor in Atlanta) decided that she would seriously study alternative healing systems. As she collected information, she shared it with me. I had already started to eliminate meat from my diet. This helped my upper respiratory problem, but not until I gave up milk, ice cream, eggs and other dairy products and learned how to combine foods did I really begin to feel the difference a "correct" diet makes in one's life. I was less tired; my energy level doubled almost immediately.

The major thing I learned is that by eliminating certain "foods," or better yet, junk foods, from my diet, I was able to experience better health. However, this move toward a total and balanced vegetarian life-style took a great deal of time and plenty of study, as well as trial and error experimentation with my body. Through the process of use and nonuse, I was able to measure the effects that certain foods have on me. For example, when I stopped eating white bread in the sixties, I switched to whole grain wheat bread, not realizing that I am allergic to wheat. Eventually, I changed to non-wheat bread and seven grain breads with a minimum of wheat. Also, I had very bad reactions to milk and ice cream. It was not until 1971 that I found out the milk producers' ad campaign of "Everybody needs milk" was a lie. Cows' milk is generally best for only cows. The enzyme necessary for digestion of milk is lactose, and over 80% of Black children have no lactose in their intestines.

I realize that each person's body is different. And, my search for my diet took some time to "perfect," but it was worth every minute. Ultimate health slows down the aging process. For me, the six major life necessities that preserve and build the body, reduce stress and keep one sexually alive and creative are 1) a vegetarian diet; 2) exercise, yoga and breathing; 3) productive work; 4) reciprocal love; 5) knowledge of what to avoid and what to add to one's life; and 6) slow time and introspection.

Life is too short to be slowed down with a lot of illness. Illness, in most cases, is a direct result of bad habits. We live in a culture that glorifies bad habits, from smoking and drinking alcohol to doing designer drugs. We are encouraged to run the streets at night rather than sleep. We are encouraged to raise our children on processed and fast foods, and we wonder why they can't concentrate, remain still for over thirty seconds, run a block without dying or find joy in any activity that requires them to use their minds.

Everything is connected. My search for the "correct" diet was also a search for the "correct" way of life. This search took me into other areas of study, such as the environment, conservation, population, food production, energy and health care systems. What I've learned over the past twenty years is that Western technology and science is very destructive to individuals, the society and the environment. This is not to infer that there have not been any "advancements," but it is to suggest that most of the time and money invested in Western research and development have not made people healthier — even though some people may be living longer. However, what *is* certain is that the "health" business is healthier and wealthier.

We can't drink the water in urban or rural areas. To breathe the air in Los Angeles or New York City during most hours is a guarantee of upper respiratory problems. Most processed foods, which make up the majority of American diets, are robbed of their nutritional value. Ninety percent of medical doctors are ignorant of the benefits or hazards of diet. According to John Robbins in *Diet for a New America*, out of the 125 medical schools in the United States, only thirty have required courses in nutrition, and the training in nutrition received during four years of medical school by the average U.S. physician is 2.5 hours. More often than not, the average American diet consists of "fast" foods from "fast" restaurants, which leads to fast deaths.

Any time a nation allocates over 40% of its national budget to defense rather than to the betterment of its people's lives, something's wrong. Any time a nation *gives* over $150 billion to private enterprise — the savings and loan industry — and can't come up with a fair, yet comprehensive national health plan for its citizens, that nation is uncaring, insensitive, incompetent and, yes, capitalist. Welcome to America. Money before people is the creed and policy in the U.S. If a culture or society is to be humane, it must be people-oriented with much of its resources going toward the care and development of its people — especially the young and elderly. This is not an impossible task, and since the U.S. is not going in that direction, individuals, families, groups, communities and organizations must act on their own.

What is a Vegetarian?

There are several types of vegetarians. Most people think that vegetarians eat all raw food, including flowers and hay. The simplest definition of a vegetarian is a person who doesn't eat anything that runs away. Vegetarians avoid flesh or warm-blooded animals. A complete vegetarian diet consists of plant foods only: fruits, grains, legumes, nuts and seeds. *Lacto-vegetarians* include milk and the products of milk, like cheese and ice cream in their diet. *Lacto-ovo-vegetarians* include milk and eggs in their diet. There are other variations, but the only one that may be of importance to most people is the *vegan*. A vegan is not only a total vegetarian but one that does not use any products made out of animal parts, such as leather or wool.

Health

There are over thirteen million vegetarians in the United States, and according to Gary Null in his *The Vegetarian Handbook*, "Throughout most of the world, vegetarianism is the rule, not the exception." Many people changed their diets because of failing health. They recognized that the "traditional" balanced diet recommended by the American Medical Association was not healing them. Many of these people may not be able to articulate the reasons for change, but they realized that change was necessary. They knew that there must be another way because the food they were eating did not help to eliminate asthma, colds, sore throats, depression, arthritis, constipation, ulcers, teeth problems, obesity, fatigue and many other degenerative diseases brought on by improper diet, stress and lack of exercise.

Ethics — New Values

I am against any kind of killing. The killing of animals for food is barbaric and *not necessary* to feed all the people on the planet. Meat, for most people in this world, is a luxury. However, in the West, meat and other flesh is the main course, and vegetables have been reduced to side dishes. According to John Robbins' *Diet for a New America*, the industries of the Great American Food Machine (also known as the meat, dairy and egg industries) "don't want you to know how the animals have lived whose flesh, milk and eggs end up in your body. They also don't want you to know the health consequences of consuming the products of such a system, nor do they want you to know the environmental impact." This book is *must* reading for anyone who is concerned about the life-threatening effects of meat-eating on the mind, body and environment. The inhumane treatment of animals solely for the production of a "tender steak" is horrible. As John Robbins suggests:

> Increasingly in the last few decades, the animals raised for meat, dairy products and eggs in the United States have been subjected to ever more deplorable conditions. Merely to keep the poor creatures alive under these circumstances, even more chemicals have had to be used, and increasingly, hormones, pesticides, antibiotics and countless other chemicals and drugs end up in foods derived from animals. The worst drug pushers don't work city streets — they operate today's "factory farms."
> But that's just the half of it. The suffering these animals undergo has become so extreme that to partake of food from these creatures is to partake unknowingly of the abject misery that has been their lives. Millions upon millions of Americans are merrily eating away, unaware of the pain and disease they are taking into their bodies with every bite. We are ingesting nightmares for breakfast, lunch and dinner.

Economics and Conservation

Common sense tells us that fruits, vegetables and grains are more economic than beef, chicken or fish. If one increased his or her vegetable intake proportionately to his or her decrease in the consumption of flesh, the savings would be substantial. Patronizing the produce stand rather than the butcher shop will open up a whole new world of health and wealth. This change in life-style will also aid the small farmers in their battle against Agribusiness. According to Gary Null in his book, *The Vegetarian Handbook*, "Land is capable of supplying food for nearly fourteen times as many people when it is used to grow food for people rather than crops to feed livestock." The cost of breeding and slaughtering animals, processing and packaging meat requires up to sixteen times the energy, land, water and raw materials needed to produce the same poundage of grain.

Personal Choices

Freedom in America has its down side. Freedom to die is just as tempting as freedom to live. In fact, most Americans unknowingly choose slow death rather than illness-free life. Medical care in the United States is curative rather than preventive. The Great American Food Machine, throughout its billion dollar advertising campaign, has determined the eating plan for most Americans. American doctors' reliance on drugs and the knife to "cure" people should be a national scandal, but it is not. We all have choices. However, one's eating and exercise habits are formed early, and they are difficult to change. If a person is raised on fast food and cooked food (generally over-cooked) only, the chances of attracting that person to non-cooked fresh vegetables and fruits are few. Generally, a person has to face a serious crisis in his or her life before life-giving and life-saving changes are contemplated.

Before that crisis comes, and it will surely come if we are not caring for our bodies, let's review a few facts from *Diet For A New America*. According to John Robbins, the meat, dairy and egg industries (the Great American Food Machine) tell us that animal products constitute two of the "basic four" food groups. What they do not tell us is that there were originally twelve official basic food groups before these industries applied enormous political pressure to cut out the other non-meat/dairy foods. We are told by the meat, dairy and egg industries that we are well fed only with animal products, but what they do not tell us is that the diseases which are commonly prevented, consistently impeded and sometimes cured by a low-fat vegetarian diet include:

Strokes	Heart disease	Osteoporosis
Kidney stones	Breast cancer	Colon cancer
Prostate cancer	Pancreatic cancer	Ovarian cancer
Cervical cancer	Stomach cancer	Endometrial cancer
Diabetes	Hypoglycemia	Kidney disease
Peptic ulcers	Constipation	Hemorrhoids
Hiatal hernias	Diverticulosis	Obesity
Gallstones	Hypertension	Asthma
Irritable colon syndrome	Salmonellosis	Trichinosis

This short essay cannot possibly address all of the reader's concerns. I hope I've raised some questions and evoked an eagerness in the reader to do her/his own research. From experience and study, I learned that it is not time alone that ages the body. When the negatives outnumber the positives in one's life, watch out for illness. Improved health is found in one's saying *yes* to life. In doing so, one must cease consuming coffee (and other caffeine-laden foods), smoking (cigarettes and herbs) and drinking alcohol. Alternatively, one should seek enlightened advice and consider these ten points:

1) Get six to eight hours of sleep a night.
2) Drink at least a half gallon of *clean* water a day. Remember, most tap water is polluted.
3) Bathe everyday — seek cleanliness.
4) Exercise *at least* forty-five minutes, four times a week.
5) Start each day with fifteen minutes of deep breathing; try to bring life-giving oxygen into your stomach.
6) Avoid, if possible, most processed foods. Move toward a 50/50 diet, 50% uncooked and 50% cooked. Start each day with fruit and fresh juices. Always under-eat rather than stuff yourself.
7) Be creative — creativity and longevity go hand in hand. Emotional and spiritual health aid in physical health.
8) Make sure that there is continuous *love* in your life. Make your family a priority.
9) Practice reciprocity — try to give and receive with an open heart and mind.
10) Study — always seek life-giving and life-saving information. *Be disciplined.*

The following is a list of holistic practictioners across the country: Johari Amini-Hudson, D.C. — Decatur/Atlanta, GA; Thabiti H.N. Cartman, D.C. — Chicago, IL; Ndugu Khan, N.D. — Houston, TX; Paul Goss, N.D. — Los Angeles, CA; Roland Sydney, N.D. — Chicago, IL; Alvenia Fulton, N.D., Ph.D. — Chicago, IL; Jifunla C.A. Wright, M.D. — Detroit, MI; Asar Ha-Pi — Chicago, IL

Remember, "You are what you eat" is not just a hip slogan to throw at friends; it's common sense at its highest. What's food got to do with it? Everything.

REFERENCES

Benjamin, Harry. *Commonsense Vegetarianism*. England: Health For All Publishers Co., 1950.

Boyd, Billy Ray. *For the Vegetarian in You*. San Francisco: Taterhill Press SF, 1987.

Giehl, Dudley. *Vegetarianism: A Way of Life*. New York: Barnes & Noble Books, 1979.

Goss, Paul. *Forever Young*. Published by author, 1985.

Gregory, Dick. *Dick Gregory's Natural Diet for Folks Who Eat: Cookin' with Mother Nature*. New York: Harper & Row, 1974.

Kondo, Nia and Zak. *Vegetarianism Made Simple and Easy*. Washington, D.C.: Nubia Press, 1989.

Lappe, Frances Moore. *Diet for a Small Planet*. New York: Ballantine, 1971.

Lappe, Frances Moore and Collins, Joseph. *World Hunger: Twelve Myths*. San Francisco: Grove, 1986.

Null, Gary. *The Vegetarian Handbook*. New York: St. Martin's Press, 1989.

Robbins, John. *Diet for a New America*. Stillpoint, 1987.

Ten Ways to Live Longer by the editors of *Prevention Magazine, 1982.*

Vegetarian Times magazine, one of the best sources of current and accurate information on vegetarians.

The Five Daily Battles that Most
Black People Fight in America

Denial of reality is a psychological problem. People who are not in control of their lives are taught to abuse themselves mentally and physically. However, this abuse is often defined as adapting, accommodating, going along with the program, or, as the brothers say, "being real." Being real or not, the pain that all Black people have suffered in this country would fill volumes of horror stories. Briefly, these are five wars that are fought daily by most Afrikan Americans:

1. *Color*

I started writing this piece on October 19, 1987 — the day of the modern stock market crash that was named "Black Monday." The fact that it was called "Black Monday" rather than "white Monday" is a lesson for those who are willing to listen. The stock market worldwide is an economic game that many white people play. There are very, very few Black players. The point is that when anything bad happens in the white world, it is always a *Black* day. Color, unlike class, religion or country of origin, has defined Afrikan American people in the West. Everyday, in and out of the Black community, we are confronted with the reality of race. (See "Nothing Black but a Cadillac.") Color determines reality for Black people in America far more than anything else.

2. *Poverty*

America was built on the backs of enslaved Afrikan people. After Emancipation the Afrikans were promised forty acres and a mule. White people did not deliver on the promise. Not given a "fair" or "equal" chance to catch up, Black people have become almost totally dependent upon the state or national government. White people kept Afrikans in chains for four hundred years, forcing us to help build an empire; then they took the chains off one day and told us to compete with them, the very people who profited from our labor. It is just about impossible to catch a people with a four hundred-year head start without resources, institutions, education, finances and land. The poverty of Afrikan American people in the United States is not of our own making. Traditionally, Black people have been a land-based people that used the land and its gifts wisely. The move from land to concrete has disrupted the lives and institutions of Black people. Black people are truly the real miracles in the West. However, poverty persists and it is now taking its toll on the best and the brightest of our youth.

3. *Hair*

Anytime the vast majority of a people spend a good part of their days, weeks and months changing the texture, color and style of their hair into the texture, color and style of a people unlike them, this speaks volumes about that people. Black people *battle* with their hair every day. When babies are born into the Black community, the two things that are immediately noticed, after the sex of the baby, are the *color* and *hair texture*. The hair is watched and groomed very carefully, in hopes that it will not turn "bad." Again, if one is told all one's life that his/her hair is "bad," then it shouldn't be uncommon that most Black people, women and men, spend *productive* hours trying to change and accommodate their hair to the prevailing fashion. We should teach our children very early that Europeans have European hair, Asians have Asian hair and Afrikans have Afrikan hair. Many women change their hair not only because they've been taught to, but also because their Black male partners demand it. The men change their hair because they are confused. To take the hair of Afrikan Americans, brutalize it and try to change it into "European" hair cannot be anything but a lifelong losing battle.

4. *Fear*

Fear in the Afrikan American community is the great equalizer. The use of terror by white people has been a very effective war strategy. Any serious study of European history reveals that the major threat they hold over the people they control is "death." White world supremacy could not maintain its control if it were not for the fear shared by oppressed people worldwide. Such fear manifests itself in a number of ways: death, imprisonment, loss of jobs, loss of material possessions, loss of status or fame, loss of financial resources, etc. White people have the power, will and determination to keep Afrikan American people in their "place." This "place" will always be subservient to whites. Only a few negroes will be able to escape, and they will generally be used as the examples of what is possible. Black people have been the glue holding white people together; we have been the reason there has not been a second civil war in the United States. "A white dog does not bite another white dog when Black dogs are present," goes the Afrikan proverb.

5. *Language*

This is the most subtle battle we fight. Most Afrikan American people are without their indigenous language. Language is crucial to identity and culture. The language used by Blacks in the United States is almost 100% English. However, it is "Black English," a language that has grown up in the Black community and is a legitimate and effective communicative tongue. The in joke in most English departments (college and high school) around the country is that Black people are incapable of speaking, writing or creating in English. Of course, this is not true, but misinformation is not uncommon among ignorant and arrogant people. Most professional Black people are bilingual; they speak "Black English" and the languages of their respective professions. Most of them understand the necessity of both languages and have adapted their speech accordingly. Just like other cultures, the way Black people communicate within their community is legitimate and, more importantly, it is *right*. But, when we move in and out of other communities, we will be more effective if we speak their languages — whether their languages are French, German, Hindi or English. Language has been a major tool that whites have used to deny Blacks entrance into corporate America. The key to language is to understand that even though Europeans and Americans have used it to belittle other cultures, no people has a monopoly on the spoken or written word. The influence of a language, to a large degree, depends upon the *power* of the nation advocating that language.

Black people are often captives of false arguments. The five "battles" are not insurmountable. They require that we face and conquer the individual and collective doubt in us. Self-knowledge cures self-fear. The capacity of a people to succeed in battle depends, in part, upon its own definitions and its ability to actualize such definitions on a broad scale. European-Americans have been quite successful at doing this. Afrikan American people must understand that "he who lives with an ass makes noises like an ass." Such noises are not our destiny.

The S Curve, Double Circle or Infinity: Serious Solutions for Serious Men

Cracking the Code, Finding the Key. What is the Hook?

There are many ways of looking at the world other than those methods taught in the West. There are, in fact, universal truths such as love, non-love, violence, happiness, poverty, health, sickness, hunger, greed, wealth, struggle, politics, ignorance, etc., which are contemplated daily in all cultures by women and men seeking more beautiful and beneficial ways of life.

The limitations of vision, the inability to rise above the restrictive barriers of a culture and the conforming expectations of peers and family are each partially responsible for the lack of individual and group development among Afrikan American people. Learning to accept and deal with failure does not make one a failure. However, knowing only failure in one's self and in others close by doesn't speak loudly for other possibilities.

In the United States it is much easier to accept success — in all of its various forms — because most people, from birth to adulthood, are taught directly and indirectly to expect and seek success. Success in the West generally is measured by the possession and control of people and things (i.e., ownership). Therefore, if one doesn't have homes, cars, gold credit cards, property, clothes, fame, money (not the kind earned from weekly assembly line pay checks) and lots of "beautiful" and "successful friends," one is not really considered materially substantial in the Western context.

However, this type of "success" without a measured understanding of one's wholeness in relationship to the earth, its people, its animals and vegetation is just about impossible — if "success" is only defined by the acquisition or ownership of people and things. Success in an Afrikan and humane context is not defined by joining the killers of the world. Success, redefined, is the ability of our people to negotiate *difficulty* and deliver answers, resources and bright possibilities for ourselves as well as the majority of the world's people.

211

Often the secrets of life are so clear and simple that we refuse to accept them because such insights didn't cost a minor fortune or levitate from some European brain factory. For example, a great many people in this country abuse themselves on a daily basis by consuming unfiltered, polluted tap water and sugar (in all of its forms) without question. That such consumption of tap water and sugar is harmful is an accepted fact among *knowers*, but such simple knowledge is hard to find in the literature read by "everyday" people. Moving "everyday" people to the status of *knowing* is the challenge and is part of the responsibility of those who know. *We all do what we've been taught to do* — I've written this in most of my books from *From Plan to Planet* (1973) to *Killing Memory, Seeking Ancestors* (1987). Moving from ignorance to knowledge, from unknowing to knowing, is very *complex* at one level and quite *simple* at another. However, it is certain that such travelling will require much more than a good rap from a knowledgeable person — though it may start there. Generally, the knowers among us are everyday people in our communities. Many of them are unappreciated, little known, overworked and often three steps from poverty and despair.

I

If one *thinks* and *feels* in a historical context — that is, weighing both the negative and positive forces that influence certain events — one's analysis and interpretation of experience will more often than not be closer to the truth. In thinking about the truth, one also *feels* the truth — gut reaction is important here. A historical mode of *thought* and *feeling* enables the *thinkers* and *feelers* to go beyond the limiting acts of present day arrogance and self-righteousness.

If one possesses in-depth knowledge of other times, places, cultures, and peoples, chances are that one's perception and analysis of past, present and future events will be more accurate. Historical *reasoning* and *feeling* provide one with a context in which to search for *content*. Two excellent examples of this are Dr. Chancellor Williams' *The Destruction of Black Civilization* and Ayi Kwei Armah's *Two Thousand Seasons*. These two books could not have been written without a passion for historical reasoning and an understanding of *feeling* as an analytical tool, especially since most scholars and serious writers are taught to be empirical and objective without introducing their emotions into a work. The enlightened concept

212

of history speaks to an intimate and non-superficial awareness of *culture* — that is, culture in its most liberating definition, which would include an understanding of the interconnections that, love, health, history, education, literature, food, politics, religion, nationalism, economics, sports, entertainment, language, war, peace and race have to each other locally, nationally and internationally.

If cultural history is presented properly, that is, in a way that doesn't dull the mind, it may produce students who will be less likely to jump to easy conclusions and misguided judgements. A critical selection of data and a serious study of cultural and historical facts can heighten one's interpretation and understanding of local, national and world events. Also, a raw, undisciplined evaluation of data outside of cultural/historical knowledge will probably lead to ill-defined answers, easy solutions and long tomorrows absent of beauty or truth. The study of culture/history in a context of logic (reason) and feeling (emotion) can sharpen one's mental skills and heighten one's appreciation of cultural/historical differences and political and economic realities of all people, whether they be rural, urban or a mixture of other unknown qualities.

However, the real significance of cultural/historical study is that it places cultures, peoples, nations and the world into a frame-of-reference that explains a people's current place in the universe. For example, it is helpful to know that Ethiopia was not always on the doorstep of starvation but once was a world leader in the production of food and knowledge. It also is useful to understand that this beggar's mentality that has crept into the Black community is recent and does not have a historical precedent prior to our coming to the Western Hemisphere. The Chinese have a saying: "Fool me once shame on you, fool me again shame on me." It has been stated also that two types of intelligence exist: intelligent intelligence and stupid intelligence. Where are we? I think that many of us have turned our lives over to "experts" and "specialists," thereby refusing to attack the difficult questions in our lives because of fear, ignorance and the acceptance of the recent history of Afrikan American failure and disappointment in America.

II

Life is definitely rough when ignorant people talk about how ignorant other people are. In measuring the noise in our community, we must be

213

able to distinguish between the false and the real. Too often we will accept men in $2,000 tailored suits with 10¢ tailored minds because our definitions of good and valuable are distorted. Our values often are misplaced and focused on how one dresses, the car one drives, the size and location of one's house or where one vacations, rather than on those things that *really* matter.

We all have our horror stories. Few of our people are exempted from the brutality of America. As the end of the 20th century approaches, one is not assured by the forecast of the future of Afrikan American people. It is easy to overlook the obvious in the United States: three million plus homeless people, sixty million functional illiterates, historically high unemployment, a deadening drug problem, an environment that's losing its ability to withstand pollution, etc. Men and women make their own history, but they do it within the cultural climate of their time (i.e., the historical, political and economic realities that allow or discourage such movement). For example, Afrika is poor and not as productive as it has been or should be because of internal difficulties (nation by nation), but also because of its colonial past and present. And, yes we are aware of the fact that it is much easier and less embarrassing to place most of the blame on former colonialists or, as in the Afrikan American case, former slave masters, than to *take hold* and transform ourselves. For example, if one were to look at today's Uganda in its utter devastation and desperation, a quick unknowing answer to its problem would be, "It suffers the legacy of colonialism." The answer is partially correct. However, a closer look also would take into account the last thirty-plus years of "independence" under Milton Obote and Idi Amin, two Afrikan men who abused power as if it had been ordained. The continued slaughter of Uganda's people and destruction of the land intensified under Black leadership. This example is not the exception. All over the Black world, from the Sudan to Chicago, Black men (and some women) abuse position and influence at the expense of their people and others.

It is instructive and painful to note that unlike other non-Afrikan former colonial or occupied nations (such as Singapore, India, China, South Korea and Japan), there is not one sub-Saharan Afrikan nation that produces or supplies to the Western world *any* refined Afrikan produced product that is used daily in most homes. For instance, VCR's are 100% Asian, much of the cotton clothing sold in the U.S. comes from India, and the U.S. automobile industry has been crippled by cars coming from Japan.

214

My point is the decline that Africa and its people have experienced over the last 1,000 years has not stopped, and her children who have been scattered worldwide have not been much help in bringing about such a reversal. Unlike the Jews, Arabs, Japanese, WASPs and others, Afrikans have few, if any, international effective structures working *unselfishly* for Black people. This is partially because the standards which most of us live by have been compromised to the point that in many quarters mediocrity is viewed as advancement. Concepts like integrity, morality, honesty and excellence are given lip-service as many of our teachers and leaders outdo the world in saying one thing while they do the destructive other.

III

The S Curve, Double Circles, or Infinity: Solutions

When a woman or man moves to a level of *knowing*, she or he ceases to be *reactive* and becomes *proactive* (i.e., a positive worker and an example). This is important because our people have enough talkers and rappers. The ability to inspire a crowd or congregation temporarily to do good work is not necessarily a great art; the key is to produce many people and leaders who internalize good work concepts and constantly and consistently do productive and developmental work.

In thinking about this, the letter "S" continues to jump in and out of my mind. In doubling the "S," as in man and woman (or partners) facing each other in a position of love-making, you get double circles or the sign of *infinity*. A man reaches a level of completeness only with a woman of like mind. If a man or woman is with a partner of unlikeness, only confusion can result. Therefore, our journey takes on another path when a partnership of completeness is made. The curve of the "S" is also important from a cultural standpoint because we are a circular people. That is, our lives revolve around the rejoining of the circle (families, communities, the Afrikan world), whereas the unbroken line of the circle represents our people in this land as well as the diaspora.

Therefore, if we concentrate on the S curve of double circles, we see that there exists a value-based system — a system of thought and action that can break the chains that have tied us to Europe and other false concepts of squares, sky scrapers, greed, individualism, sexism, selfishness, silliness and separation.

215

The S Curve (short definitions)

Source — For all people there are beginnings, in-betweens and endings that are renewing themselves.

Soil — Earth as life-giver, receiver, and renewing energy.

Seeing— Has very little to do with eyesight. Vision, insight.

Soul — The third eye of knowledge, where imagination dwells, where strength dwells.

Self— Faith in one's self is not egocentric pop psychology but is only an extension of one's willingness to accept and seek growth that leads to self-esteem.

Spirit — The willingness to fly into the face of denial. Spirituality, the connecting of the inner-self with the negative and positive temptations of the world.

Strength — Secure in one's history, traditions and present. Responsible. Standing up to evil and corruption.

Structure — All people, especially children, need order and predictability in their lives.

Searching — Trying to find meaning in all questions. Self-knowledge as a starting point.

Security — Knowing, feeling, giving and receiving love from family and extended family.

Study — A way of life that is as important as eating and breathing. Understanding that fruitful study is the foundation of a *knowing* person.

Student — Ongoing, for life. A seeker of knowledge.

Serious — Approaching the world with an attitude of understanding that goes beyond the normal or expected.

Space — One's private place for regeneration.

Stop-time — A time for contemplation and change. A point of reevaluation.

Smile — Laughter, the healing mechanism that is free but seldom understood or used.

Simplicity — An appreciation of the quiet; the search for quality within the unnoticed. Not moved by brand names.

Silence — Quiet time. Slowing running to a walk. Understanding one's internal needs for the absence of noise. Learning to listen.

Stillness — Ability to hear the heartbeat of one's future. A photograph or music that slows one's pulse.

Solitude — Aloneness. Welcomed isolation, a pacing that opens one up to other possibilities.

Sharing — Social network, family, children. The interaction of social institutions that impact on one's quality of life.

Saving — Frugality. The putting aside of resources for the future.

Service — The giving of one's talents to those less fortunate.

Specialness — The feelings one has for one's self and those one loves.

Support — Putting oneself in a position to offer knowledge or resources as needed.

Subtle — A way of functioning that does not underestimate another's intelligence.

Stimulate — Ability to pull the best from others and self. Self-motivated and sure starter.

Struggle — The only way to approach life in the United States. Without struggle, one is only an observer and victim. Conscious organizing.

Shining — Having touch with an internal light.

Saneness — A quality of being that allows one to function intelligently under all circumstances. Always trying to make practical sense.

Speaking — Multilingual. Watching one's words carefully. Avoiding perpetual talking. Having something to say and knowing when to say it.

Skepticism — Always questioning. Not accepting the easy answers or people who perpetually smile with their hands out.

Substance — A quality of being for which we must strive. Quality. Knowledge. Wisdom.

Success — The maximization of one's natural gifts and talents for a fruitful and meaningful life for one's self, family and people.

Steady and ready for Sisters — Having internalized the S curve and more.

Negatives

Siege — People under siege very seldom can create.

Separation — Individuals who are separated from each other, their history and culture will only invite confusion.

Shame — When everything is everything, nothing is nothing — a state of life where values cease to have meaning and anything goes. Honor is replaced with pleasure.

Stress— The psychological beating of the mind and body. A *major* killer of Black people.

Stale — Rotting. Mental retardation. Backwardness beyond saving.

Silliness — Jerri curls on men and women who are supposed to be able to think for themselves. Adults who play rather than think. Superficiality in values and knowledge.

Sameness — The melting pot theory that continues to burn Black people.

Sexism — The idea that men are the center of the universe and that women exist to serve men, children and dogs.

The S Curve (long definitions)

Source:

For all people there are beginnings, in-betweens and endings that continue to renew themselves, and in the absolute spread of time, there are only seconds separating the three. Very few people understand all three. Where one comes from is as important as where one is now or will be tomorrow. Afrika is not an accident of nature. Therefore, Afrikan people — wherever they may sleep — are there for a purpose. The scattering of Afrikan people around the world is not a punishment but an unfocused and improperly defined mission. The meaning of the mission will not and cannot become clear unless we return to the understanding of the *source*. This returning is not necessarily a physical journey because Afrika itself is in a state of questioning. This journey is a movement toward acceptance, acknowledgment and discovery (or finding); also it is one of admitting ignorance and questioning surroundings. The true meaning of Afrikan people in America is much more profound than a quest for food stamps or the Presidency. Our being here is more of an answer than a question. It is clear that the energy of Afrikan American people flows throughout the rivers and sunsets of America and the world.

Soil:

Earth is life. One of the most obvious misunderstandings of earth as life-giver is when an adult or child's answer to the question "Where does fruit come from?" is, "The *supermarket*." Indeed, the answer — most certainly, in the child's context — may be correct. However, in the overall order of life, it is an uninformed answer. Few people have abused the earth like Europeans. The rush to Western technology and industrialization has reeked serious damage on the earth in the name of progress. Soil (earth) as the provider of life is without question. We need to understand the life cycle of plants, animals and insects if we are to become more responsible in our approach to food. When people are raised on concrete rather than soil, their lives take on other shapes. Often their lives are full of crack(s); not only are their days drowned in drugs, they are defined by breakage. When one loses the connection to the earth, the land becomes like any other commodity — something to be bought, sold and used for making money rather than saving lives. From the damaging effects of acid-rain to the greenhouse effect, it is clear that the current rulers of this earth are sleepwalking toward *dust and dirt* rather than Black, bountiful soil. Remember, the only thing that nobody, anywhere is making any more of is *land*.

Seeing:

Most of us do not see; we are looking. *Seeing* has very little to do with eyesight. In fact, if eyesight is necessary for seeing, why are there so many intelligent blind people? Seeing, in this context, has more to do with *vision*, the type of vision that Stevie Wonder and Ray Charles possess. *Vision.* That's how a people escapes the trap of mediocrity. Not that mediocrity on occasion is dangerous, but the problem arises when mediocrity becomes the accepted norm or goal. Seeing means eclipsing *sameness* and being able to meet the challenges of life at a more meaningful level. *Seeing* is the encouragement of creativity and the actualization of one's personal gifts or talents. Often, such seeing comes in the form of poetry, novels, music, drama, visual arts and dance. The seers that produce visionary works in America often are destroyed because the populace cares more about the sayings and doings of entertainers, sports figures and news anchor people than those of writers, artists and thinkers.

The seers, the prophets in the United States, generally are those persons who have been systematically locked out of the benefits of the nation.

Soul:

The insight of any people can be seen in its creations. Soul, in its most representative form, in fact, is the essence of a people. Soul is, indeed, a special food, but it is not pork chops with white rice and gravy. Often the unexplained energies we receive that get us through the day or week have to do with what is inside. The ultimate soul is the knowing and forgiving soul. Within the soul is the third eye of knowledge. It is where imagination dwells. Imagination is as close as one can get to creating something out of nothing. If one has soul, she/he has balance, heart, hearing, unknown capacities and vision. Soul is the voice in music, the speaker in poetry, the narration in fiction, the feet in dance and the language in drama.

Self:

Belief in one's self should be subordinate only to belief in one's people and in a higher order that regulates all of us. One must develop a reasoned humbleness about one's own powers because it is clear to the knower that something else is working in this universe. Therefore, faith in one's self is not egocentric psychology but is only an extension of one's willingness to accept and seek growth. One's faith in self should be intuitive. It is also the perception and understanding that there is an order in life — a sense of wholeness with a special direction. Intuitive faith or belief allows for change and encourages a certain flexibility in one's actions. Therefore, faith or belief in one's self has a profound and far-reaching psychological effect. Faith or belief in one's self is the basis for all good work. Faith in one's ability allows one to become centered and focused in a direction that will provide fruit for self and others. The major and most rewarding approach to the self is to determine how best to become a creative and productive person as part of a self-reliant community. Self-knowledge means a gut and an intellectual understanding of one's self in connection to other peoples, cultures and races. Self-knowledge, if it is working, means self-love.

Spirit:

This is the brilliant force that has sustained our people all over the world. It's the articulate answer that rides the drumbeat throughout the Black world. Spirit focuses on the will to fly into the face of denial. Spirit provides the stimulus to live and create. Spirit is that quality in all of us that pushes us beyond the expected. It's the fighter's, dancer's, performer's secret weapon. It is spirit that takes the ordinary and makes it look like talent. When we talk about a person with *spirit*, we are talking about that which is extraordinary in a person's actions, heart, giving, beliefs and example.

Strength:

Saying no to weakening pleasures. Discipline. Avoiding the easy, the quick, get-over attitude. The ability to go deep into one's self for energy and fire. The ability to accept responsibility for ideas and actions that advocate that which is good, just and right. Ongoing mental and physical development, from lifting weights to lifting one's mind. Firmness in the mouth of evil opposition. Seeking ways to work for a functioning future. Learning from one's errors. The ability to admit mistakes and apologize for one's negative transgressions against self, family and people. Healthy and ready to support and encourage the good in all people. The ability to smile and show serious compassion and love for children. Processing the *will* to tackle the difficult obstacles in one's life. Not giving in to the quick fixes, unhealthy temptations and smiling lies. Always fighting corruption and deception.

Searching:

Trying to find meaning in all questions. Knowing that looking is far more than having one's eyes open. Seeking a purpose in life that is beyond the meaningless quest for material things and quick fixes. The defining of relationships: people to people, woman to man and children, man to woman and children, humans to animals and vegetation. Seeking answers through continuous study. Knowing that imperfect questions will only lead to incorrect answers and confusion.

Study:

Study is the contemplative search for the betterment of self and others. This involves quiet meditation on things that are valuable and necessary for human development. To be is to know. Knowing is a process. The most important parts of the process are 1) wanting to know; 2) understanding where knowledge and information can be found; 3) having the ability to distinguish between useful and non-useful knowledge; and 4) allowing useful knowledge and information to have a positive impact on one's life. Daily study is the key to knowing. If you have valuable knowledge, the world will come to you.

Student:

One who seeks and is open to life and its many secrets. A receiver of magic, garbage, hope, possibilities and bright tomorrows. Ongoing for life. One who questions most things and will not settle for easy answers or easy solutions. A book to the student is like food to the hungry. Questions to the student are like chalk to a blackboard or a basketball to the NBA.

Serious:

An approach to life that denotes an understanding of the complexity of the world. A person is serious when she or he accepts responsibility for making life better and more rewarding for self, family, extended family, community, one's people and the world. Seriousness is the necessary attitude for action. Knowing when to act is the compliment to a serious attitude. One who possesses this quality approaches the world from the position of a builder and developer.

Space:

A place to regenerate: home, temple, church, mosque or center where one's energy is restored. Nature-parks, libraries, museums, areas where one can meditate and contemplate one's place in the universe. One's private area, an area that is an extension of one's personality, where one

223

seeks strength, knowledge and peace. A place to which one wants to return often. One's space can be personal or collective.

Smile:

Laughter heals. Smiling often and at the right time makes life easier. Life cannot be serious twenty-four hours a day. One must learn to relax and let go. Do things that make one happy, such as spending time with children. Laughter and smiles will surely come if one is around children enough. Be careful about taking one's self too seriously.

Simplicity:

Learn conservation. Walk sometimes rather than ride. Take trains or buses rather than airplanes. Read books rather than watch television. Look for answers in the unexplained. Barter rather than buy all things. Simplicity lies in the enjoyment of art, music, literature, drama, dance, nature, learning and other activities that cost little or no money. It is the quality within the quiet and the unnoticed. Simplicity means back to basics; seeking the natural order of life; moving toward less complication in one's life. One who is simplistic seeks the true and renewable fundamentals of a functional life.

Silence:

Listening to one's own heartbeat. The absence of noise. The ability to communicate without words. A new level of hearing. An appreciation of calmness. A quality of hearing that is regenerative.

Solitude:

Without distraction. Building one's internal self; aloneness. Welcomed isolation. Meditation. Prayer. Clearing the mind. Connecting the mind to the body and spirit. Restoring order in one's life. Thinking time. Invaluable spacing.

Sharing:

Giving when least expected. Reciprocity with community, mate and children. The realization that giving is the best way to receiving. One cannot contribute positively to a functioning community unless one is willing to share beyond the limited expectations of others.

Struggle:

Life is not easy, never has been. To struggle means to reject the victim's role. One who struggles is a rejuvenated fighter — lifelong. She/he is organized, prepared and multi-talented. To struggle is to understand complexity; to pick one's own battles. There cannot be fruitful progress without struggle.

Skepticism:

We were born wanting to know. The art of questioning is lost or developed very early. Most people accept style over substance, junk food over nourishment. We must return to the difficult questions — and expect serious answers. Beware of people who have all the answers to every question without skipping a beat. To have doubts is healthy.

Substance:

A person's actions will ultimately define him/her. Words are fine, but as they say on the block, "You can't beat the drum without hitting it." Be slow to give answers, quick to be the example of the answer. Value knowledge. Realize that wisdom comes from study, work, building, creation and production.

Steady and ready for Sisters, family, community, people and world. Understanding the S curve and other philosophies of life. Mastering the S curve. Seeking and accepting quality and excellence as normal. Looking for that which compliments and encourages beauty in relationships. Able to lead and accept leadership. Loving the sisters, their music and motion. Willing to work for their happiness. Knowing that their happiness will make us happy. Realizing that our women represent source and smile. Knowing that the two selves must connect and grow as one. Maintaining a spirit that stimulates the soul, which gives strength to serious students of love, life and saneness. Avoiding silliness and shamefully sexist acts with a passion. Subtle and simplistic in one's approach to our women and to life. Speaking with wisdom in acknowledging the specialness of Afrikan women.

Finally, I must emphasize several points. We must be skilled doers in this world — walking and working with a humility that is focused on wellness. "Research shows that people who are driven by ambition, goals, and achievements only are more prone to illness than those who place more stock in *harmonious* relationships." Secondly, we must take responsibility for the wellness of ourselves and our people. This means that we must free ourselves from sickening doctor/patient relationships and be careful about looking to other so-called experts to make us well. We must become more adult-like and responsible in *attacking that which is not right* in our lives and communities. Thirdly, we must eat correctly — that is, we must take responsibility for everything that goes into our bodies and our children's bodies, as well as make sure that our families, extended families and friends are aware of life and life-giving alternatives. The most appropriate diet that I've chosen for myself is based on the correct use of fruits, vegetables, whole grains, beans, sea vegetables and clean water. To that I add daily study, yoga and meditation — to connect one to a higher inner self, to exercise the inner and outer body with the mind. Also, a good program of physical exercise is necessary. I suggest walking, cycling and swimming.

It is clear also that one must have an unwavering faith in one's self, our people and the possibilities of the future. This cannot be a blind *faith* but one based upon adherence to study and creative production. This can happen by developing support networks that include but go beyond the extended family. Such networks as sisterhoods, brotherhoods, child-care centers, schools, political organizations, food co-ops, businesses, boys' and girls' clubs must be committed to life. If they are to function in our best interests, each will approach life in a way that fosters optimum benefits for its members. For example, we must be political, but we do not have to become politicians.

It is beauty, security, health, love, enlightenment and happiness we seek. We can only find such music in a functioning social familyhood whose members are aware of its source, soil and soul, and who are able

to see themselves as searchers for spiritual strength — coming as serious students to a space for study and reflection, devoid of stress or staleness, absent of people who find value and energy in sameness that produces silliness without stop-time. Our laughter should be smiles promoting a healing simplicity, rich in silence, stillness, solitude and silver that encourage sharing, saving, service, support and intellectual specialness. All subtly stimulating a shining, sure saneness that makes sense for our struggle, while speaking firmly and skeptically with substance to the promised success we so heartfelt need and
work for
making us steady and ready for
sisters,
family,
extended family, community
world.

MOTHERS

for Mittie Travis (1897-1989), Maxine Graves Lee (1924-1959),
Inez Hall and Gwendolyn Brooks

"Mothers are not to be confused with females
who only birth babies"

mountains have less height
and
elephants less weight than
mothers who plan bright futures for their children
against the sewers of western life.

mothers making magical music miles from monster madness
are not news,
are not subject for doctorates.

how shall we celebrate mothers?
how shall we call them in the winter of their lives?
what melody will cure slow bones?
who will bring them worriless late-years?
who will thank them for hidden pains?

mothers are not broken-homes,
they are irreplaceable fire,
a kiss or smile at a critical juncture,
a hug or reprimand when doubts swim in,
a calm glance when the world seems impossible,
the back that america could not break.

mothers making magical music miles from monster madness
are not news,
are not subject for doctorates.

mothers instill questions and common sense,
urge mighty thoughts and lively expectations,
are impetus for discipline and intelligent work while
making childhood exciting, unforgettable and challenging.

229

mothers are preventative medicine
they are
women who hold their children all night to break fevers,
women who cleaned other folks' homes in order to give their children
     one,
women who listen when others laugh,
women who believe in their children's dreams,
women who lick the bruises of their children and
give up their food as they suffer hunger pains silently.

if mothers depart their precious spaces too early
values, traditions and bonding interiors are wounded,
morals confused, ethics unknown, needed examples absent and
crippling histories of other people's victories are passed on as
     knowledge.

mothers are not broken-homes,
they are gifts
sharing full hearts, friendships and mysteries.
as the legs of fathers are amputated
mothers double their giving
having seen the deadly future of white flowers.

mothers making magical music miles from monster madness
are not news,
are not subject for doctorates.

who will bring them juice in the sunset of their time?
who will celebrate the wisdom of their lives,
the centrality of their songs,
the quietness of their love,
the greatness of their dance?
it must be us,
able daughters, good sons
their cultural gift,
the fruits and vegetables of their medicine.

We must come like earthrich waterfalls.

III. Worldview

"We still need the essential Black statement of defense and definition. Of course, we are happiest when that statement is not dulled by assimilationist urges, secret or overt. However, there is in "the souls of Black folk" — even when inarticulate and crippled — a yearning toward Black validation."

Gwendolyn Brooks
from "Requiem Before Revival"

Why Foreign Policy Is Foreign
to Most Afrikan Americans

International affairs has to do with relationships, the reasons these relationships exist, and in whose interest they exist. It also has to do with power — raw, unadulterated force and fear, the kind of fear that makes men piss in their pants and blow their brains out. Such power has forced nations to spend 60% of their national budgets on weapons systems, as their people seek nourishment from the garbage of tourists. In the last quarter of the 20th century, on the heels of modern computer technology and satellite communication, the conducting of foreign policy is still the game of running the world.

Simply stated, the relationship that one country has with another country or countries is defined as its foreign policy. A nation's foreign affairs can range anywhere from trade to "constructive engagement," from scientific, cultural and educational exchange to war. Generally speaking, the foreign policy of a nation is set by its ruling body — in the United States, the executive branch. In effect, the President is charged with the formation of a foreign policy that must be, at some point, confirmed by the Congress. To really understand a nation's foreign policy, serious study is required. Most people in the United States, whites as well as Blacks, do not have any idea about what this country is doing around the world, with the possible exception of its "War on Terrorism" that is explained in the thirty-second slots each night on the evening news. This country's foreign policy is calculated in body counts as the sophisticated theft of nations goes unnoticed. The roles the CIA and KGB play in the world's destabilization seldom are explored in the popular press.

The citizen-consumer in the United Stated plays checkers and video games, while the world-runners (politicians, businessmen, military and academia) continuously restructure the world's chessboard. Unlike the game of chess learned during youth, opponents on the world stage do not start with equal chances to checkmate. The game of world-running is fixed according to Holly Sklar's book, *Trilateralism*. The stakes are too enormous to be left to the skill or luck of a single player. These are gigan-

231

tic gang wars in which the combatants fight without referees or rules. The major gangs are the United States and the North Atlantic Treaty Organization versus the Soviet Union and the Warsaw Pact. Each gang, with some consultation with its membership, has carved up the world into "Spheres of Influence."

What is clear but not talked or written about in great detail is that white people, who are less than 9% percent of the world's population, *run it all,* and that all others fall into one of the two camps or into the ineffective nonaligned nations. White world supremacy, operating in the areas of business, law, education, language, religion, sports, entertainment, military and foreign affairs, is the most serious problem facing Afrikan Americans and other people of color, argues Neely Fuller in the *The United Independent Compensatory Code/System/Concept.*

The function of a gang is to acquire, develop and protect one's turf (its economic market). Thus, the analogy of a nation to a gang is not too far-fetched. The old Anglo-Saxon proverb, "The only successful war is the one that is won," operates daily in the Pentagon and on the streets, which is why the United States can, with a confident arrogance, ignore the World Court's decision condemning its activities in the not-so-"secret" war against Nicaragua. This is also why the USSR and the USA can, with little difficulty, tie up those votes in the United Nations that they feel go against their best interests. The United States and the Soviet Union are modern gangs that, in the final analysis, listen only to each other. And even though each country speaks a different language and operates out of dissimilar cultural imperatives, each one's message is the same, *we run it.*

To fully understand the foreign policy of the United States, one has to have a lot of time and an appreciation for serious money. The major stimulants for the foreign affairs of the United States are its "national security" and profits. Imperialism may be a little understood word on the block, but for most of the world it is a dangerously nonnegotiable reality. The large gap between rich and poor countries; the involvement of politics and international economics; and the effective use of economic and military power to create dependency, exploitation and dominance speak to the type of imperialism (economic control) at which the United States is the reigning master. The foreign policy of the United States is predicated on three principles: 1) expanding markets; 2) national security and anti-communism; and 3) global, economic and political hegemony. At one level, this is deep stuff which will require the average person to give up evenings, weekends, holidays and even dating to grasp its meaning. But, on the other hand, there are some close-to-home and recent observations that may help clarify the crippling influence of U.S. foreign policy.

Ferdinand Marcos, the recently deceased former dictator of the Philippines, ruled that country by using force and crony capitalism for more than twenty years. Marcos, on a salary less than that of the lowest paid state governor in the United States, amassed a fortune that is estimated to be somewhere between $3 and $19 billion. Only his widow, mistress, accountants and lawyers know the exact amount, and they are talking only to each other. Today, 72% of the Philippine population lives in poverty, compared with 27% in 1965. In twenty years of dictatorial rule, Marcos killed, imprisoned and politically crushed his opponents with the aid and blessing of the United States government. What did the United States get out of this deal? The use of land in the Philippines for U.S. military bases. From Lyndon Johnson to George Bush, U.S. foreign policy in the Philippines has been structured around the needs of the U.S., at the cruel expense of the Filipino people.

The poorest country in the Western Hemisphere is Haiti. Jean Claude "Baby Doc" Duvalier and his father before him ruled that small nation like a family business for over a quarter of a century. The poverty is so great in Haiti that fresh water in one's home is viewed as a luxury. The military and economic oppression was so effective that most people involved in progressive political actvity could expect instant imprisonment, torture or death if caught. If a young person cried for food, work and education, she or he was in danger of being branded a communist. The United States provided millions upon millions of dollars in aid to Haiti; little, if any, went directly to the people. Trickle-down economics has not arrived in that part of the world.

The way Baby Doc showed concern for his people was by driving through town with his wife, throwing coins to the populace. However, in February of 1986, the "Baby" and his family fled in the night, with the United States providing the taxi service. Before he left, he had robbed the country white. According to *The New York Times*, he left less than $1 million in the central bank. Corruption in Haiti was a prerequisite for success. The former dictator's wealth is estimated to be between $300 and $900 million, all stolen from the Haitian people. He and his wife are believed to have real estate and monies stashed throughout the West, mainly in the United States, France, and Mexico. Marcos and Duvalier are both looking for a home, and they're doing it in style.

The final example is South Afrika. The history of South Afrika, in broad terms, closely resembles that of the United States. George M. Frederickson, in his book *White Supremacy: A Comparative Study in American and South African History,* draws many cogent parallels. The most obvious is that Europeans settled both lands and on each continent, slowly but effectively instituted a reign of terror designed to reduce and subjugate the indigenous population. In the U.S., the term "genocide" would be a polite description of the "success" Europeans have had in reducing the indigenous population and securing the North American continent. The white South Colonialists of South Afrika, with much help from their Euro-American brothers, still are working at stealing Afrika.

What is obvious, however, is that the annihilation of Afrikan people has not worked and will not work. What has worked is the effective neutralization of many Afrikan people and their reduction to a dependent people in their own land. Also, the whites, through the use of rewards and punishment, have been able to divide the Blacks into battling factions that fight each other rather than the true enemy. This is the classic victim's reaction to oppression. The white colonialists, with their ideology of white supremacy, have developed a system of calculated terror that functions like a well-oiled machine twenty-four hours a day, 365 days a year. Presently, there are over 7,000 Black Afrikans who are being detained in South Afrikan prisons without charges or legal representation.

The white minority (about four million of the population) has structured a completely separate and unequal system that is designed to totally contain the movement and development of the country's majority Black population (25 million plus). The national government has classified and segregated everything from education to housing, politics to food production, employment to sports, entertainment to health care. This system of hatred and social disease flourished in part because of the United States and other Western nations' support and, in particular, through the use of multinational corporations such as IBM, Ford, General Motors and others. The bottom line is that the U.S. chose to fight communism by instituting a boycott against Poland and initiating a private war against the people of Nicaragua, but all it can do for Afrikan Blacks, in the wake of ten Black deaths a day and indescribable oppression, is talk. The major excuse the administration gives is that "constructive engagement" is working, but few actually give the real reasons why this country continues to back such a racist regime.

First, the whites of South Afrika and white Americans are blood brothers. Secondly, the U.S. imports from South Afrika over $1 billion a year in chromium, manganese and platinum for its industrial, economic and military uses. The human rights of people of color are secondary to the national defense and profits of the United States. Bantustans of South Afrika are similar to the Black ghettos of the United States. The racial and economic deprivation our brothers and sisters suffer in South Afrika actually exists in the U.S. but at a much more subtle yet effective level. In fact, many Afrikan Americans do not believe that they are oppressed. To fully explain this will require another essay. However, it is clear that America's Black "permanent underclass," with its high unemployment, frightening illiteracy, enormous prison population, homelessness and huge addiction to drugs and alcohol, is a dependent and enslaved people. To truly comprehend the state of Black America would require a social science course in itself (see Pinkney's *The Myth of Black Progress*). Blacks here are just a boat ride away from the type of enslavement that exists in South Afrika. Think about this: people in the U.S. seldom, if ever, talk about a permanent white underclass. The racist duplicity and contradictions of U.S. foreign policy can be easily illustrated by examining U.S. actions in Grenada, Libya, the Middle East, Chile, Ghana and other nations. The U.S. actions in the Philippines, Haiti, Israel and South Afrika represent state terrorism at its highest stages. The people of the Philippines and Haiti actively are initiating change that has little to do with the corrective actions of the United States. This country jumped on the train of the Haitian and Filipino people when it saw change in the wind. South Afrika remains a serious problem that has Third World War possibilities if substantive changes do not come soon.

There are several observations here for Afrikan Americans: 1) all people do what they've been taught to do, and most of them act in the way that they perceive is in their best interest; the basis for these actions are both cultural and biological; 2) Black people in the United States, most certainly since 1865, have been concerned mainly with surviving and developing in the Western Hemisphere. The majority of Black people have forgotten their holocaust — the middle passage. Many Black people also have forgotten the genocide committed against the indigenous people of this land, those persons renamed Indians or Native Americans. Most

Blacks understand by now that treaties and contracts with the Western world are like sports records — made to be broken.

Generally, the Afrikan American's view of the world is colored by his or her view of himself or herself. That is, acculturation has prepared Blacks to see what they have been taught to see and to believe what they have been taught to believe. The saying "It is easier to believe than think" is quite apropos for the Black situation in the United States. Foreign policy is foreign because most Afrikan Americans have been too busy trying to master, translate and understand domestic policy.

Whereas serious struggle is multifaceted, most Blacks are still one-dimensional and strait-jacketed to a European-centered worldview. Many Blacks are like smokers who believe the warning label on the package is for someone else. Death and taxes are indeed certain; but for the chained mind, slavery is too. It is difficult to win a war when people have to buy weapons from the enemy. Most buyers will never be sold or given weapons from the top of the line. Nations are not taken seriously when they can't do fundamental things like feed themselves. Imperialism has reached its highest stage when the sons and daughters of a given nation, mainly from the First World (Afrika), study abroad and choose to stay and participate in the building of that nation, rather than return home. The brain drain from the First World is unbelievable and crippling to that continent.

The war, whether on the battlefield or in the classroom, is with ideas. Actually, ideas run the world. Foreign policy is fashioned in the popular as well as the national culture. We can see this from the foreign policy of the Catholic Church, where every few months the Pope goes on diplomatic trips around the world. And, most certainly, we can see it in the popular culture with such movies as *Red Dawn*, *Rambo*, *Rocky IV* and the popular *Top Gun*. Ideas are important. Two bad ideas are 1) the view of Black people as a minority people in the world; and 2) the suggestion that Afrikan countries should continue to tie their currency and development to Europe (i.e., the West). My point is that Black people represent over one billion people in the world; if Blacks cannot recognize our own strength worldwide in terms of numbers, land mass and resources and cannot organize such vast wealth, we are lost. Cheikh Anta Diop, in his book *Black Africa*, calls for the formation of a United Black Africa into a single economic and cultural federated state. It is quite clear that white people are organized at a world level for the perpetuation and continuation of their rule. Afrikan people can do no less.

236

Very seldom will an Afrikan trained at Harvard Business School or the London School of Economics create self-reliant ideas out of that academic experience unless he or she is a Kwame Nkrumah, W.E.B. Du Bois, Nelson Mandela or Patrice Lumumba. The only time a great many Black people get involved in U.S. foreign policy is in its implementation as foot soldiers in foreign wars. Black people are the people who fight the wars for this country against other people of color around the world. Recent examples are Vietnam and Grenada.

If Afrikan Americans ever are to have a serious impact on U.S. foreign policy, accurate information is needed. At the end of this essay, there is a list of books, newspapers, magazines and quarterlies with which the interested reader can start. The major rules to follow in gathering data about the world are 1) do not depend on *one* source of information; 2) be flexible by studying materials of both right and left political views; 3) take political science courses at local universities; 4) travel whenever possible to other nations; 5) make friends with foreign students, visitors and citizens; 6) start a personal library; 7) work with progressive Black organizations; 8) attend foreign policy lectures that are open to the public; 9) form foreign policy study groups; 10) don't become overwhelmed with what you will discover; and 11) watch and consult legislators on foreign policy issues.

The attitude one brings to this subject is crucial. Don't be afraid to admit ignorance. The world we live in is very political and extremely complicated. Most things in this world are political, from the food one eats to the clothes one buys. The Western world is Eurocentric, racist, sexist, class-conscious, and youth-oriented. If a person is Black, conscious and living in America, one thing is absolutely certain — he or she is *fighting daily* or has been defeated.

The United States uses over 60% of the world's natural resources but is the home of less than 7% of the world's people. Much of those resources come from Afrika. If one cannot see the inequality in this arrangement, it only confirms the effectiveness of Western acculturation and the dominance of the Eurocentric worldview. The most important foreign policy issue facing Afrikan Americans is our relationship to Afrika. Blacks in the U.S. must pressure the State Department and Congress to pursue a just and balanced policy. We can learn from the Polish and Jewish people in their capable lobbying for Poland and Israel. Afrikan Americans will remain powerless pawns in the international chess game unless Afrika and its future become central in Black thought and action. The 21st century is upon us. Memory is calling, and this generation will truly be judged by its children — if they are alive and productive. Using the knowledge and technology of the present, we must pull from the wisdom and vision of our foreparents to issue on this earth a better world.

REFERENCES

Any bibliography of this inexhaustible subject can only be very selective

Agee, Philip. *Inside The Company: CIA Diary*. New York: Lyle Stuart, 1984.

Aliber, Robert Z. *The International Money Game*. New York: Basic, 1987.

Barraclough, Geoffrey. *The Turning Points in World History*. London: Thames Hudson, 1979.

Biko, Steve. *I Write What I Like*. San Francisco: Harper & Row, 1986.

Brown, Lester R., et al. *State of the World 1986*. New York: Norton, 1986.

Cline, Ray S. *Secrets, Spies & Scholars*. Washington, DC: Acropolis, 1978.

Cohen, Benjamin J. *The Question of Imperialism*. New York: Basic, 1973.

Diop, Cheikh Anta. *Black Africa: the Economic & Cultural Basis for a Federated State*. Chicago: Chicago Review, 1987.

_____ . *The Cultural Unity of Black Africa*. Chicago: Third World Press, 1987.

Dower, John W. *War Without Mercy: Race & Power in the Pacific War.* New York: Pantheon, 1986.

Dunnigan, James F. and Bay, Austin. *A Quick and Dirty Guide to War.* New York: 1986.

Fallows, James. *National Defense.* New York: Random House, 1981.

Franck, Thomas M. and Weisband, Edward. Eds. *Secrecy & Foreign Policy.* London: Oxford University Press, 1974.

Frederickson, George M. *White Supremacy.* New York: 1981.

Fuller, Jr., Neely. *The United Independent Compensatory Code/System/ Concept A Textbook/Workbook for Thought, Speech and/Or Action For Victims of Racism* . Washington, DC: published by author, 1984.

Garwood, Darrell. *Under Cover: Thirty-five Years of CIA Deception.* New York: Grove, 1985.

Hanlon, Joseph and Omond, Roger. *The Sanctions Handbook.* New York: Penguin Books, 1987.

Herman, Edward S. *The Real Terror Network.* Boston: South End Press, 1982.

Kolko, Joyce. *America and the Crises of World Capitalism.* Boston: 1974.

Kwitny, Jonathan. *Endless Enemies.* New York: Congdon & Weed, 1984.

Nalty, Bernard C. *Strength For The Fight: a History of Black Americans in the Military.* New York: Free Press, 1986.

Nkrumah, Kwame. *Neo-Colonialism.* New York: International Publishing Co., 1966.

Pinkney, Alphonso. *The Myth of Black Progress.* Cambridge: Cambridge University Press, 1984.

Sampson, Anthony. *The Money Lenders.* New York: Peter Smith, 1988.

Sklar, Holly. Ed. *Trilateralism.* Boston: South End Press, 1980.

Smith, Anthony. *The Geopolitics of Information: How Western Culture Dominates the World.* New York: Oxford University Press, 1980.

Stockwell, John. *In Search of Enemies.* New York: Norton, 1984.

Williams, Chancellor. *The Destruction of Black Civilization.* Chicago: Third World Press, 1989.

Wright, Bobby E. *Psychopathic Racial Personality and Other Essays.* Chicago: Third World Press, 1989.

Newspapers

New York Times	*Philadelphia Inquirer*	*The Final Call*
Washington Post	*Chicago Tribune*	*In These Times*
Wall Street Journal	*Miami Herald*	*The New York Sun*
Los Angeles Times	*The Buffalo Challenger*	*Christian Science Monitor*

Quarterlies and Magazines

Foreign Affairs	*The Nation*	*Commentary*
Foreign Policy	*The Progressive*	*Black Scholar*
The Return	*The New Republic*	*Mother Jones*
New African	*The National Review*	*New International*
West African	*Black Books Bulletin*	*Covert Action*
African Concord	*African Guardian*	*Zeta*
Essence	*African Commentary*	*Focus*
New York Review of Books	*Crisis*	*North Star*

BLACKS AND JEWS:
THE CONTINUING QUESTION

I was asked by a friend to participate in a forum concerning Black/Jewish relations in Chicago. I refused because I do not believe that such forums are useful without fundamental changes in economic and political relations in this city. My friend then requested that I make a few comments about Black/Jewish relations as I see them, to be broadcast over Chicago public radio. I said yes for four reasons: 1) a friend requested it; 2) there are other views from our community that have not been articulated, 3) this subject is not new to me; and 4) our children deserve more than we are receiving on this question from our leaders and the media. (See the recent *Esquire* article, "The Uncivil War," by Taylor Branch — 5/89.)

To say that Blacks are anti-Semitic is as absurd as saying that Jews are anti-Israel. This issue of Blacks and Jews in Chicago has been blown all out of context and has put some Blacks in an undefensible position of responding to the statements of one man that were, at best, ill-informed and insensitive. The larger issue is not one of Blacks and Jews but of Blacks and white people. The historical, racial, political and economic (i.e., cultural) relationship of Black people to white people, of which Jews are an integral part, has not been approached or analyzed in a reasoned manner in the media or back rooms.

To isolate the gigantic problem that Black people face worldwide, that of white world supremacy, to a fight between Blacks and Jews is to support and legitimize the victim's approach to Black struggle and world realities. Often the victim's approach to a question is ahistorical; it's like saying the holocaust didn't happen, when, in fact, there have been many holocausts throughout history. One such holocaust was the rape of Afrika by Europeans and the scattering of Afrikan people around the world to provide free labor for Europe and her colonies. And according to Chancellor Williams' *The Destruction of Black Civilization*, Walter Rodney's *How Europe Underdeveloped Africa* and George Padmore's *Africa: Britain's Third Empire*, over 65 million Afrikan people perished during the Euro-Asian trade in Afrikan men, women and children. Another ex-

241

ample was the European colonization of the Western Hemisphere that destroyed nations of indigenous people (over twenty million); those who are left in the U.S. occupy reservations and a new name, "Native Americans" — sounds like something generic. The German's killing move against its own citizens, mainly Jews, is the holocaust with which most Americans are familiar. The Jewish holocaust remains on the consciences of most literate people because the Jewish people — and rightly so — will not let the world forget. This non-forgetting strategy, along with a Jewish armed force, collective white guilt and aid, helped to create the modern state of Israel, which occupies land that used to be Palestine.

One of the most effective weapons the Jewish people have at their disposal is the labeling of a person or group as anti-Semitic. It is no secret in the Black community that many Blacks will take up Jewish battle before even thinking of their own because, all too often, many Blacks see the Jewish struggle and the Black struggle as one and the same. The quickest way to be designated a surefire, out-in-the-open anti-Semite is by openly confronting the Jewish influence in America, especially in regards to Israel. History, facts and the search for truth often are backseated to long-held positions that allow little room for change, compromise or peace. In an enlightening article, "The Illusion of Jewish Unity," in the June 16, 1988 issue of the *New York Review of Books*, Rabbi Arthur Hertzberg examines the geopolitical nature of the Jewish question. Rabbi Hertzberg states that taxpayers in the United States, of which Black people are a significant part, support Israel to the sum of over three billion dollars a year. This may, indeed, be new information to a great many Black people because prior to Rev. Jackson's raising the right questions in his run for the Presidency, it was assumed that foreign policy of the United States was not the concern of Afrikan Americans. The Jewish influence on the foreign policy of this country is awesome, especially when it comes to Israel. See Paul Findley's *They Dare Speak Out*; the former Illinois congressman dared to criticize Israel, and the Jewish lobby, the American-Israeli Public Affairs Committee (AIPAC), was instrumental in seeing that he did not return to Congress. Another important contribution to this ongoing debate is Edward Tivnan's *The Lobby: Jewish Political Power and American Foreign Policy*. Mr. Tivnan makes it very clear that the job of AIPAC — the only registered lobbyist for Israel on Capitol Hill — is to push and advocate pro-Israel legislation and to soften, intercept and quiet all criticism of Israel.

However, the Jewish need to be involved with the "Black Question" has always been strong. From the Herbert Apthekers to the Theodore Drapers, from the Irving Howes to the Herbert Gutmans, from the Norman Podhoretzs to the Norman Mailers, the Jewish influence over "Afrikan-American" scholarship and ideological development is unbelievable. Their input is unrelenting, and many of the current problems of the Black struggle are a result of our becoming too dependent on Jewish, WASP and other people's interpretations of Black history, life and culture. One of the most recent Jewish contributions to this is Weisbord and Kazarian's *Israel in the Black American Perspective* (Greenwood, 1985).

My argument is not against the Jews bringing forth their own worldview around the Afrikan American question. *My concern is the uncritical acceptance of their worldview and the inability of the work of Black thinkers and activists to find its way into print.* The majority of Afrikan American people are basically left with a Eurocentric, white Judaic-Christian analysis of Black struggle, and any discussions of politics, race, economics, education, religion, politics, culture, law, etc. generally are clouded by this limited perspective.

Such a perspective distorts the Civil Rights and Black Power movements of the sixties. There is no Black/Jewish coalition or alliance in existence among the majority of Black and Jewish people, and there never has been. That *some* Blacks and Jews have worked and struggled together is unquestionable. However, if one understands the concept of coalitions/alliances, one talks about a combining of equals, partners or cooperating decision-makers. This state of affairs never has existed between the majority of Blacks and Jews or between Blacks and any whites. The participation of Jews in the Black struggle of the fifties and sixties was more image, money and decision-influencing than anything else, according to Harold Cruse in his important study, *The Crisis of the Negro Intellectual*. Cruse and others point out that Blacks represented (and still do) a buffer zone for the Jews in regards to their Anglo-Saxon-Irish-Italian-Polish-German (i.e., white) brothers. The Blacks' move toward liberation (which some define as civil rights), after careful inspection, clearly points out that the Black struggle aided Jews and other ethnic whites to a much greater degree than it did Black people. According to Lewis A. Coser and Irving Howe in their book, *The New Conservatives*:

The American negroes have served as a kind of buffer for American Jews. So long as deep-seated native resentments and hatreds were taken out primarily on blacks, they were less likely to be taken out on Jews. If Jews have been the great obsession of Christianity, blacks have been the great obsession of America. And as long as this condition existed, both organized and spontaneous hatred in America concentrated on blacks and only secondarily on Jews.

This should not be odd or earth-shattering if one truly comprehends the type of war that is being waged daily in this country and in much of the world against Black people. Jews have sophisticatedly linked the Black struggle to theirs, and it has worked beautifully for the most part. This linkage began to unravel in the sixties when S.N.C.C. (Student Nonviolent Coordinating Committee) began to question the international nature of Jewish struggle, especially in its relationship to Palestine and South Afrika.

Is there a Jewish conspiracy to rule the world? I don't know. But Jewish-Americans, WASPs, Irish-Americans, Italian-Americans and Polish, Japanese, Greek and French-Americans actively participate in world and domestic capitalism. And the Fortune 1000 companies haven't been dismantling industrial America and shifting much of its manufacturing to European and Third World countries because of altruism. The controlling of world markets and resources is nothing new to global capitalism or socialism. The capitalists just do it better. The major capitalists in the world are white. There are Jews among them.

In an analysis of the annual *Forbes* lists of the 400 richest Americans, Edward S. Shapiro in the winter 1987 issue of *Judaism* makes it very clear that the Jewish presence in monied America is significant but not dominant. Of the *Forbes* 400 richest American families, over 100 are Jews. Therefore, "twenty-five percent of the richest Americans comes from a group which is less than three percent of the general population. By contrast, the *Forbes* list contains only a handful of Italians, no Hispanics, one Black, and a couple of Eastern Europeans, groups which outnumber Jews." Mr. Shapiro also states:

...a disproportionate number of America's ordinary millionaires are also Jewish and the per capita income of American Jews is also far higher than in that of the general population...Furthermore, of the fourteen American billionaires, at least four are Jewish: Marvin

244

Davis, the Denver oil mogul and former owner of Twentieth Century Fox; Leslie Wexner, America's leading merchant and head of the Limited, Inc. women's apparel shops; and the Newhouse brothers, Samuel and Donald, who control America's greatest privately owned newspaper, magazine, and book publishing empire.

Does such wealth control America or the world? No! Mr. Shapiro also points out that Jews are "still rare in corporate America where power is in the hands of the insurance companies, banks and industrial corporations that are controlled by non-Jews." However, such wealth does have immense influence in America and, in particular, Black America. Much of the wealth in Jewish America, according to Gerald Krefetz's *Jews and Money: the Myths and Reality* and Stephen Birmingham's three books, *Our Crowd, The Grundees* and *The Rest of Us*, comes from real estate, retail, publishing and entertainment. *All four areas impact daily on the lives of Black people in terms of where we live, what and where we shop, what we read and who makes it in the entertainment field,* one of the few areas that Black people dominate as performers. (Also see, Neal Gabler's *An Empire of Their Own: How the Jews Invented Hollywood.*)

Blacks can appreciate and understand the Jewish dilemma. (See the May 24, 1988 issue of the *Village Voice*, in which a discussion moderated by Nat Hentoff, "What's a Jew to Do?" explores the issue of Israel, United States, South Afrika and the world.) However, Blacks never have had the luxury of actually making the complete separation of Jews from other whites. The Jews in their day-to-day associations with Blacks, in many cases, have not allowed this. In fact, there are constant reminders of Jews not only being Jews but white also. James Baldwin in his essay, "Negroes are Anti-Semite Because They're Anti-White," states:

> ...the Jew is singled out by Negroes not because he acts differently from other white men, but because he doesn't. His major distinction is given him by that history of Christiandom, which has successfully victimized both Negroes and Jews. And he is playing in Harlem the role assigned him by Christians long ago: he is doing their 'dirty work.'

Many Jews are in an identity crisis; however, this is generally among the young and is not a problem for the Jews that make life and death decisions. Since Jews have used Blacks as buffers for so long, many now feel threatened by those Blacks who question the actual meaning of such a relationship. Those Afrikan Americans that do question such a relationship are in the acute minority. Few, if any Black publications explore the relationship with any type of seriousness. When the question is raised publicly, it is generally a reaction to a Black calling Jews out of their name or questioning their influence in Black affairs.

Several things need to be emphasized:

1) We live in a global world, and just as Jews are concerned about Israel, the Irish about Ireland and the Polish about Poland, Blacks too must be concerned about Afrika, specifically South Afrika where the descendents of Europe rule with gestapo tactics. And South Afrika's continued existence as a white supremacist nation, in part, is dependent on the United States, Western Europe, Israel, Japan and a few Afrikan nations.

2) For Blacks to advocate Black or Afrikan American nationalism is not odd or racist or unusual in a world context. In fact, most people — Jews included — who are in control of their own cultural imperatives act in a self-protecting and self-reliant manner that is a form of nationalism and may have either religious or secular roots. In fact, that which is odd, racist and unusual is that there are not more Black people advocating Black nationalistic ideas. This, of course, has to do with the effectiveness of the acculturation/seasoning process and the Black commitment to the American promise of integration and fairness, even as such misconceptions destroy many Black people daily.

3) Jews and most white people who negotiate with the Black community at a policy level are informed and have done their homework. Often the criticism of whites and Jews that comes from the Black community is personal and highly emotional — which in itself doesn't make it less valid, but in the political arena such responses are less effective if they can't be immediately documented or collaborated, thereby leaving them open to counter-criticism and dismissal. The study of other cultures and people cannot be left to academia, who are often too removed from the Black community or have been co-opted and thus are not effective. If we are to confront our critics and/or adversaries, we must know them well.

4) This issue of knowing and not forgetting one's history is of paramount importance. The self-protecting manner in which Jews define, project and carry out their own worldview is another lesson we can learn from them. The power of Black people is diluted and often not actualized because of forced amnesia. Whether Blacks reside in Brazil, the United States, the Caribbean, Asia or Afrika, the two grains that divide us are non-communication (i.e., language and contact) and other people's definitions.

One of the many strengths of the Jewish people — and they must be admired for this — is that they build institutions. Therefore, when a response is needed to a particular problem, question, or attack, they are able to act quickly and decisively at an individual and institutional level. And this response comes from many quarters, such as the pages of *Commentary, Midstream* and *The New York Times*; as well as organizations like the Anti-Defamation league of B'nai B'rith and the American Jewish Congress. That former President Reagan and Jesse Jackson took the human rights issue, which was first raised in reference to the Black situation in the United States in the sixties by Malcolm X, to the U.S.S.R. is another sign of Jewish determination. Mr. Reagan and President Bush have yet to be as forceful about the human rights and majority rule of Blacks in South Afrika.

It's time for Blacks to stop being the pawns in the word-games of others. Our youth are wasting away in imitation schools, overloading the few drug programs available, filling up the prisons, being forgotten in mental institutions and dying faster than the statistics can record their forgotten bodies. The Black testing time has passed. Does this mean that some Black people and some Jewish people cannot work together, grow together and struggle against evil together? Absolutely not, this has happened in the past and will undoubtedly continue. However, *Chicago Sun-Times* columnist Vernon Jarrett is correct in pointing out the Black/Jew double standard in the Jewish criticism of Blacks without restraint. Therefore, it is very difficult for many informed Blacks to forget the Jewish anti-Black feelings expressed by Jewish leaders such as Norman Podhoretz. His now infamous position, "My Negro Problem — and Ours," appeared in the February 1963 issue of *Commentary*.

> The hatred I still feel for Negroes is the hardest of all the old feelings to face or admit, and it is the most hidden...by the conscious at-

titudes into which I have succeeded in willing myself. It no longer
has, as for me it once did, any cause or justification (except, perhaps, that I am constantly being denied my right to honest expression of the things I earned the right as a child to feel)...Color is indeed
a political rather than a human or a personal reality and if politics
(which is to say power) has made it into a human and a personal
reality, then only politics (which is to say power) can unmake it once
again. But the way of politics is slow and bitter, and as impatience
on the one side is matched by a setting of the jaw on the other, we
move closer and closer to an explosion and blood may yet run in the
streets.

The difference between Blacks and Jews is that we do not see Norman
Podhoretz as the only spokesperson on Jewish thought and, therefore, do
not go off half-crazy because of his racism and ignorance.

It is clear to most Blacks in the United States that the majority of Jews
are not rich, not politically influential and not in control of U.S. media,
science, education, economics or legal system. They have influence, yes,
but not control. (See G. William Domhoff's *Who Rules America Now?*)
This is important because Israel could not *exist* without the aid (some call
it welfare) from the United States. Israel received over $3 billion in aid
in 1988 from the U.S. This comes to about $10 million each working day.
This money doesn't include the millions of dollars that are raised by the
various Jewish organizations. My point is that Afrikan Americans contribute through taxes and as individuals to the upkeep, survival and development of Israel. I've yet to hear a *thank you* from Jewish leadership. If
Afrikan Americans received $3 billion a year from any source, we would
not have too many problems that couldn't be solved.

There is a lesson in all of this: 1) Jews take care of their own, using
monies and resources from wherever they are available; 2) they are a highly literate and political people that keeps their struggle in the minds-eye
of most people worldwide; 3) regardless of the criticism, they are always
on the offense; 4) they have stopped apologizing for being Jewish and
have developed visible Black spokespersons like Julius Lester and Sammy
Davis, Jr. to advocate their cause.

A final point that often is overlooked is that violence against Jews by
Afrikan Americans is just about nonexistent. I am not aware of any Black
people in the U.S. organizing to do harm to Jewish people or Jewish institutions. Nor am I aware of any organized or individual acts of violence

by Black people against Jews or their institutions. It seems to me that the rift between Blacks and Jews is mainly verbal.

In the Black community of the eighties and nineties, Jews have been replaced on the front line (commercial) by Arabs and Koreans; if we criticize them, are we anti-Arab or anti-Korean? Like the Jews, Poles, Italians and Irish, we must elevate our struggle to a world level and seek life-giving and life-saving answers that will positively resurrect our communities. As long as we are reacting to other people's definitions and programs, pro-action among the knowers in the Afrikan-American community will be futile. Today Afrikan American people in the United States are *a majority people with a minority complex*, and this comes from the uncritical acceptance of other people's ideas, dreams, visions and definitions. However, there is a significant number of Afrikan American people that will never go back to acting out the definitions of others. Change is in the wind and a whole lot of people are upset, not only Jews.

Malcolm X: Diamond in the Coal

There is not a day in my life that I do not think about Malcolm X. His picture, along with those of Garvey, King, Lumumba and Hoyt Fuller, rests on the wall above my desk. It often reminds me of the influence he had on me and millions of other Black people of my generation. To have become conscious in the early sixties is to have been touched by the truth of Malcolm X. That is beyond question. He was the man that gave my generation a *voice*. His presence, his example, his stand against the greatest human evil to confront our people — *white world supremacy and its creation, negroes* — is stamped upon my mind forever.

The short life Malcolm X, formerly Malcolm Little, was ended as El-Hajj Malik El-Shabazz. His travel from a self-hating victim to a politically conscious and learned spokesman-organizer for Black people via the Nation of Islam (under the guidance of the Honorable Elijah Muhammad) is what legends are made of. His journey from the streets to prison to proactive statesman in Afrikan American struggle is well chronicled in his *Autobiography of Malcolm X*, written with the assistance of Alex Haley. His autobiography should be read by all Black people, especially the young. It was Malcolm X who understood that what one could change does not need to be eliminated. Most certainly, he saw in himself and in Black people eminent possibilities for positive and lasting change (i.e., development).

There are many images that define Malcolm X. His unique articulation of Afrikan American struggle without bowing, scratching his head or tap dancing is the clearest. He lived with facts, and in all of his confrontations (and that's what they were) with reporters, media hosts, public officials and others he gave more than he got. The clarity and conviction of his arguments helped to unglue many negro-minds from the myth and hypocrisy of white people and Eurocentrism. He handled himself and the language like a young, undefeated fighter. He was *always* reading; seldom did we see Malcolm X without a book, magazine or newspaper. He was, what is called today a "quick study."

He received the respect of younger and elder brothers, not because they feared him but because he had proven himself time and time again; he had

251

tested fire. How could one not remember the photograph of Malcolm X at the window of his home, with weapon in hand, guarding his family? Betty Shabazz and their girls — Attalah, Qubilah, Ilyasah, Gamilah Lamubah, Malikah Saban and Malaak Saban — all quiet and sincere, engaged (in their own public and private ways) in a battle that was still being defined, a war that was/is often beyond explanation or comprehension, yet very dangerous. Malcolm X as student, teacher, spokesman, organizer, leader and family man represented the type of man that did not put style before content, image before thought or reaction before analysis. His suits were not tailor-made; nor were his ideas or actions. His message was clear water and music for a thirsty people searching for a new dance.

Malcolm X was not perfect; he made mistakes and on many occasions, to friend and foe, admitted error. But, who among us during the difficult sixties did not error? The Malcolm X difference was that he did not allow his mistakes to destroy him; he learned from them and took succeeding steps with careful deliberation. No, he was not perfect, but he was moving toward a kind of working perfection. Whether or not he would have arrived we do not know. However, the odds are it would have been a well-fought battle. El-Hajj Malik El-Shabazz was cut down—brutally murdered in the prime of his life by negroes blinded by a self-righteous ideology that created in them (and others) a killing-field mentality. For them, the easiest and quickest answer to serious and embarrassing questions was to kill the questioner; bury the message and messenger.

The short life of El-Hajj Malik El-Shabazz is without parallel in Afrikan American struggle. His impact is immeasurable, his message undying, his integrity legendary, his commitment unquestioned and his significance and contribution are still growing. In fact, it was Malcolm X and the Nation of Islam that first popularized the using of Black as the correct designation for people of Afrikan descent in America. It was also Malcolm's Organization of African American Unity that made the ultimate connection between Black people here and Black people in Afrika, Asia, the Americas and elsewhere. Somehow I don't feel that the current debate over what we should call ourselves would have taken up too much of his time. Black and Afrikan American had entered his lexicon already married, and a divorce seemed unnecessary. Ossie Davis, a man who is usually careful with his adjectives, called him our "Black Shining Prince." He did shine, as in illuminate, and the light that glowed behind his ever present glasses should always burn in us, our children and their children until the evil that killed him and *continues to kill* millions of our people yearly is plowed into the earth never to rise again.

Malcolm X, the name most people remember him by, was the complex, serious, multifaceted, quick-smiling man who doubted and questioned, doubted and questioned until inaction would have been viewed as endorsement of the hypocrisy with which he could no longer live. He tried in his own unique way to give answers to those difficult and murderous times. To forget and not honor his contribution is to give quarter to the enemies of Black people and, in effect, bury memory and history in an unmarked grave.

Our commitment to Black world struggle, and Afrikan American struggle in particular, ideally should be no less than his. To not try and reach his level of seriousness is to acknowledge our own failure and, just as important, would be a confirmation of Black impotence. Such inaction will confine us to the garbage bins of history, and people worldwide will continue to use Black people as the catch-line in their jokes. If anything can be said about Malcolm X, it's that he was not a comedian and he didn't sell wolf tickets.

A common saying in the Black community is "If you don't know where you are going, any road will take you there." Remember that the ideal may not be the "mountain top," but may be the path to the top; life is, indeed, a process. Certainly, El-Hajj Malik El-Shabazz never stopped learning and he, unlike most of our leadership, truly respected and believed in the ground-rooted and untouched power of Black people. It is good that we can now talk of Martin Luther King and Malcolm X in a way that is not conflicting. They both loved Black people and gave the ultimate gift that one could give to our people, their lives. Jeff Stetson in his very powerful play "The Meeting" examined the possible connection between the two of them. It is clear that the work of Dr. King will be remembered and advanced. To remember and celebrate the life of Malcolm X is fine. However, I believe it is time that a nationwide effort is launched to build a living memorial or institution for the life-work of this monumental man. The form that such a structure would take is not for me to say. All I can do is join the call for it and be willing to be a part of a national effort to make it a reality.

Malcolm X, El-Hajj Malik El-Shabazz, our Black Shining Prince, the diamond in the coal, did not "know his place" in America or the world.

As a consequence, he was dedicated to making "other places" for all people, especially those of Afrikan descent. His short, yet beloved journey into our lives marked his presence as true prophet and insightful seer. His heartfelt fight should still be our fight; his preparation and seriousness must be duplicated in Black communities across this land. In doing so, we not only rejoice in what he left us, but we also appreciate the genius of his vision because when the *word* is finalized, we know — without doubt or hesitation — that Malcolm X, El-Hajj Malik El-Shabazz, gave us *a way*; and he often smiled while doing it.

New Steel Screaming in the Wind:
Hoyt W. Fuller

Clearly there are losses that are irreplaceable, examples that are indispensable. Hoyt W. Fuller has joined our ancestors. Hoyt W. Fuller died in March of 1981. His journey is an early and unexpected one, is a hurting exodus, but in any language *gone means gone* and as to the thousands of people and students he touched, as important as some of them are, none will occupy the chair of the teacher. So it is. What remains are memories of a unique *Afrikan Freedom Fighter*, his magnificent body of written work, scores of his ideas that need acting on, and an army of people that his spirit of urgency connected with and transformed.

I have not met many "true" Black men in my time, and therefore without concrete images of what Black manhood is, I have had to study and reconstruct a definition that is consistent with 20th century realities. In my estimation, some of the qualities that best exemplify new Black manhood are cultural and moral integrity, competence, psychological security and stability as a Black man, sensitivity to the needs of one's people, a strong work ethic, a culturally-based mindset, an unquenchable thirst for knowledge (truth), a winner's attitude toward life, an insatiable love for Black people (especially the children), revolutionary unpredictability, and an unstoppable willingness to struggle against any odds for the liberation of Black people. This was Hoyt Fuller, Black man extraordinaire. His credo was a simple one: *Liberation for Black people is possible*.

Yet, too, he knew that liberation was indeed unlikely without strong Black men and women whose first obligation was securing their own vision and historical direction. He understood the complexity of the human heart and realized the extent to which many Black men and women had made the "easy compromise," resulting in their effective neutralization. He was not one to hide behind excuses:

> But what clogs in the heart is that Black men know what they do.
> They know. The flight to Kappa-Omega is not blind. If red blood
> deserts the veins, then substitute tomato juice. When white men

deride the manhood of those they degrade, what they mean is this: men do not beg for freedom, men take their freedom. Only fearful fools confuse real manhood with slapping backs and guzzling booze...These are games children also play...Far too many Black men lack seriousness. They are content being slaves. "Making it" is the religion, and "success" is the god we worship. It is no cliché. What do we "make it" to?...they know. The only source of power in the race is in the people, the plain ones. Marcus Garvey knew that. Elijah Muhammad knows..."Power lies in the People." (*The Turning of the Wheel*, I.P.E., 1972, Chicago)

Hoyt Fuller knew the power of the Black collective, yet he was also the example of the fired-up, conscious individual. He felt that a people's Liberation was indelibly tied to individuals and their institutions. Acceptance of the status quo was never in his game plan. For him, a people's liberation was not only a material reality but was mostly reflected in their day to day spiritual and political (i.e., cultural) development. He represented the epitome of the paradoxical man. He was tormented and imprisoned, yet he was free. He would often comment, "I am not home in America," as he fought daily against the piles of excrement that America forced on his people. Actually, the world was his prison, even though there were places in this world where he was less hurried, more relaxed and constantly productive. However, the larger questions remain: How was this man different? Did his passage among us impact our lives positively?

Hoyt was analytical but not aloof, an idea man but not actionless. He constantly involved himself with the daily construction of a means toward an end and seldom was confused in his ideas or acts as to the ultimate end: liberation. He profoundly understood that the lack of action infecting the great majority of Black people, especially the men, is not genetic or biological. Rather, it is the result of hundreds of years of special, intensified conditioning, which also destroyed other cultures, such as the indigenous people of the Americas. He knew deep inside that constant and consistent motion toward the affirmative is absolutely necessary. Not to act, not to function consciously in the best interest of one's people was, to Hoyt, unthinkable and merely a way of accepting the world on the terms of others.

In essence, Black inaction was acting against Black action. Do nothingness, translated into negative acts, has left us terminally confused and frightened. However, in this precarious existence, Hoyt dared to see potential in us, and based upon much study, enormous travel, and his own varied life experiences, he seldom fell prey to false expectations. His truths were continuous and earthshaking:

> The American educational system, as it is, is not designed for the benefit of Black people, who are oppressed by that system; it is not designed to facilitate the regeneration of a people it has calculatedly debased; it is not designed to liberate the spirit of the sons and daughters of Africa nor to enhance that spirit nor to thrill at its soaring; the American educational system is not designed to encourage the destruction of the American political and economic system, no matter how cruel and debilitating embattled minorities may find that system.

> The American educational system, as it is, is designed to benefit and to maintain the status and well-being of the white middle-class majority; it is designed to train the personnel and to maintain the ideology which will ensure the perpetuation and endurance of the American political and economic system, which is now, and always has been, hostile to the ultimate aims of the Black minority which serves it. (*Black World*, May 1974).

His motion was to change and upset, to dethrone current Euro-American interpretations and correct them with a perspective (his word) that spoke to the realities of his people and other people of color. For certain, he was not seeking to replace a white falsehood with a Black one. Intellectual honesty and an accurate reading of history would not allow for such nonsense. He knew that the process of freedom was always open to debate and interpretation.

Nor was he a fighter for some vague notion of universality or world humanism. He was too culturally grounded to be sidetracked into never-never land. Plainly stated, he was a Black (Afrikan) man first, and then a citizen of the world. He, as far as I know, never apologized for this honor, but functioned for the seventeen years of our friendship in a way that forced Afrikan Americans either to accept themselves and work toward our collective self-interest or crawl back into the closets of scientific slavery. He was not one to avoid confrontation and fought very well with words and fists. If anything was truly important to him, it was not to make truth out of lies. His commitment to authenticity and to facts was unquestionable, and is exemplified in his editorship of *Black World* and *First World* magazines, and in his only published book, *Journey to Africa*, (Third World Press).

Unlike most of us, Hoyt Fuller seldom chose the easy route. He was a warrior of the first rank and did not pick false battles. He sought the eye of the needle. He knew that one cannot reason with the majority of white people (and their negro lackeys); therefore, they are to be feared and organized against. He felt that Black murder in the United States had become legitimate, yet our best responses to it were ribbon wearing and promises not to make such murder a political issue. Hoyt was not an excuse maker and often stated:

> ...power makes concessions only when challenged by counter-power...But we know what we do and what we fail to do. After nearly 400 years of racist subjugation, Black people have no justification for repeating the cycle of hope and disillusionment. If we do not seize the instruments of power and use them, we must admit that it is our terribly conscious choice. (*Black World*, December, 1972).

He was the classic race man, not superficially wearing his culture on his back, but carrying it within him to the point where if you were in his presence, and an enemy of our people, the racial and cultural intensity of his personality would force reactions from you, in the positive or the negative.

There is an uneasiness among our people. Contrary to misinformed belief, Ronald Reagan is not a dumb actor; he is in fact a superb screen writer, director and an integral part of the Western production team that is bent on the absoluteness of their emerging order. Hoyt prepared some of us. These new interpreters voicing opinions disguised as facts will be resisted with the forces of volcanoes and the strength of the elephants.

The fight against this white conservative and neo-conservative united front was Hoyt's special project. He warned us. Well, it's for real, and above ground. Cowboys, American pie, and Real Stuff are back in force with another crop of "new negroes," led by the likes of Thomas Sowell, Samuel Pierce, Mel Bradley, Arthur Fletcher, William O. Walker, Thad Garrett, Martin Kilson, Glenn C. Loury and Wilson J. Williams. These preachers and posing princes, clowns in scholar's roles, will not have an easy time of it. Hoyt had often stated that the "task is monumental, and it is not easier by the diversionary tactics of the game-player. It is imperative that the Black Community know the difference between the committed and the comedians." His truths could devastate. Hoyt is not to be mourned but emulated, his actions duplicated a thousand times:

He will be missed, not lost among papers
remembered in midnight study cells
and early morning runs.
remembered as an originator of
wisdom
from a vision that was sound and sane
steadfast and tempered
Tempo between songs and dance   between
fist and articulation   call him
fresh music
screamingly dangerous

Sang beauty first
notice the eyes of children
locate their living and eating space
try and smile now.
run with and against the common wind
do damage for damage   be
unpredictable with map and compass
and weapons pressed against the cheek
Catch fire and fire
notice
there is an uneasiness among us
window shades are drawn,
people talk in nods and whispers
babies are again born in homes,
people are picking up books and nails
and anxiously listening to grandparents.
there is sunrise on the horizon
Pass this word quickly and quietly
there are rats in the streets.

Poison is needed.   Now.

Bobby Wright:
Genius in Honest Search

How does one measure greatness?

There are few Black men or women today in the "right" place, or position, asking the penetrating questions and demanding answers and corrective actions to the racial situation in the United States and the world. Generally, Black people are viewed as pitiful pawns in an international game of control and manipulation, and our worldwide misuse is an accepted by-product of business as usual.

The loss of Dr. Bobby E. Wright is magnified a hundredfold because he was the constant swimmer, the energized professional, the concerned and loving family man, the Garveyite race man; always a step or two ahead of the accepted theories masquerading as insight and knowledge. Dr. Wright was a man who had fought to get to the "right" place in order to ask the "right" questions and demand and force the "right" actions.

It is true that we do not recognize greatness among us. Our measurements of importance are generally faulty and speak mainly to the superficialities of life e.g., from where one lives, the type of clothing one wears, the car one drives, to the number of bodyguards that one employs to carry bags and open and close doors. Dr. Wright cut through dishonesty with a passion. He, as a clinical psychologist, understood the mind of an enslaved people. He knew the mental state of a people caught in a world stolen and remade for Europeans. His view was that the high Afrikan standards that gave the world civilization were now confusing or nonexistent. Dr. Wright was a visionary with standards, values, integrity and convictions. In essence, he was a man who valued Afrikan traditions and culture.

He died in the prime of his thinking. He was involved in honest search. His presence was a stabilizing force for all people who had recently become anchored to video machines and sightlessness. He understood the power of ideas, and was constantly cutting through nonsense and mediocrity. His concern was for the widening distance between the haves and have-nots, the job-givers and job-seekers.

Bobby's love was conditional and selective. He had been burned often by the call of "Blackness" and "Brotherhood." His work, more than most in his profession, is a telling indictment of white world supremacy, and within his multidimensional approach he recognized and gave us a way of dealing with this evil. However, Bobby could not talk as fast as he was thinking, even though he often tried. It seemed that his mind was always rushing, going jet-like from idea to idea, leaving most people on the bus of a wasted Western culture. He was fire and energy, thoroughly original, possessor of a monumental mind in a sea of lobotomized small thinkers.

He focused and unsettled us. In his short life, he seldom spoke of his own future. He knew of a death worse than personal physical passing, that of a people unaware of their own promise. Dr. Wright was a thorn in the brains of Black men and women posing as leaders. In many of them he diagnosed a deep dishonor that disqualified them for their trusted positions. His last words were a warning to his friends and associates, "Watch the leadership, especially those proclaiming *their* God-given answer to the problems of Black people."

He was a fighter within the eye of the volcano,
a listener in the midst of the hurricane,
a lover unafraid of giving tears of laughter,
a scientist seeking bright and moving moments,
a deliverer of truth within the truth,
a tree displaying roots and beauty,
a good and honest man,
carrying wisdom,
carrying future.

It is an honor to publish him.

My introduction to Dr. Wright's collection of essays, *Psychopathic Racial Personality and other Essays.*

Nothing Black but a Cadillac:

Color, Power and Identity in America

Color, economics and other cultural manifestations are what separate people in the United States. Most people of color, regardless of consciousness, see the pigmentation of their skin as the major reason for exclusion, denial, stereotyping, caricature, bigotry and racism. People of Afrikan descent are designated by people in the dominating culture in the United States as negroes, niggers, coloreds, Black so-and-sos or slaves. Generally, the "place" of a Black person is decided before his or her educational, economic or political status is known. White America and *all* of the Western world think and act in *color*.

Culture, biology and class differences are crucial definers of people. However, in the United States, a person's color impacts on his or her present and future in such a way that money, no matter how much a person has, is at best a tonic that cannot cure the disease of white world supremacy (racism); but like most "drugs," money can temporarily arrest the deadly bite. Racism has done serious damage to the psyches of all people. Whether one observes the Untouchables of Asia, the dark-skinned people of Europe and America or the Blacks and "coloreds" of South Afrika, the common battle fought by all of them on a daily basis is one of survival and development in a world that judges and categorizes them, first and foremost, by the pigmentation of their skin. This is a worldwide phenomenon, but it is most pronounced in white-dominated societies like the United States, Canada, Europe, Australia, U.S.S.R. and South Afrika.

In this century, it was Marcus Garvey, W.E.B. Du Bois, Carter G. Woodson, E. Franklin Frazier, Frantz Fanon, Malcolm X and others who articulated the duality and finality that color plays on the Western conscience. The inability of most people of Afrikan descent, (i.e., Black people) to accurately define themselves within, as well as apart from, the dominating white (Euro-American) culture speaks loudly to how victims accommodate themselves to the oppressor's worldview. Such accommodation is beyond acculturation; it's mental slavery without chains. The internalization and acceptance of white people's values, life-style, desires, worldview, (i.e., culture) with little selectivity, has been defined as *seasoning*. The clearest example of this mindset is working at a worldwide level each day as Black people battle with themselves and their biology to look like, act like and talk like white people. This is most evident in Black people's efforts to straighten their hair and lighten their skin. And, this sickness is not confined to the Western Hemisphere. Recently, the *Los Angeles Times* (12-6-88) in an article by Mawusi Afele, a Ghana-based writer, reported that "skin-bleaching continues to be popular among women in the West African country despite warnings from doctors that it is a dangerous practice." However, this bleaching of one's face is not indigenous to West Afrika; it started here in the "good old USA" by 20th century negroes.

Taylor Branch in his *Parting the Waters*, a massive study of Martin Luther King and the Civil Rights struggle, states, "...almost as color defines vision itself, race shapes the culture eye — what we do and do not notice, the reach of empathy and the alignment of response. This subliminal force recommends care in choosing a point of view for a history grounded in race." The white response to the majority of the world's people, who are not white, is indeed grounded in race. More than any other factor in the Eurocentric context, *race* defines, categorizes, tracks, destroys and redefines cultures. The color question in America has a way of driving most people into silliness and/or madness.

The word *Black* as defined by non-Black people (as well as millions of Black people) is still: devious, dark, soiled, dirty, forbidding, disastrous, amoral, evil, wicked, sinful, fiendish, inhuman, treacherous and diabolic. Many Afrikan Americans still instruct their daughters not to marry men darker than they are. Those whom many Blacks call "Black-Black" or "jet Black" men, as well as dark-skinned women, are still back-seated and made to stand in the "shadow" of light-skinned people. When some of our children are upset with each other, the invectives they call each other are often preceded by the word *Black* as in, "You Black bitch," or "Black son-of-a-bitch," or "You Black mother fucker," etc. Who has not heard and repeated the popular folk put-down of Black people:

> if you're white you're alright
> yellow you're mellow,
> brown stick around, but if
> you're Black step back.

264

The point of all this is that we must be very careful not to go back to the pre-sixties and let the word *Black*, the description we selected for ourselves, revert without question or opposition to its most common negative uses. "Black" for us is a *political designation*. We've always said that "Black" is synonymous with Afrika and, therefore, represents a particular history and culture.

The argument that no one is really white or Black is irrelevant when culturally the color symbols have reached the height of political myths, and these myths have been accepted as truths. To exclusively define Black people in the United States as Afrikan American only denies history, culture and reality. If one truly understands the multi-ethnic, multilingual, multi-religious (i.e., multi-cultural) continent that Afrika is, one realizes that what is really called for are accurate definitions. If we are really Afrikans — as I believe we are — what does that mean?

In terms of cultural diversity, Afrika is at the apex of complexity. Afrika is not homogeneous. From the Arab-dominated north to the European-controlled south to the Afrikan-populated middle, Afrikans have yet to reach a consensus on something as vital as a continent-wide workable definition of Pan-Afrikanism. However, the question for Black people in America is, "What part of Afrika do our foreparents come from?" Are we Nigerians, Ghanaians, Tanzanians, Kenyans or Ethiopians? Are we the daughters and sons of Algeria, Libya, Chad, Zambia, Angola, Zimbabwe or Liberia? What language(s) have we lost? Is our natural tongue Fanti, Ga, Hausa, Ibo, Swahili, Shona, Tswana, Zulu or Kamba? According to Kofi Awoonor in his *The Breast of the Earth*, there are about 800 major languages in Afrika. Yes, Blacks in America are Afrikan people, but is there, or should there be, more to that definition? I think the answer is that we don't know. Therefore, do we accept and identify with all of Afrika? I think the answer to that is yes, but it still is an incomplete answer.

When white people in the United States recognize their respective ethnic backgrounds, they are Polish Americans, Irish Americans, Italian Americans, Jewish Americans, etc. Most of the time they simply refer to themselves as white, but they do not see a conflict in using both terms. Seldom do white Americans define themselves as European Americans. Most whites in America do have some memory or connection to their former homelands and wouldn't dare define themselves as something as ambiguous as the entire continent — European Americans. In fact, if it weren't for Black people, whites in the United States — if we can believe their history — would be at each other's throats. The glue that keeps white people "together" is Black people. Toni Morrison, in a recent *Time* interview (5-22-89), states it this way:

> ...black people have always been used as a buffer in this country between powers to prevent class war, to prevent other kinds of real conflagrations. If there were no black people here in this country, it would have been Balkonized. The immigrants would have torn each other's throats out, as they have done everywhere else. But in becoming American, from Europe, what one has in common with that other immigrant is contempt for *me* — it's nothing but color.

The point I'm trying to make is that "Black" as a designation of a people, of course, is not accurate if we naively conceive of the Afrikan American presence here without a specific history and racial context. However, the historical, political and cultural reality of the United States is that color has always been *the* overriding issue here and in much of the world. Therefore, if Black is, indeed, a political reality rather than a "human" one, should not Black people control such a reality? And politics, in the final analysis, is the acquisition, use and distribution of power. It seems to me that our focus should be on taking any political reality that affects us and making it work for us, on our own terms. This is partially what the struggle of the sixties was about — *redefinition*.

People who have dark skin, which is a genetic and biological condition, have been defined as negative by white people worldwide. Would it not be in Black people's interest (especially that of their children), and in keeping with today's geopolitical construction, to take such a reality and make it *positive*? Most certainly white people, who are European, are not giving up or running from "white." Why? They've defined "white" as *the best of everything*, and most of the world has bought into their political definition. Poet and thinker Gwendolyn Brooks put this perspective in a manner that we all can understand in her essay "Requiem Before Revival:"

> I give whites big credit. They have never tried to be anything but what they are. They have been and will be everlastingly proud proud proud to be white. It has never occurred to them that there has been or ever will be ANYthing better than, nor one zillionth as good as, being white. They have an overwhelming belief in their validity.

266

Not in their "virtue," for they are shrewdly capable of a very cold view of *that*. But their validity they salute with an amazing innocence — yes, a genuine innocence, the brass of which befuddles most of the rest of us in the world because we have allowed ourselves to be hypnotized by its shine.

The key, of course, is that all political realities in part depend upon how a people, any people, defines itself and struggles to actualize a worldview it considers *necessary for its development or beauty*.

Dark-skinned people, Black people, if you will, should be moving toward greater accuracy and extension. We are an Afrikan people that has been scattered and brought to this land. We must not ever forget that the horror perpetuated on us was not only an economic move by white people, but our people also represented the exact opposite of the white (European) worldview. In their destruction and denigration of us, white people found themselves, for we, in color and life-style, did not and could not fit the European (white) model. The two things that people of Afrikan descent share are *color* and *negative experiences with white people*. Whether we wish to accept it or not, our Blackness is now a political, historical (i.e., cultural) reality in this land. Not using "Black" doesn't mean that it will go away.

We cannot give up "Black" as long as it is not redemptive and as natural and/or lifegiving as water. We must use "Afrikan American" because it does connect us to land, history, culture that do represent our source, spirit and soul. We are an Afrikan people, but we are also part of a larger Afrikan community worldwide that has suffered mainly because we are Black. It was Gwendolyn Brooks who stated, "I share *Family*hood with Blacks wherever they may be. I am a *Black*, and I capitalize my name." If Afrikan people controlled the images of this world, this perspective wouldn't be necessary. Until that day, the choice is not either/or but an intelligent use of both, "Afrikan American" and "Black" with a capital "B."

Final Words/World

Question: Do I think all white people are racist, evil, bad and corrupt? No, but those who are are clearly in the majority and are the ones who hold power and determine the future of my children and my neighbors' children. The oppressed in the United States have the unusual quality of looking evil in the eye and denying its existence. This quality is not genetic, it is learned. To be a part of an oppressed culture is to be hidden from knowledge, from knowing.

Wendell Berry's *The Hidden Wound* confirmed for me that there are some white men of good will who are quietly and loudly talking to their own people about the "wound" of racism. However, talk is fine and books attacking racism are great, but the key to enlightenment is to interest the majority of white people, especially those who have power, in looking at their own history as honestly and as brutally as possible and initiating life-giving and life-saving corrections. I know that the great majority of whites cannot and will not do this, and herein lies the problem; enlightened words are like tear drops in a desert if they are not heard.

Four recent books (*Racial Matters: The FBI's File on Black America, 1960-1972; The Silent Brotherhood: Inside American's Racist Underground; With Justice For None;* and *Brotherhood of Murder*) confirm the validity of my position: white America would rather destroy itself from the inside than share power, wealth or influence with "former slaves." The FBI's annual "Uniform Crime Reports" clearly points out that the main criminals in the United States are white people. From drugs to white collar crimes, from homocide to organized crime, white men are the reigning kings. Yet, Black men are portrayed day after day on television, in newspapers, and in magazines as the chief thieves and boogiemen in the country. That's like saying the main predator of the elephant is the mosquito.

I hope that this book has been helpful to the reader in his/her consideration of another point of view concerning the status of Black people. I would like to think that my views are realrooted. I didn't have a grant or research monies to write this book. Eleven years (off and on) of work went between these covers. After completing *Enemies: The Clash of*

Races in 1978, I was "whitelisted." Speaking engagements and poetry readings across the country were cancelled, and I found myself without employment for about a year. Whether or not I'll be whitelisted as a result of this book doesn't really matter. Sometimes change only comes after a shaking up. I'm reminded of the words of Doris Lessing from her book, *Prisons We Choose to Live Inside*:

> It is particularly hard for young people, faced with what seem like impervious walls of obstacles, to have belief in their ability to change things, to keep their personal and individual viewpoints intact. I remember very clearly how it seemed to me in my late teens and early twenties, seeing only what seemed to be impregnable systems of thought, of belief - governments that seemed unshakeable. But what has happened to those governments like the white government in Southern Rhodesia, for instance? To those powerful systems of faith, like the Nazis, or the Italian Fascists, or to Stalinism? To the British Empire ... to all the European empires, in fact, so recently powerful? They have all gone, and in such a short time ... It is individuals who change societies, give birth to ideas, who, standing out against tides of opinion, change them. This is as true in open societies as it is in oppressive societies...

As a revolutionary poet/activist/intellectual, it is my responsiblity to challenge the state, to point out contradiction and hypocrisy, to offer solutions and to, if possible, be an example of one who lives an honorable life. I've grown tired of men who only demonstrate respect for Black women when they are trying to get something out of them. It is important that we be able to admit error (especially to Black women), learn from our errors, apologize if necessary, and keep on growing.

I'm not optimistic about the reception of *Black Men: Obsolete, Single, Dangerous?* because I do not think that America, in relationship to race, has matured very much since the sixties. Many people, Black and white, will deny the deadly role white world supremacy (racism) plays in the world and in the destruction of Black people. Hopefully, I have not excused the transgressions and limitations of my own people in this regard. We still have mountains to climb. The power of conscious and committed individuals is our major hope. Don't give up; remain activists. People are naturally innovative and creative. The beauty of jogging uphill is being able to run down the other side. I'm going to try to write some new poetry

now, continue to publish new and innovative Black writers, try to inspire
new students
and each day
meet the
sun with a
smile
as I attack
this ever present
mountain.

one love,

H.R.M.

Yes

for those that want:
every woman a man
every man a woman,
every person an education and willing work,
for all people
family, food, clothing, shelter, love,
frequent smiles and children swimming in glorious happiness.

for every elder a home, blooming health, few worries,
good teeth and fun-filled thank you's.
for all people,
liberating culture,
the full love of laughing children who
have been bathed in the caring eyes of
family, friends, nation.

for all people,
the inner glow that radiates peace and wisdom,
the confirming smiles of knowledge known,
the confident walk of music heard,
the quiet presence of having accepted and created beauty.

for Afrikan people
an unspoken understanding that
this is the center we gave the world

this is civilization.